The Six Marine Divisions in the Pacific

The Six Marine Divisions in the Pacific

Every Campaign of World War II

George B. Clark

McFarland & Company, Inc., Publishers

Jefferson, North Carolina, and London

All photographs courtesy Marine Corps Archive and Special Collections.

LIBRARY OF CONGRESS CATALOGUING-IN-PUBLICATION DATA

Clark, George B., 1926–
The six Marine divisions in the Pacific : every campaign
of World War II / George B. Clark.
p.   cm.
Includes bibliographical references and index.

ISBN-13: 978-0-7864-2769-7
ISBN 10: 0-7864-2769-8 (softcover : 50# alkaline paper) ∞

1. United States. Marine Corps — History — World War, 1939–1945.   2. United States.
Marine Corps — Organization.   3. World War, 1939–1945 — Campaigns — Pacific Area.   I. Title.
D769.369.C63   2006   940.54'5973 — dc22   2006020690

British Library cataloguing data are available

On the cover: Marines of 3/23 on Iwo Jima, February 27, 1945
(Courtesy Marine Corps Archive and Special Collections)

Manufactured in the United States of America

*McFarland & Company, Inc., Publishers
Box 611, Jefferson, North Carolina 28640
www.mcfarlandpub.com*

Contents

Acknowledgments

This book, like so many others, would have never been completed were it not for the support, without condition, of my wife of more than a half century, Jeanne J. D. Clark. So, if you don't like what you find within, blame her.

My son, Patrick T. Clark, has been most supportive of my meager efforts for many years.

While most of the material you will find below has been derived from Federal publications in my own collection there are several people who have helped and encouraged me over the years. The list must include James T. McIlwain, M.D., a friend and historian of many years; Col. Richard "Rich" Hemenez, friend, historian and author *also*; Harry Tinney, a real support group all by himself; Comdr. Neil Carey, USN (ret.) a friend of Marines, who, along with Gen. Merrill B. Twining, created that marvelous tribute to the 1st Mar-Div on Guadalcanal *No Bended Knee;* and another long-time pal of mine; Lt. Col. "Pete" Owen, one of the Corps' Finest and a splendid author himself; Col. Walt Ford, *Leatherneck's* editor, and his colleague, Col. "Jack" Glasgow of the *Marine Corps Gazette*, who have helped when asked; Gunnery Sgt. Richard "Dick" Gaines, who spreads the word; Maj. Gary Cozzens, who has kept me in business; and my MANY friends who also find the USMC in World War I fascinating.

I cannot and must not forget two of my support group who made some of the enclosed photographic material available: Mr. Michael Miller, director of Marine Corps Archives and Special Collections; and his *most able* assistant, Mrs. Patricia Mullen, Marine Corps Archivist. As with so many times in the past, whenever anything is needed, that fine group is always available.

Thanks to all.

Preface

World War II has been over for more than sixty years and, except for aficionados who read anything printed on the subject, the Pacific war is almost all but forgotten. Most people know that the United States became engaged in the ongoing war when it was attacked by the Imperial Japanese Navy at Pearl Harbor in Hawaii on 7 December 1941. They are also very familiar with the "D-Day" landings on the French coast by the U.S., British and Canadian armies on 6 June 1944. However, not much else is known by the general public. "I was never very good at history" is the common remark made when engaged in discussions about the war.

Certainly the Pacific war and the part played by U.S. forces in the bloody campaigns to defeat Imperial Japan has been, for the most part, virtually ignored in recent years. The actual "players" are dying off (for the most part they are at least 80 years of age) and their story will eventually die with them. The campaigns were horrendous in the number of casualties that occurred in each battle, American and Japanese. Additionally, the struggle was so dreadful and the Japanese troops so intent on not giving way when obviously defeated, that as casualties mounted so did the intense racial hatred. The hatred was unlike the attitude toward the other main enemy, Nazi Germany. The German soldiers at least knew when they were defeated and it appears that most G.I.'s respected their enemy and didn't hate them. Consequently, the U.S. forces in the Pacific war were forced to rely heavily upon weapons of horror to dislodge the enemy. Finally the ultimate horror weapon, the atomic bomb, had to be dropped in order to save as many lives as possible from the million or so casualties that were anticipated in a battle for the Japanese home islands.

This book concentrates upon the Marines' war, all of which was fought in the Pacific save a few isolated experiences in other theaters. It is organized somewhat differently than anything previously published. It is a brief history of each of the six Marine Divisions, concisely describing each campaign, as well as providing an order of battle for the campaign. The part played by other military/naval/air organizations in each campaign is not entirely ignored but certainly kept to a minimum. Each Marine division will be covered in its entirety in its own campaigns. However, the ancillary Marine units, service and support, are virtually ignored. But they too played an important and essential part in the war so please consider them as very busy along with their infantry comrades.

The U.S. Army also had its share in the entire Pacific war and they suffered, died, and were also victorious wherever they fought. MacArthur's campaigns were usually fought on major islands (New Guinea or the Philippines), whereas other army units fought the island campaigns, many times alongside their Marine comrades. The Americal Division served with the 1stMarDiv in the Guadalcanal campaign and later relieved the Marines to assume responsibility of the final conquest of the island. A battalion from the 145th Infantry and another from the 148th Infantry, both of the 37th Infantry Division, served in the Central Solomons campaign where several Marine Raider Battalions were also engaged. The Army was very actively engaged with the Marines in the Marshall campaigns, especially the 7th Infantry Division. The 27th National Guard Infantry Division served on Saipan with the 2d and 4th MarDivs, and the 77th Infantry Division on Guam with the 3dMarDiv. The Marines of the 1stMarDiv were very glad to get support from the 81st Infantry Division on Peleliu, and of course the Tenth U.S. Army was also composed of three MarDivs on Okinawa. This is not to ignore the contributions of the U.S. Navy in the various islands. Their support was mainly medical or spiritual but also included the fighting "SeaBees" (Naval Construction Battalions) in many campaigns. The Marines on scene had a saying: "Don't make fun of a seabee, he may be a Marine's grandfather," while they replied by calling Marines "Junior SeaBees."

Consequently, it seemed time to produce a general history of each campaign of the six Marine divisions, and to provide an order of battle of each, for each campaign. Included is as much TO&E detail as I could uncover in each campaign, finally being able to provide, during the Okinawa campaign, the commanding officers down to company level. For all the other battles, the units' lowest senior ranking officers are generally limited to the unit "3" (Operations) officer, though division, and usually regimental, will routinely show the other staff positions. See below for brief descriptions of their numerics and tasks. Because this work is about the Marine divisions in the Pacific war it will, intentionally, ignore the U.S. Army's great contribution to winning that war. However, it will also ignore contributions made by smaller formations of Marines. Those would include the Defense Battalions, various Corps (i.e., IMAC, IIIMAC, and VAC), Marine air, and their ancillary services. The text concentrates upon the infantry units of the divisions almost to the exclusion of the artillery, engineers and other service type units. Other units which participated, like the various Raider Battalions, air units and all FMF units (i.e., laundry, service and supply battalions, island command units, depot companies, ammunition, bakery, tractor battalions, and others) are mentioned briefly or not at all.

During the war, occasionally, titles changed. Examples would include the naming of a regiment a *Combat Team*. This happened to the 1st MarDiv when it landed on New Britain. The 1st Marines became *CT B* (Combat Team B), the 5th Marines *CT A*, the 7th *CT C*. The battalions became *BLT 15* (1/5), *BLT 25* (2/5) and *BLT 35* (3/5). The same thing happened to the other regimental battalion teams. There were several other alternate names, but, for consistency's sake, I have retained the old familiar *Marines* with the unit numeric.

The coverage of each division is basically general, with limited details. To attempt the detail necessary for full coverage would require a huge separate volume for each division. What has been set down is mostly an overview of where each was, and what they did, with emphasis on the heroes and other individuals who make up history. Artillerymen and engineers were usually in the heat of each campaign so please accept their presence at all times. Especially note that the USN Corpsmen were always right up front, taking as much punishment as their infantry comrades they saved and sometimes more.

Sometimes a battle is covered separately under two or even three Marine divisions. Frequently it was difficult to avoid explaining what another division was doing while "our" division was fighting a battle. Nonetheless my concentration was always on the division under consideration. Okinawa was especially difficult as were the other island campaigns where U.S. Army divisions provided important services. But I did not intend to write a general history of the battles, but rather of each division in that battle. Hopefully I missed very little important material.

Regiments (i.e., Marines) were important, as was the total history of their formation. Some, like those of the 4th Marine Division, were nigh impossible to reconstruct since they were created from various Marine Reserve units brought together. Sometimes battalions, but frequently companies, were not merged together until brought on active duty. I believe that most of the other regiments' histories were sufficiently compiled for a better understanding of their backgrounds.

Because I believe that people make history and as such should receive more coverage than a mere mention I have added a section on Persons. Each person listed was, to my mind, important to the story being told and should be given a brief biographical sketch. There are numerous maps, some of which are quite detailed and others less so. Because a map may be useful for two or even more divisions, details for one division may confuse when used for another. Primarily, they are to show the general outline of the island, not all the highlights covered within the text.

Words used by Marines and their Corps are oftentimes different from common usage. A brief glossary of some of those words readers will encounter within may be useful, especially for those not well versed in Marine Corps language.

Airdale— Naval or even a Marine aviator.

BAM— Broad Assed Marine. Women Marines, who did not take kindly to the insult.

BAR— Browning Automatic Rifle. A quick-firing weapon that found great favor amongst Marines and soldiers. At the time, the major automatic infantry weapon.

Boondockers— Field shoes. To be worn out in the boondocks.

Boot— A Boot Camp trainee.

CMC— Commandant of the Marine Corps. Also labeled as "MGC" for Major General Commandant, or other rank.

Corpsman— A Marine trained to give first aid and minor medical treatment. Corpsmen saved many a Marine's life.

Cruise— Means, usually, a four-year enlistment.

Defense Battalions— Origins were in 1937 when it was deemed essential that the Corps provide coast defense and anti-aircraft protection for naval stations. Heavily utilized at the beginning of the war but later recognized as a less valuable usage of manpower. Their greatest contributions during the war were at the defense of Wake and Midway Islands.

Detachment— Nearly any size group that didn't easily fit in ordinary designated units like company, battalion, regiment, division. In use for a long time, with no parameters, up or down.

Fire Team— A formation utilized late in the war. It consisted of four men, a leader and three subordinates, one of whom carried a BAR. Three FT's were a squad, three squads a platoon.

Fleet Marine Force (FMF)— Originating in the Advanced Base Force concept, in the early years of the 20th century, it was essentially a defense force to protect, with artillery and infantry, captured Navy installations. On 7 December 1933 it evolved into an amphibious strike force and was called by its current name, and most frequently by its initials.

Gunny— Term for a gunnery sergeant, the most popular sergeant.

HAM— Hairy Assed Marine. The verbal response to "BAMs," launched by women Marines.

JASCO— Joint Assault Signal Company. A group of Marine, Navy, and sometimes Army units to provide air-sea fire control to serve landing forces ashore.

Marines— Used to denote a regiment, or perhaps individuals, or collectively a group of Marines.

Mister— Term used addressing junior Marine officers. Mister Brown, etc.

Navajo Code Talkers— Intelligent use of original Americans (Indians) for communication between ground units in their language, which the Japanese had failed to learn.

Pack-Howitzer— Lightweight artillery piece, designed to go anywhere that Marines could go. They were often, at the beginning of the war, the only artillery the Marines had.

ParaMarines— Paratroops designed to provide services behind enemy lines. Usually there was little, if any, depth behind the enemy. They were, like Raiders, lightly armed and usually unable to contribute more than courage to an engagement. They were phased out early in the war.

Raiders— Formed as a result of Roosevelt's decision to satisfy Winston Churchill's desire to see the United States emulate the Commandos of Great Britain. Understaffed and under-weaponed, they performed miracles and paid the price for doing it.

Replacements— Those Marines that were brought in to replace those brought out.

Reserves— A valuable addition to the expanding Corps. The first genuine Marine Reserves was established on 29 August 1916 but didn't come into its own until the postwar period. Then the unpaid reserves were generally scattered around the country in company formations. Its history is too complex for this space; however, they provided great value in World War II and have ever since. The 4th Marine Division was heavily composed of reserves.

Samoan Marines (Reserves)— Formed in that island group from natives around a cadre of Marines on 1 July 1941 to defend the island from any foreign (Japanese) invasion.

Seabees— Naval Construction Battalions ("CBs") mainly created from a stock of older but well-trained construction workers, whose help during tough times the Marines genuinely appreciated.

Skipper— A term used for a company commander. Origins are obviously nautical.

Introduction

During World War II, the U.S. Marine Corps, a small military service, a modest population of officers and men, expanded from 55,000 to 480,000, including approximately 17,000 women Marines. Only once before had the Corps greatly expanded and that was during World War I when it climbed from a "massive" 1916 total of 10,500 to reach an unheard-of total of 53,000 officers and men, plus a few women. Each time the U.S. Army was vocally and vibrantly opposed to those increases, and each time they were voted down by the Congress. Sometimes the Navy also wasn't thrilled. Each time the Corps managed to fulfill its responsibilities, and ofttimes with media encouragement became the darling of the American public. That incensed the U.S. Army even more.

The United States Marine Corps has had a distinguished record of service to the nation for well over two centuries. Mostly, during its history, it has been an auxiliary to, but not a appendage of, the U.S. Navy. Frequently the two services have had considerable difficulty concerning that issue. On several occasions, however, the Corps has been assigned by the president of the U.S. to the Army for ground service. The most recent of these assignments was during World War I. But when that service ended, Marines always came back to the Department of the Navy. It is a sea service and its members are frequently addressed as sea soldiers. In fact, Army officers often complain that they "look like soldiers" but "talk like sailors." During the period covered by this book, the U.S. Marine Corps was not assigned for duty with the Army but instead retained its quasi-independence under the direction of the Secretary of the Navy.

The leaders of the Marine Corps (and the Navy) had, following the end of World War I, determined that the next war would probably be fought in the great Pacific against Japan and be of an amphibious nature. They were understandably gratified when that vision proved dead on target following the attack at Pearl Harbor by the Imperial Japanese Naval forces. The effort and training indulged in by Marines, and to a lesser extent the U.S. Navy, for the better part of twenty years would now pay off.

There had been more than just training. In fact the powers that be had barely scratched the surface, since no nation had a successful history of amphibious warfare and there was much to learn. A major amphibious effort at Gallipoli, by the British and French in World War I, had failed drastically. But the Marine Corps was convinced that amphibious warfare was doable and because they trained for it, were way ahead of the USA on that score. They would be better prepared to fight that kind of a war than the latter. The Corps had somehow inveigled several industrialists into developing and creating seagoing craft intended for assault from the sea. That too was an ongoing effort when war came but initially the Marine Corps and Navy were somewhat better prepared than the Army for what was to come. The USN had been almost a willing partner in amphibious warfare preparation from the very beginning, which was essential.

The Corps had begun to seriously prepare for amphibious war in the early 1930s when they formed a concept they called the Fleet Marine Force or FMF. It was a struggle to even conceptualize a formation of any type requiring great numbers when the Corps was so limited, like the other services, in manpower. But the leaders and their subordinates worked on that concept, developing plans and planning imagined equipment for at least a ten-year period. The required manpower was considered to be secondary to thought and skill development. They would be available when needed and they were.

At the beginning of the war, from December 1941 until the first amphibious assault landing in August 1942, the U.S. military/naval forces were pulling themselves together to fight a two-front war. But it was to be mainly in Europe, the war against Nazi forces, the front given the primary focus by the president. The Pacific War was secondary; ultimately to recover from the initial setbacks and to face an all-conquering Japan.

When the Pacific War began, the Army and Navy each demanded complete control over how and where the war would be fought. This created a hostile environment that took the wisdom of Solomon to settle. Actually, it never was quite settled to the satisfaction of the Army, but they learned to live with the ultimate solution. The decision of the Joint Chiefs of Staff in Washington (with the concurrence of the president) was that the matter was so complex that they would, essentially, command that war. Their agents, Army general MacArthur and Navy admiral Nimitz, would have control over segments of the Pacific region. MacArthur commanded the Southern Pacific area, which would include Australia north to the Asian coast. Within that domain would lie New Guinea, the Philippines, and the large group of the Solomon Islands. Nimitz's rule would include most of the islands of the Pacific: the Gilberts, Marshalls, Marianas, Volcano, Bonin and Ryuku groups, plus others, to be identified later. Therefore, when the 1st Marine Division landed on Guadalcanal in August 1942, and the other Solomon Islands, their overall commander was technically General Douglas MacArthur. In fact he would be overheard several times calling the 1st MarDiv "my Marines." Most of the Marine divisions, fighting in the central and northern Pacific, however, would be under the overall command of Admiral Chester W. Nimitz.

The Marines and the Navy had several discussions about who was really running the war after an actual landing was made. The Navy senior officers believed that they were in overall command, from beginning to end. In others words, they were admirals at sea and generals on land. The Marine senior officers believed the Navy commanded until the Marines were ashore, then the Marines took over. Holland McT. Smith had a few "pleasant" exchanges with his Navy counterparts over that subject, never having it settled to everyone's satisfaction. Somehow it all worked, sometimes better than other times.

In addition to those Marines in the various divisions, all ground troops, we might add that they were frequently supported by both Marine air and Navy air, the former more than the latter during the later engagements. Their assistance was always beyond the call of duty. Close air support helped the Marines win most of their battles. It was a concept that was worked out during the Nicaraguan "troubles" and brought to a successful conclusion during World War II.

Perhaps it would also be useful to provide a chronology of the war in the Pacific, including those battles that are not covered within this book. Primarily the dates below concern the Marine participation, if any, with an abbreviated listing of units engaged.

Pearl Harbor, December 1941. Detachments of Marines.

North China, December. Detachment of Legation Guard Marines on Embassy Duty, Peking, China.

Defense of Guam, December. Detachment of 122 Marines.

Defense of Wake Island, December. Elements of the 1st Defense Battalion and Marine Fighting Squadron 12. Help was provided by a few sailors, a dozen or so Army radio personnel and some, but not all, of the civilian construction workers.

Defense of the Philippine Islands, December 1941–May 1942. 4th Marines at Bataan plus Navy and Army reinforcements (to create a 4th Bn) on Corregidor.

Defense of Midway Island, June 1942. 6th Defense Bn, 2d Raider Bn, Marine Aircraft Group 22.

Guadalcanal, August 1942–February 1943. 1st and 2d MarDivs, 11th Defense Bn, USA Americal and 25th Divisions.

Makin Raid, August 1942, 2d Raider Battalion.

Russell Islands, February to March 1943. 3d Raider Bn, USA 43d InfDiv, various Seabee units.

New Georgia, June to December 1943. 4th Raider Bn, USA 43d, 37th, and 25th InfDivs.

Bougainville, October 1943–March 1944. 3d MarDiv, 2d Raider Regiment, USA 148th Infantry, various Seabee units.

Gilbert Islands, November 1943. 2d MarDiv.

New Britain, December 1943–March 1944. 1st MarDiv.

Marshall Islands, January to March 1944. 4th MarDiv, USA 106th Infantry, assorted Navy and Army support units.

Saipan, June to August 1944. 2d MarDiv, 4th MarDiv, USA 27th InfDiv.

Tinian, July to August 1944. 2d MarDiv, 4th MarDiv.

Guam, July to August 1944. 3d MarDiv, 1st Marine Provisional Brigade, USA 77th InfDiv.

Peleliu, September to October 1944, 1st MarDiv, USA 88th InfDiv.

Leyte, October to December 1944, VAC artillery, USA 7th and 96th InfDivs.

Iwo Jima, February to March 1945. 3d MarDiv, 4th MarDiv, 5th MarDiv.

Okinawa, April to June 1945. 1st MarDiv, 6th MarDiv, USA 7th InfDiv, 27th InfDiv, 77th InfDiv, 96th InfDiv, 20th Armored Group, various USA support units.

Japan, August 1945. Planned 2d, 3d, 5th MarDivs. Various actual units involved including 4th Marines (Rein) plus USN and numerous USA.

Northern China, September 1945. 1st and 6th MarDivs.

Units of the U.S. Marine Corps were recipients of both the *Presidential Unit Citation (Navy)* and those listed for the *Army*. Following is a listing by campaign with unit, including other than Marine divisions.

US NAVY AWARDS

1st Defense Battalion, Wake Island.
Marine Fighting Squadron 211, Wake Island.
Marine Aircraft Group 22, Midway Island.
1st Marine Division (Reinforced), Guadalcanal.

Marine Fighting Squadron 214, Guadalcanal and environs including Munda, Northern
    Solomons, Vella Lavella and Cape Torokino.
2d Marine Division (Reinforced), Tarawa.
4th Marine Division (Reinforced), Saipan and Tinian.
3d Marine Division (Reinforced), Guam.
1st Marine Division (Reinforced), Peleliu, Ngesebus, and Palau.
Marine Aircraft Group 12, Philippines.
Assault Troops VAC (Reinforced), Iwo Jima.
1st Marine Division (Reinforced), Okinawa.
6th Marine Division (Reinforced), Okinawa.
Marine Observation Squadron 3, Okinawa.
2d Marine Aircraft Wing, Okinawa and Ryukyus.

U.S. ARMY AWARDS

4th Marines (Reinforced), Philippines.
4th Marines (Reinforced), Manila.
Marine Night Fighting Squadron 541, Philippines.

Marines were awarded 82 Medals of Honor, 1,026 Navy Crosses, 3,952 Silver Stars, 606 Legion of Merit, and 354 Navy and Marine Corps medals.

Sometime in 1952 the Marine Corps made a final calculation of its casualties during the Pacific War. Killed in action, died of wounds, missing and presumed dead, 21,242. A group that died in Japanese POW camps totaled 348. Another estimated 5,000 died in non-combat related situations. Marines who were wounded but survived during the war totaled 67,207.

Navy personnel assigned to the Marine Corps that were killed, died of wounds, or missing — chaplains, doctors, and enlisted Corpsmen — totaled 2,462 with another 5,153 wounded in action. Without those men of the Navy, the Marines would have found their job impossible. One other group that should be mentioned were the members of the Construction Battalions (SeaBees) who were also indispensable.

Abbreviations

AAA = AntiAircraft Artillery
ABMC = American Battlefield Monument Commission
ADC = Assistant Division Commander
Adm = Admiral
AG = Aircraft Group
Amph = Amphibious
Arty = Artillery
AWC = Army War College
BBD = Battleship Division
BG = Brigadier General
Bn = Battalion
Brig = Brigade
Btry = Battery
Capt = Captain
CG = Commanding General
CNO = Chief of Naval Operations
CO = Commanding Officer
Co = Company
Col = Colonel
CoS = Chief of Staff
Chem = Chemical
Comm = Communications
DB = Defense Battalion
Demo = Demolition
Det = Detachment
Div = division
DMO = Division Marine Officer
DOW = Died of Wounds
D, P&P = Director, Plans & Policies
DUKW = amphibian truck
EBS = Engineer Boat & Shore
Eng = Engineer (ing)
ExO = Executive Officer
FA = Field Artillery
FMO = Fleet Marine Officer
1stLt = First Lieutenant
G = General
Grp = Group

H&S = Headquarters & Service
Hdqs = Headquarters
HQMC = Headquarters Marine Corps
Hosp = Hospital
How = Howitzer
IG = Inspector General
IJA = Imperial Japanese Army
IJN = Imperial Japanese Navy
IMAC = I Marine Amph Corps
Inf = Infantry (USA Regiment)
InfDiv = Infantry Division (USA)
Intell = Intelligence
JAG = Judge Advocate General (USN)
JASCO = Joint Assault Company
KIA = Killed in Action

LANDING CRAFT

LC, Mk II = landing craft, mechanized
LCI = landing craft infantry
LCM = landing ship medium
LCP = landing craft Personnel
LCT = Landing Craft Tracked
LCV = landing craft vehicle
LCVP = vehicle or personnel
LST = landing ship tank
LSV = landing ship vehicle
LVT = landing Vehicle Tracked
LVT (A) = amphibian tank
LG = Lieutenant General
Lt = Lieutenant (USN)
LtCol = Lieutenant Colonel
Main = Maintenance
Maj = Major
Marines = Marine Regiment
MarDiv = Marine Division
MAW = Marine Air Wing; any variant
MB = Marine Barracks

MCS = Marine Corps Schools

MD = Marine Detachment (anyplace)

Med = Medical

Mess = Messenger

MIA = Missing in Action

MOS = Marine Officer's School

MP = Military Police

MT = Motor Transport

Mun = Munitions

NAD = Naval Ammunition Depot

NAS = Naval Air Station

NWC = Naval War College

ONI – Office of Naval Intelligence

Ops = Operations

Ord = Ordnance

Pion = Pioneer

Plt = Platoon

Prov = Provisional

QM = Quartermaster

RA = Rear Admiral

RB = Raider Battalion

RCT = Regimental Combat Team

Recon = Reconnaissance

Rein = Reinforced

2dLt = Second Lieutenant

Serv = Service

Sgt = Sergeant

SHIPS, AMPHIBIOUS

AK = cargo ship

AKA = attack cargo ship

AP = transport ship

APA = attack transport ship

Sig – Signal

SNLF = Special Naval Landing Force

Sp = Special

Sup = Supply

IIIMAC = III Marine Amph Corps

Tk = Tank

Trac = Tractor

Trp = Troop (Usually USA)

USA = United States Army

VAC = V Amphibious Corps

WIA = Wounded in Action

The numbers G-1 through G-5 mean the following:

"1" = Personnel   "4" = Logistics

"2" = Intelligence   "5" = Government

"3" = Operations

Preceded by: B = battalion, R = regiment, D = Division, C = Corps, and W = Wing. Eventually, by the end of the war, Marine units were using G for division and S for battalion, the same style utilized by the U.S. Army.

Biographies

With highest rank attained and Marine Division associated with

Ames, Evans Orchard, Major General. 3d MarDiv. Ames was born 12 April 1895 in Boston, Massachusetts. Studied law at the University of San Francisco. Appointed a 2dLt of Marines on 6 Feb 1917 from California. He served at many posts, including the MB, Guam, MB, Mare Island, Haiti, Quantico, the Philippines, and China. Attended MCS, served with MD's aboard ships, was FMO, Asiatic Fleet in 1940. Was at MCS, Quantico when the war began. Colonel and command of the 21st Marines in the 3d MarDiv at Cape Torokina, Bougainville on 1 November 1943. Became CoS and deputy commander of the Supply Services, FMF, Pacific, from March 1944 to January 1946. During that period he was promoted to brigadier general on 9 May 1945. He retired as a major general in February 1947. His decorations included two Legions of Merit and a Bronze Star.

Charles Dodson Barrett

Barrett, Charles Dodson. Major General. 3d MarDiv. Born on 16 August 1885, in Henderson, Kentucky. He was commissioned a 2dLt of Marines on 5 Aug 1909. He had the usual schooling at the MOS then postings at MB, Boston, sea duty with MDs aboard ships, at Vera Cruz, Mexico in 1914, aide to MGC Barnett, brief service with the AEF, then in Santo Domingo. Schooling at the *Ecole de Guerre* in Paris, MCS and instructor at Quantico, later at HQMC with War Plans Section, then Director, Office of Plans and Policies, after which at CNO from 1936 to 1939, CO, 5th Marines, and then Assistant Commandant of the Marine Corps in November 1941. Brigadier General in command of the 3d Brig at Samoa, followed by CG, 3d MarDiv until September 1943. CG, IMAC until he died from a fall on 8 October 1943. He was buried in Arlington National Cemetery with full honors. His decorations included a DSM as well as campaign medals.

Blake, Robert. Major General. 3d MarDiv. Blake was born on 17 August 1894, in Seattle, Washington. Earned a BA, on June 1917, from the University of California. He was appointed a 2dLt of Marines on 10 Aug 1917. Went to France as a platoon leader with the 17th Co, 1/5 and fought at Belleau Wood, Soissons, and St. Mihiel. Earned DSC, NC, and Silver Star, plus two Croix de Guerre for heroics on Hill 142 on 6 Jun 1918. Led the 66th Co, 1/5, at the Meuse River and into Germany 1918–1919. After the war he served at various posts; MB at Mare Island, Instructor at MCS in 1920; CO, MD, USS *Pennsylvania*; CO of 2/5, 2d Brig in Nicaragua and with the electoral mission in 1929;

HQMC; Embassy duties Paris and Madrid; MCS at Quantico; Special Service Squadron; ONI ; NWC in July 1940. CO of the Tenth Defense Bn; CoS of the 3d MarDiv until 1 Feb 1944. CO of the 21st Marines to 20 Apr 1944. In 1944, BG, retroactive to 2 Oct 1942. Deputy island commander of Guam, to May 1945. Deputy CoS of Tenth Army on Okinawa between June and November 1945 then CG of occupation forces. Various post-war posts, major general upon retirement in June 1949. His other decorations included Gold Star in lieu of 2d Navy Cross for Nicaragua, Purple Heart, Silver Star, Legion of Merit and Bronze Star. General Blake died on 2 October 1983.

Bourke, Thomas Eugene. Lieutenant General. 5th MarDiv. Born on 5 May 1896, in Severna Park, Maryland. A BS degree from St. John's College in 1916. Enlisted service in the US Army in 1916. Marine 2dLt on 18 Nov 1916. Naval station, St. Thomas, Virgin Islands, 1917–1919; Served at MB, Quantico; MD, American Embassy, Nicaragua; then MB, Washington, D.C.; Field Artillery School, Fort Sill, OK; 2d Brig in Nicaragua; 1931, War Plans Division at HQMC; Field Officers course and the AWC in June 1936; Pearl Harbor until July 1940; MB, San Diego; Colonel 1 Nov 1939; first CO of the 10th Marine Artillery Regt on 27 Dec 1940. BG in June 1943 while he was the CG of 24th Corps Artillery (US Army) 1943–1944. BG Bourke became the first CG of the 5th MarDiv at Camp Pendleton on 21 Jan 1944. Promotion to MG in February 1944. ADC with the division and served at Iwo Jima. CG of 5th MarDiv June 1945 into 1946 in the occupation of Japan. He retired in November 1946 and upon retirement was promoted to lieutenant general. His decorations included the Legion of Merit and two Bronze Stars. General Bourke died on 5 January 1978.

Bruce, Andrew D. USA, Major General. 77th InfDiv. A native of Missouri and a graduate of Texas A & M in 1916. Accepted commission as a 2dLt USA in June 1917. During World War I he was a member of the 2d Division's 5th Machine Gun Bn, of the 3d Infantry Brig. He served with the unit from the Troyon Sector (Verdun), at Chateau Thierry, Soissons, St. Mihiel, and at Blanc Mont. He served in the occupation of Germany. Following the war he held a mixed command, staff and school assignments. He was a LtCol upon the war's outbreak in Dec 1941 and headed the USA's tank-destroyer school at both Camp Meade and later at Camp Hood. He assumed command of the 77th Infantry Division 1 May 1943. He and it served at Guam in the southern landing with the 1st Prov Marine Brig. Then landed at Leyte and fought during the Philippines campaign. He and his division once again fought with Marines on Okinawa beginning in April 1945. LtGen Bruce retired from the US Army and died in 1969.

Buckner, Simon Bolivar, Jr., USA, Lieutenant General. 10th Army. Born in Mumfordville, Kentucky on 18 July 1886. Attended Virginia Military Institute then West Point, graduating in 1908. Service in Texas, Philippines, Washington, DC, Aviation section of Signal Corps at Kelley Field. Postwar was an instructor at West Point, Graduate of the Infantry School, C&GS School, Leavenworth, AWC, LtCol in 1932, Col in January 1937 and assumed command of 66th Inf. CoS of the 6th InfDiv October 1939, then to Alaska to command all army troops there. BG October 1940, MG August 1941, two regiments, Battalion of infantry and regt of artillery successfully retook Attu and Kiska. To Hawaii in June 1944 to organize and command the Tenth Army. Landed on Okinawa and led IIIMAC and USA XXIV Corps until KiA on 18 June 1945.

Carlson, Evans Fordyce. Brigadier General. 2d MarDiv. Carlson was born in Sidney, New

York on 26 February 1896. Son of a minister, he began a varied and exciting life which included service in the USA beginning in 1912 at age 16. Served in Hawaii and the Philippines and was a "top sergeant" when his four

year term ended. Again with the USA in 1914 Mexico; 2dLt USA in France, WiA; Occupation of Germany. Resigned commissioned and in 1922, enlisted as a private in the Marine Corps. Commissioned a 2dLt in 1923; duties included Culebrea; Pacific Fleet; tried aviation; in China from 1927 to 1929. Nicaragua in 1930; Navy Cross; then acted as chief of police, in Managua. In 1933 to China at MD, Legation Guard, Peiping; Chinese language student; MCS, back to China in 1937 as Observer with Chinese forces. To US in 1938 and resigned commission to write his observations. Reentered Corps in 1941 and in 1942 CO of 2d Raider Bn. Led raid on Makin with Gold Star in lieu of second Navy Cross. Same happened on Guadalcanal where he led Raider Bn on long march in November 1942 and was awarded another Gold Star. Tarawa as an observer, then WiA at Saipan, Gold Star in lieu

Evans Fordyce Carlson

of a second Purple Heart. On his retirement, 1 Jul 1946, he was advanced to brigadier general. His awards besides those listed included, Legion of Merit, Presidential Unit Citation with three stars, Victory medals from two wars, expeditionary medals galore. Carlson died at Portland, Oregon on 27 May 1947.

Cates, Clifton Bledsoe, General and 19th Commandant. 1st MarDiv; 4th MarDiv. Born on 31 August 1893, in Tiptonville, Tennessee. Educated at Missouri Military Academy and B.L. degree from University of Tennessee in 1916. A 2dLt of Marines on 24 May 1917. Joined the 96th Co, 2/6, as a platoon leader. To France and DSC at Belleau Wood, with an Oak Leaf Cluster for his refusal to leave his men though wounded and seriously gassed. WiA at Soissons; served at St. Mihiel, Blanc Mont, and the Meuse Argonne. Awards included several Silver Star citations and Navy Cross. Occupation of Germany. CO the Marine company in the 3d Composite Regt, sometimes known as "Pershing's Own." A aide to the President in 1920 and to MG Commandant George Barnett. His other appointments included Dept of the Pacific; recruiting duty at Spokane; and the ABMC in

Clifton Bledsoe Cates

March 1928.; Education included MCS, USA Industrial College, AWC; With troops, 7th Marines at Quantico, the 4th Marines at San Diego, later in Shanghai and the 6th Marines in China. LtCol Cates served War Plans Section, Div of Ops & Trng at HQMC; Director of the Basic School. May 1942. Col Cates, CO of the 1st Marines, at Guadalcanal, Legion of Merit with a combat "V." Commandant of the MCS at Quantico until June 1944. BG, 3 Apr 1943; MG 23 Jun 1944; CG, 4th MarDiv, fought the division in the Marianas and Iwo Jima. Awarded Navy DSM for Tinian, and a Gold Star in lieu of a second for Iwo Jima. Post-war he served in various capacities including as General Commandant of the Marines Corps 1 Jan 1948. On 30 Jun 1954 he retired as general. His other decorations included two Silver Stars, and two Purple Hearts. He died on 4 June 1970.

Cauldwell, Oscar Ray. Major General. 3d MarDiv. Born on 24 August 1892, in Nyesville, Indiana. Graduated the Naval Academy, commissioned a 2dLt of Marines on 3 Jun 1916. Duty with 1/6 already in France. Capt 26 Mar 1917 and CO of 95th Company, 1/6, at Verdun and Belleau Wood, WiA on 2 Jun 1918. Back for Soissons. Post-war he served as an instructor at MCS, Quantico until June 1921 and again in 1927. Education included Army Infantry School at Benning; MCS and USA C&GS at Leavenworth; NWC; AWC. Troop service First Brig in Haiti until February 1926. LtCol Cauldwell, assigned to the war plans section, FMF, then as a staff officer at the NWC to March 1942. Colonel on 1 July 1939. CO of the Third Marines to August 1942. BG on 26 Aug 1942 and ADC of the 3d MarDiv from 15 Sep 1943 to January 1944 participating in the Bougainville campaign. Back to US to become the CG of Training Command, FMF, from April 1944 to May 1946. Upon retirement in May 1946 he was promoted to major general. His decorations included the Silver Star and Purple Heart. Major General Oscar Ray Cauldwell died on 8 Sep 1959.

Craig, Edward A. Brigadier General. 3d MarDiv. Craig was born on 22 November 1896 in Danbury, Connecticut. Graduated St. John's Military Academy, Delafield, WI. Commissioned a 2dLt of Marines, 23 Aug 1917. Served with the Eighth Marine Regt; to Haiti, April 1919, 2d Prov Brig, Dominican Republic. Craig served in "every clime and place" including Olongapo, Philippine Islands, Shanghai and Peking China, Nicaragua plus sea duty with the troops. As an aide to MG Commandant Lejeune, classes at the MCS, Quantico, Staff positions with CO, Aircraft Battle Force, USS *Yorktown* and *Enterprise*, and the NAS, Pearl Harbor, July 1941. In World War II he was CO, 2d Pioneer Bn, 2d MarDiv. ExO, 9th Marines June 1942, CO Service Troops, 3d MarDiv, CO, 9th Marines, at Bougainville, November 1943 and at recapture of Guam, where he was awarded Navy Cross. Corps Operations Officer with VAC, planned and participated in the landing on Iwo Jima in February 1945. CoS of the Marine Training Command, San Diego. Post-war he served nobly at Pusan and Inchon as ADC of the 1st MarDiv. Retired a BG on 1 June 1951. In addition to the above listed awards Craig earned numerous expeditionary and campaign medals. Craig died on 11 Dec 1994 at his home in El Cajon, California, at the age of 98.

Crowe, Henry Pierson. Colonel. Born in Boston, Kentucky on 7 May 1899. Attended local schools and enlisted as a private in the Marine Corps on 28 Oct 1918. Served in Santo Domingo; in Nicaragua; and on sea duty, among many posts within the US. Was notable as a shooter on teams that won national cups and earned the distinctive and coveted Distinguished Marksman Medal. "Jim" Crowe, his nickname, was also a notable football player for the Quantico Marines. Became a commissioned Marine Gunner in September

1934, and later served in the Legation Guard, in Peiping, China, 1936. After his return served with 6th Marines then the 8th Marines. At Samoa in January 1942; promoted to captain then major; then to LtCol in January 1944. CO, Regimental Weapons Co on Guadalcanal. Known for saying "Goddamn it you'll never a Purple Heart hiding in a foxhole! Follow me!" They did. Later, CO 2/8 on Tarawa; at Saipan, where he was WiA. Stateside for repairs. Training Officer, FMF, Pacific. Post-war he served in many places including China with the 29th Marines and the Inchon landing in 1950. He remained active until his retirement in March 1960. Among his many awards was the Navy Cross at Tarawa and later in Korea two Legion of Merit's, one USA the other USMC. Jim Crowe died at age 92 on 27 June 1991.

Cumming, Samuel Calvin. Major General. 4th MarDiv. Born in Kobe, Japan, on 14 October 1895. Earned a BS, Virginia Military Institute in 1917, commissioned as a 2dLt of Marines on 10 Aug 1917. To France in 1917 with the 5th Marine Regt, platoon leader with the 55th Company, 2/5. WiA on 11 Jun 1918 at Belleau Wood. CO of 51st Co, 2/5, at Blanc Mont and again at the Meuse River campaign. His post-war services with troops included, 1st Brig of Marines in Haiti and the *Garde D'Haiti*; in China with the 3d Brig Jul 1928; MB, Navy Yard, Puget Sound, WA; MB, the Virgin Islands; MB, Quantico. Education at C&GS, Leavenworth, on 1 Aug 1932; then AWC; MCS, Quantico until 1936. FMO in the Scouting Force to May 1939. To HQMC, between 1939 and 1943. Col Cumming on 1 March 1941; CO of 25th Marines, 4th MarDiv, July 1943 to April 1944; Kawajalein Atoll, promoted to BG on 19 Sep 1942; ADC, 4th MarDiv, at Saipan and Tinian between April and September 1944. CoS of MB, HQMC, between September 1944 and November 1946; MG upon retirement that month. His decorations included 4 Silver Star medals, three during World War II, plus two Purple Hearts from wounds received in France. Major General Samuel C. Cumming died on 14 January 1983.

DeCarre, Alphonse. Major General. 2d MarDiv. DeCarre was born on 15 November 1892 in Washington, D.C., appointed as a 2dLt of Marines on 13 Nov 1913. 1st Brig of Marines, Haiti, 30 Jun 1915. MD, USS *New York,* landed at Oriente, Cuba in 1916. Captain 26 Mar 1917. CO of HDQS Co, Fifth Regt. France. At Belleau Wood, captured an enemy machine gun company of 180 officers and men. Earned a DSC and Silver Star citation. At Blanc Mont, earned French Legion of Honor and Croix de Guerre, with Palm. Post-war he served at MB, Philadelphia Navy Yard; Peking, China Legation Guard; FMO with Scouting Fleet; Haiti; various US posts with MB; and HQMC. Education at MCS, Quantico; and NWC. Colonel on 5 Sep 1938 and in June 1939 assumed duties of CO, the Naval Prison at Portsmouth, NH. CO of the MB at Puget Sound, WA, 21 June 1941— July 1942. BG retro to 22 Mar 1942. ADC of 2d MarDiv; then Acting CG Guadalcanal in 1942 (See Marston below) and CG of all Marine ground units in the continuing campaign. Major general upon retirement in June 1946. DeCarre's decorations besides those earned in France included the Navy Cross, DSM, Silver Star and Purple Heart plus numerous campaign medals. He died on 3 May 1977.

Del Valle, Pedro Augusto. Lieutenant General. 1st MarDiv. Born on 28 August 1893, in San Jose, Puerto Rico. Graduated from the Naval Academy in 1915 and accepted a commission as a 2dLt of Marines on 5 Jun 1915. Service with the troops; 1st Prov Marine Brig in Haiti; CO 9th Artillery Co. Santo Domingo; MD, USS *Texas*, British Grand Fleet in World War I; Quantico, adjutant of the 10th Marines; CO, MB, NAD, Dover, NJ; *Garde d'Haiti* ; Second

Brig of Marines in Nicaragua; sea duty; other duties: Aide to MG Joseph H. Pendleton; at HQMC between 23 Jun 1938 and 1941. Education: MCS, Quantico then as instructor; AWC; LtCol on 29 May 1934. Assistant Naval Attaché to Rome, Italy between October 1935 and June 1937. With Italian army invading Ethiopia. Wrote observations for the Navy and a commercial book. Colonel on 1 Jun 1939 then in Cuba, CO of the 11th Marines. Guadalcanal, 7 Aug 1942. BG as of 15 Sep 1942; hurt in airplane accident, returned to the US in 1943. Back to the Pacific to train and lead the artillery of the newly formed IIIMAC, retaking Guam in July 1944. MG, effective 10 Jan 1944, CG, 1st MarDiv on Pavavu for the next trial at Okinawa. Post-war, first Marine Corps IG. Retired, promoted to LG on 1 Jan 1948. His decorations included, among many others, DSM, Legion of Merit, Gold, and the Navy and Marine Corps Medal, plus numerous campaign medals. He died on 28 Apr 1978.

Pedro Augusto Del Valle

Edson, Merritt Austin. Major General. 1st MarDiv, 2d MarDiv. Born on 25 April 1897, in Rutland, VT. Attended the University of Vermont, member of the National Guard called to active duty on the Mexican border in 1916. Commissioned a 2dLt of Marines in September 1917. Platoon leader with B Co, 11th Marines, 5th Marine Brig. France in October 1918. Post-war, became a Naval Aviator on 12 Jun 1922. To Guam with Scouting Squadron 1 (VS-

Merritt Austin Edson

1M) until June 1925. Depth perception problems ended his aviation career. Varied career included MCS, Quantico; MD, USS *Denver*. CO of Coco River patrol, in Nicaragua, earned the Navy Cross. Depot of Supplies; HQMC; 30 Apr 1936, Senior Course at Quantico. 4th Marines at Shanghai, on 19 Jun 1937; HQMC in June 1939. Wrote *Small Wars Manual*. On 27 May 1941 formed the 1st Raider Bn out of the 1st Bn, 5th Marines. CO of the Bn to September 1942. At Guadalcanal earned the Medal of Honor for his leadership of the defense of the airfield on the night of 13–14 Sep 1942. Second Navy Cross for Tulagi. Colonel 21 May 1942 and BG 1 Dec 1943. 2d MarDiv as ADC, at Tarawa. CoS of FMF in Hawaii, planned Okinawa invasion. US Army were trying to force amalgamation of the Corps with the Army. Edson retired, to "speak his mind" in any collisions between the two services and the Congress. He retired to Vermont as major general on 1 August

1947. His other awards were numerous and included a Silver Star and two Legions of Merit with Gold Star. He died on 14 Aug 1955.

Erskine, Graves Blanchard. General. 3d MarDiv.
Born on 28 June 1897 in Columbia, Louisiana. Attended Louisiana State University; service in the Louisiana National Guard on the Mexican border. Commissioned a 2dLt of Marines on 15 Aug 1917, MOS, Parris Island, SC. To 79th Co, 2/6 as a Platoon Leader. Verdun and Belleau Wood, WiA on 6 June going to Bouresches. Captain on 19 July at Soissons; WiA at St. Mihiel. Silver Star medal. Hospitalized in the US in October 1918. Upon release, MB, Norfolk, VA; recruiting duty at Kansas City, MO; First Prov Brig in Haiti. Inter-wars he served at sea, with QM Dept; 2d Brig at Santo Domingo, attended USA Infantry School, Ft. Benning, GA, Instructor at MCS; Nicaragua with 2d Brig; instructor at Basic School, Philadelphia; C&GS School, Fort Leavenworth. Taught MCS, Quantico; Exo, MD, Legation Guard, Peiping, China, until 21 Jun 1937. To Quantico to begin a three year assignment as section chief at MCS. Colonel, 1942, CoS Amphibious Corps, Pacific Fleet in San Diego; duty in Alaska in July and August 1943. BG, the youngest in the Marine Corps; Deputy Commander

Graves Blanchard Erskine

of VAC. For meritorious services at Kawajalein, Saipan, and Tinian, received two Legion of Merit awards, both with combat "V." MG in September 1944 and in October, CG, 3d MarDiv, Iwo Jima, awarded DSM. Started vocational training schools for his Marines in order to facilitate those going back to civilian life. Became CG when 1st MarDiv returned from China. His post-war duties were considerable. Retired in June 1953 and took post as Asst to Sect of Defense. He died on 21 May 1973.

Roy Stanley Geiger

Geiger, Roy Stanley. General. Born on 25 January 1885 in Middleburg, Florida. Graduated from Florida State Normal, with LL.B. from John B. Stetson University in 1907. Enlisted in the Marine Corps on 2 Nov 1907. Commissioned a 2dLt of Marines on 5 Feb 1909. Sea duty and recruiting duty in NYC; Nicaragua, 1912 with 2d Bn, Artillery Co E, 1st Prov Regt. Camp Elliott in Panama; 1st Marine Brig, Cavite Navy Yard; Legation Guard, Peking, China until January 1916. Aviator trainee at Pensacola NS; Captain on 29 Aug 1916, Naval Aviator #49, (USMC Aviator # 5) in June 1917; CO of the Aeronautic Detachment, now First Marine Aviation Force, led command to Brest, France, CO, Sqd A, 1st Marine Aviation Force, a.k.a. Marine Day Wing of the Northern Bombing Group. Bombing runs over German positions France and Belgium. US on 12 Jan 1919, Navy Cross. Office of the JAG, USN. Education: CG&S, Leavenworth; MCS; AWC; NWC; Naval Attaché for Air with British in 1941. With troops: 1st Prov Brig in Haiti; MB, Quantico on 19 Feb 1921. With aviation: CO 4th Sqd, 1st Aviation Group at Brown Field, Quantico. Organized flight of four bombers from San Diego to Brown Field, a major feat. CO, Observation Sqd, VO-2M. Aviation Section, Division of Ops & Trng, HQMC. CO of Marine Corps aviation, East Coast Expeditionary Forces. Replaced deceased Col Thomas Turner 6 Nov 1931 at HQMC. CO of Aircraft One, FMF. Critical report on the performance of the RAF in general. On 20 Aug 1941, CO of the 1st Marine Air Wing; 1 October he was BG. Led "Cactus Air Force" to 4 Nov 1942, during the Solomon's campaign, awarded a Gold Star in lieu of a second Navy Cross. HQMC in May 1943 to become Director of Marine Aviation. MG Geiger as of 8 Sep 1942. Led the IMAC during the Bougainville operation. Awarded a DSM. Re-designated as IIIMAC in April 1944 which he led in the recapture of Guam in August 1944, then in October in taking Peleliu; awarded two Gold Stars in lieu of more DSM's. Led IIIMAC at Okinawa, and as Assistant 10th Army CG. CG upon Gen Buckner's death. In July 1945 CG, FMF, Pacific. Marine Corps representative at the Japanese surrender aboard the USS *Missouri*. HQMC, still in command of the FMF. His other decorations included the Distinguished Flying Cross and Air Medal in addition to numerous campaign medals. Geiger died on 23 Jan 1947 at the Naval Medical Center, Bethesda and was buried at Arlington National Cemetery. Promoted to general posthumously by the 80th Congress in January 1947.

Hall, Elmer Edwards. Brigadier General. 2d MarDiv. Born in Rocky Bar, Idaho, on 20 Apr 1890, attended the University of Oregon, 1910 to 1913. Hall enlisted as a private in May 1917; accepted a commission as a 2dLt on 15 Aug 1918. As of 25 Sep 1918 in France with the 13th Regt, until July 1919 when returned to the States. MB, Mare Island Navy Yard on 1 Oct1919 where he played football for the Mare Island Marines in the 1919 Rose Bowl game. Then a recruiting officer in Salt Lake City; playing for the Quantico Marines football team. Legation Guard, Nicaragua; With the 2d Brig of Marines, Nicaragua; sea duty June 1931. San Diego, Marine Officer's class for company junior officers. HQMC 1934. Two years later, major. June 1938 returned to Quantico as head coach of the football team; and graduate from the Field Officers Course. LtCol effective 8 Jul 1940 and colonel on 21 May 1942. CO of the Second Engineer Bn at Pearl Harbor; CO of the 18th Engineers, 2d MarDiv. CoS of the division then Regt commander of the 8th Marines at Tarawa. BG effective 1 Aug 1944 and on that same date he retired for incapacity based on service injuries. His awards included the Legion of Merit for several events, including Tarawa, between 1 May and 15 Dec 1943. Navy Commendation Medal. He died on 22 September 1958.

Hanneken, Herman Henry. Brigadier General. Born in St. Louis, Missouri, on 23 June 1893. Enlisted as a private of Marines in July 1914, and after five years attained the rank of Sgt. Appointed a 2dLt in December 1919 while in Haiti, after he had killed Peralte in a daring raid upon his headquarters. His reward was a Medal of Honor. Hanneken returned to the US in 1920 and schooling at MCS. After return from the Brazilian Exposition he went to sea. At the NAS, Lakehurst, NJ then the MB, Philadelphia Nav Yard. In December 1928 he was in Nicaragua with the 2d Brig and in a month had captured Sandino's CoS, Gen Jiron, earning a Navy Cross. More MCS, CO at NAD, Hingham, MA. More sea duty. With the 7th Marines at Guadalcanal, and recipient of a Silver Star. At Peleliu he was CO of the 7th Marines earning a Legion of Merit. Postwar he served as CO of the Staging Regt, Trng & Replacement Command, Amphib Forces, Pacific Fleet. To BG when he retired on 1 July 1948. In addition to the medals listed above, he held a Bronze Star, Presidential Unit Commendation, and numerous expeditionary and Hanneken died 23 August 1986 at the Veteran's Hospital, in LaJolla, CA.

Herman Henry Hanneken

Hart, Franklin Augustus. General. 4th MarDiv. Born on 16 September 1894, in Cuthbert, Georgia. Awarded a B.S. from Alabama Polytechnic Institute in 1915; served in the Alabama National Guard in Mexico, 1916. Accepted a commission as a 2dLt of Marines on 6 Feb 1917. Sea duty in the Atlantic Fleet. "Skipper" of Company B, 5th Machine Gun Bn, in France on 10 Nov 1918. Occupation duty in Germany. With the troops: 2d Brig, Santo Domingo; skipper of the 77th Machine Gun Co, 2/5, Quantico; adjutant to MB, Washington, D.C.; CO of three MDs aboard cruisers; ExO of MB, Norfolk Navy Yard; *Garde d'Haiti*; CO of First Bn, Eighth Marines. Administrative: HQMC in the War Plans Section, Division of Ops and Trng in 1937; Planning Section at Marine Corps Base, San Diego June 1939 — July 1940. Education: Army Infantry school, Benning; Instructor to Basic School, Philadelphia MB; Instructor, MCS, Quantico; Senior Course at MCS; AWC, until June 1939. Naval Attaché and Special Naval Observer in London from June 1941— October 1942, staff of the Chief, Combined Operations (British) as an instructor in amphibious warfare. Colonel on 1 Dec 1941. Dieppe Operation July 1942, specially commended for outstanding conduct by Lord Louis Mountbatten, Chief of Combined Operations. US in October, on the staff of the Commander-in-Chief, US Navy, as Chief of the Future Plans Section, from October 1942 to June 1943. CO of 24th Marines, 4th MarDiv until August 1944. Marshall's campaign led Combat Team 24 earned Navy Cross. BG and ADC of 4th MarDiv from August 1944 to September 1945. Saipan and Tinian islands awarded Legion of Merit. Awarded Bronze Star with Combat V, Iwo Jima. September 1945, Director of Reserves, at HQMC. His post-war duties were extensive. Retired in August 1954 after 37 years as a Marine and at that time advanced to general. His other decorations, include a Presidential Unit Citation with a Bronze Star, for Saipan and

Franklin Augustus Hart

Tinian; Navy Unit Commendation, Iwo Jima 1945; and various campaign medals. Hart died on 22 June 1967.

Hermle, Leo David. Lieutenant General. 5th MarDiv. Born on 30 June 1890 in Hastings, Nebraska. Attended University of California, receiving a B.A. and J.D. in 1917. Appointed a 2dLt of Marines on 27 Aug 1917. Joined the 74th Co, 1st Bn, 6th Marine Regt in France. At Verdun, his company nearly wiped out by gas attack on 13 April Captain Hermle, back at Blanc Mont and leading his company went up the hill on 3 Oct 1918. In Meuse River campaign Hermle's company went forward and surrounded a large number of Germans, capturing 115 and 17 machine guns. Awarded a DSC, Navy DSM and two Silver Star citations, plus the Legion of Honor (Chevalier) and the Croix de Guerre, Palm. WiA but served during the occupation of Germany. Post-war he served at various posts. Quantico; Mare Island; HQMC; *Garde d'Haiti*, Office, JAG, USN; at sea; ExO of the 6th Marines; Colonel on 1 April 1940, and CO of the Regt in May 1941. Education included: MCS, Field Officers Course; Company Officers Course; Instructor at the MCS; AWC, graduating in June 1939. He served in Occupation of Iceland, then CoS of the 2d MarDiv. Hermle was promoted to BG and ADC on 16 Sep 1942. Ashore at Tarawa, 20 November to 24 Nov 1943. MG effective on 16 Sep 1942. January — April 1944 Administrative Deputy at VAC followed by ADC, 5th MarDiv, April 1944 to June 1945. General Rocky entrusted Hermle with the final clean-up, which he led in person. Deputy Island Commander of Guam and the Marianas June 1945 to February 1946. Hermle retired a LG in September 1949. In addition to the decorations mentioned, also awarded the Legion of Merit for services during the Tarawa campaign. The Bronze Star with V, plus a Commendation Ribbon and two Purple Hearts. Hermle died on 21 January 1976.

Holcomb, Thomas. General and 17th Commandant. Born on 5 August 1879, in New Castle, Delaware. His schooling ended after high school. Accepted a commission as a Marine 2dLt on 13 Apr 1900. His early service during the Spanish-American War was non-

Thomas Holcomb

combatant. First Marine Bn in the North Atlantic Fleet to April 1903. Commanded first Marine rifle team, served on team in 1901, 1902, 1903, 1907, 1908, leading team to victory in 1911. Adjutant, 2d Regt, Olongapo, Philippines in April 1904. MD, Peking, 1905. HQMC; MB, Washington, DC. Aide at the White House; China as CO Legation Guard in Peking. Made attaché to the American Minister to allow him to study the Chinese language. Aide to MGC George Barnett. CO, 2d Bn, 6th Marine Regt. Toulon Sector, then to Chateau Thierry. His Bn was the first Marines to arrive Belleau Wood. LtCol, second in command to Col Harry Lee, 6th Regt. Occupation of Germany. Awarded Silver Star medal and three oak leaf clusters; French Legion of Honor, Chevalier, plus three Croix de Guerre, with Palm and Gen Pershing issued him a Meritorious Service Citation. Navy Cross and a Purple Heart. CoS to BG Butler, until summer of 1922. MB, Guantánamo Bay, Cuba. C&GS school at Ft Leavenworth, KS. "Distinguished Graduate" in June 1925. Division of Ops & Trng, Washington, until June 1927. CO Legation Guard, Peking, on 1 Aug 1927. Colonel on 22 Dec 1928, Senior Course at the NWC, the AWC at Carlisle, PA, graduating May 1932. CNO on several contract boards, and on special duties performed for the CNO. CO, MCS at Quantico, put into the curriculum theoretical exercises relating to amphibious warfare. Building program at Quantico, to replace antiquated World War I temporary buildings. December 1936 made MG Commandant. Nearly eight years in the post and, arguably, was the most important man to fill that position during the Marine Corps' history. LG in 1942 and, in retirement, a full general in 1944, both ranks being the first in USMC history. The president had extended him in that post. Even in 1943 when he reached the mandatory retirement age of 64, there were serious efforts to keep him in harness. Stepped down on 1 Jan 1944, with the award of a DSM and four stars to take into retirement. Decorations included numerous expeditionary and campaign medals. He died on 24 May 1965.

Hunt, Leroy Philip. General. 1st MarDiv, 2d MarDiv. Hunt was born on 17 March 1892, in Newark, New Jersey. Schools in Berkeley, CA and at the University of California from 1911 to 1913. Commissioned a 2dLt of Marines on 6 February 1917. To France as CO of the 17th Co, 5th Regt on 22 Aug 1917. Verdun Sector in mid-March 1918, Belleau Wood, then Soissons where Hunt was WiA. DSC at Blanc Mont, Navy Cross plus three Silver Star citations. Croix de Guerre with Palm, CO of 1/5 at the Meuse River crossing on the night of 10–11 November. Occupation forces in Germany. Inter-war years he served in various capacities: recruiting; staff of the MCS; 5th Marine Regt; sea duty; CO of the Western Mail Guard unit; 3d Marine Brig to China in 1927. Bn CO, 4th Marines in Shanghai. Post Adjutant, Quantico; MCS, Field Officer's Course. *Guardia Nacional*, Nicara-

Leroy Philip Hunt

gua, CO, Northern Area and I & O Officer. US in December 1932; HQMC, 6 Oct 1933; rejoined the 5th Marines. LtCol on 30 Jun 1935, awarded two Purple Heart Medals and two Silver Star Medals, for wounds and courage in France. Registrar and ExO of the MCI, CO of the MB at Eighth and Eye. Senior Course, NWC; FMO Battle Force; Colonel 1 Jan 1940. CO of Special and Service Troops, to Iceland on 6 Jun 1941. 1st MarDiv on 9 Apr 1942, CO, 5th Marines. On 22 Sep 1942, Col Hunt was replaced by another Marine hero, Col Merritt Edson. To US and promoted to BG retro to 16 Sep 1942. ADC 2d MarDiv at Tinian, to Sep 1944. MG on 1 Feb 1944, CG of 2d MarDiv. Occupied Kyushu, Japan, 15 Jun 1946. Postwar he became a LG then General. Retired on 1 Jul 1951. His decorations are lengthy. Besides his World War I awards; he earned numerous foreign and campaign medals. Hunt died in San Francisco, CA, of a heart attack on 8 February 1968.

Jones, Louis Reeder. Major General. 4th MarDiv, 1st MarDiv. Born on 29 June 1895, in

Philadelphia, Pennsylvania. Enlisted in the Marines in 1914, commissioned a 2dLt of Marines on 15 Aug 1917. To 75th Co, 1/6; France on 6 Oct 1917. WiA at Verdun. Platoon leader with the 83d Co, participated at Soissons. Three Silver Star citations, St. Mihiel the Croix de Guerre with Palm. Led the 83d Co during occupation. Post-war services included: Naval Proving Ground at Indian Head, MD; MCS, Company Officer's course. 2d Brig in Santo Domingo; QM Dept, San Diego; Assistant QM with the 3d Brig to China on 25 Mar 1927. 4th Marines in Shanghai; Hdqs, Dept of Pacific, 30 Dec 1929. Graduated Field Officer's course MCS; Purple Heart medal and two Silver Star medals for his services in France. Instructor at MCS and LtCol following 29 May 1936. Director, MCI, at Eighth and Eye, until May 1939; CO, 23d Marines; colonel on 1 Mar 1941. At Roi on 1 Feb 1944 and Afetna Point, Tinian, on 15 Jun 1944. Awarded Navy Cross for the period of the Saipan campaign. ADC of the 1st MarDiv in October 1944. BG, effective 4 Oct 1942. In North China with the 7th Marines at Tangku on 30 Sep 1945. Post-war he held several important posts until retirement in June 1949 as a major general. In addition to medals listed he earned a third (Army) DSM in China. Jones died on 2 February 1973.

Larsen, Henry Louis. Lieutenant General. Born on 10 December 1890, in Chicago, Illinois. Commission a 2dLt of Marines on 20 Aug 1913. MOS, Norfolk, VA, 29 Nov 1913. Vera Cruz in April 1914, 4th Regt at San Diego on 6 Nov 1915. Santo Domingo then to MD, USS *Pennsylvania* on 2 Dec 1916. Capt adjutant and CO with 3/5, AEF. St. Mihiel, again CO and led 3/5 through the next two battles, Blanc Mont, Meuse River campaign, and into Germany for the occupation. Navy Cross, and a Navy DSM plus three Silver Star citations and a Croix de Guerre, with Palm. Recruiting duty at Cleveland, OH, sea duty with MD, USS *New Mexico.* Infantry School at Fort Benning, GA; MCS Senior Course in May 1925. MB, Quantico; Adjutant and Inspector's Dept on 27 March and 2d Brig of Marines in Nicaragua on 31 Mar 1928. Gold star in lieu of a second Navy Cross while in Nicaragua. HQMC in December 1930. At the *Ecole Superieure de Guerre* in France for the years 1932–1934; to Quantico. On 4 Apr 1938 to HQMC, promoted to colonel. On 22 Jul 1940 to San Diego and to BG on 22 Dec 1941. CO the 2d Marine Brig. Not long after arrival at Samoa also made commander of the New Zealand portion of the islands as well as Wallis (France) Island. Samoan duty lasted until June 1943 and, during this time to MG on 28 Sep 1942, with a Legion of Merit award. CO of Camp Lejeune, between June 1943 and July 1944. Military governor of Guam on 15 Aug 1944 would earn him a second Legion of Merit award. Retired in November 1946, as a lieutenant general, effective 28 Sep 1942. He had earned numerous awards for courage, plus the usual campaign medals. Lieutenant General Henry Louis Larsen died on 2 October 1962.

Harry Bluett Liversedge

Liversedge, Harry Bluett. Brigadier General. 5th MarDiv. Born in Volcano, California, on 21 September 1894, attended the University of California, Berkeley. Actively involved in sports in international competition. Continued playing football and in Olympic events during his Marine career. Enlisted in May 1917, commissioned a 2dLt in September 1918. Fifth Brig in France. MB, Quantico in August 1919 then Second Prov Marine Brig, Santo Domingo. Aide to BG John H. Russell, and American High Commissioner, Port au Prince, Haiti. At MCS, Quantico Company Officers' Course. Quantico until detached for duty with Third Brig in China. Aide to CG, Hdqs, Dept of Pacific, San Francisco, May 1932. CO, MD, USS *California*, June 1933 to June 1935. Senior Course, MCS, then staff at Basic School, MB, Navy Yard, Philadelphia. First Marine Brig, Quantico, 1938. Inspector-Instructor, Fourteenth Bn, Marine Corps Reserve at Spokane, WA, 1940. LtCol in August 1940, to the Eighth Marines, 2d MarDiv at San Diego. In January 1942 to Samoa, CO of 2/8. Colonel in May 1942, August, CO of the Third Marine Raider Bn until March 1943. CO First Marine Raider Regt, earning a Navy Cross between 5 July and 29 Aug 1943 on New Georgia. In January 1944, 5th MarDiv January 1944 and CO of the Twenty-eighth Marines. Awarded a Gold Star in lieu of his Second Navy Cross. Occupation forces in Japan, then to San Diego in March 1946. Post-war Liversedge held several CG posts with Reserves, among many other roles. His decorations in addition to those above included a Bronze Star and a Presidential Unit Citation plus numerous campaign medals. He died at the Navy Medical Center, Bethesda, Maryland, on 25 November 1951.

Long, Earl Cecil. Major General. Born on 4 November 1883, in Clayton, New Jersey. Attended the University of California 1901- 1905. Accepted a commission as 2dLt of Marines 5 Aug 1909. MOS, Port Royal, SC. MB, Mare Island, CA on 17 Jan 1911. On 16 Jul 1912 joined MD, USS *Denver*. Ashore at Corinto, Nicaragua to support the August 1912 activities. At Vera Cruz in April 1914. With 4th Marine Regt at San Diego. First lieutenant and captain in 1916. June 1918 to the MB, San Diego. Detailed to the QM Dept, Jan 1920. On 4 May arrived for duty at the MB, Cavite, Philippine Islands. November 1922 with the 5th Brig of Marines at San Diego. On 1 Oct 1924 he was major at the MB, Quantico. With the 3d Brig in China in 1927. HQMC, on January 1929. In November duty at San Diego. On 25 Jun 1936 to San Francisco. Colonel on 7 May 1938. Remained in San Francisco and assumed responsibilities as the Marine Corps representative to the Golden Gate International Exposition in San Francisco 1938–1940. Long was made Assistant CoS for Supply at headquarters of Dept of the Pacific 1940–1943, promoted to brigadier general on 10 Sep 1942. CG of Supply Service, for IMAC and VAC in 1943 and through much of 1944. He was then promoted to Service Command, FMF, Pacific 1944–1945 and to major general, on 7 Jan 1944. CG of Marine Base San Diego 1945–1946. Retired in August 1946. Decorations included the Legion of Merit for 3 Jan 1943 to 6 Apr 1944 and a Gold Star for 6 Apr 1944 to 30 June 1945. Retired on 1 Nov 1946.

Marston, John, III. Major General. 2d MarDiv. Born on 3 August 1884, in Somerset County, Pennsylvania. Attended the University of Pennsylvania from September 1901 to June 1904. Commissioned a 2dLt of Marines on 25 May 1908. To MB, Honolulu, HI, on 10 Jan 1909. MB, Naval Prison, Portsmouth, NH. 1stLt on 25 Mar 1911. MD, USS *Michigan;* MB, Philadelphia Navy Yard on 23 Jun 1913. With 1st Brig of Marines, Vera Cruz in April 1914. Haiti in 1915. Joined *Garde d'Haiti* ; in November 1915 with Maj Smedley D. Butler in the attack upon Fort Rivière. On 22 May 1917 promoted to major. CO of the MD, Naval Academy, 31 Aug 1918. MB, Quantico 22 Jul 1920. CO of the MD, American Legation, Managua, Nicaragua, February 1922. MB, Quantico, MCS's Field Officer's Course. Office of the Chief Coordinator in Washington; the *Guardia Nacional*, in Nicaragua; MB, Quantico on 16 Feb 1931 as head of MCS. At HQMC, Director of Personnel 13 Apr 1934. Colonel 30 Jun 1935. Peiping, 13 Mar 1937 and CO of US Marine Forces in North China. BG on 1 Oct 1939 at San Diego. On 31 Mar 1940 CoS of the Dept of the Pacific. CG 2d MarDiv in 1941. In June 1941 to Iceland to command the 1st Prov Brig of Marines. MG on 20 Mar 1942 and became CG of 2d MarDiv between 1 Apr 1942 and 1 Apr 1943. In order to maintain a relationship with the US Army, however, Marston was not allowed to accompany his division to Guadalcanal in late 1942. To the US to command the Dept of the Pacific, from 1943 to 1944. CG of Camp Lejeune from 1944 to mid-1946 and then retired in August 1946. Died on 25 November 1957.

Nimmer, David Rowan. Major General. Born on 14 October 1894, in St. Louis, Missouri. Enlisted service 1912–1918 and was commissioned a 2dLt of Marines in 1918. Served as a captain in France and later in the occupation of Germany with the Headquarters Co, 5th Machine Gun Bn. Resigned his commission in 1919 but returned to active duty at the MB, Quantico as a captain on 30 April 1921. Remained there until 29 Apr 1925 when he went aboard the USS *Mississippi* to command the MD. Instructor at MCS June 1927–1929. CO MD USS *Pittsburgh* in 1929 then duty with the Fourth Marine Regt in Shanghai 1929–1930, the American Legation in Peking, China 1931–1932, where he learned the Russian language, and as assistant naval attaché in Moscow 1932–1934. Operations officer with the 1st Marine Brig, 1937–1939. CO of Marine Corps Base, Cuba 1939–1942 then with the Ninth Defense Bn (Pacific) October 1942-April 1943. Duty with the Joint War Plans Committee of the JCS, Commander in Chief United States Fleet 1943–1944. Brigadier general in February 1944. Commander of IIIMAC Artillery 1944–1945. Major general upon retirement in July 1947. Decorations included the Legion of Merit. Died on August 23, 1975.

Noble, Alfred Houston. Lieutenant General. 3d MarDiv. Born on 26 October 1894, in Federalsburg, Maryland. Earned a BA from St. John's College in 1917. Commissioned a 2dLt of Marines in 1917. Served as the "skipper" of the 83d Co, 3/6 in France at Belleau Wood, through the Meuse Argonne earning a Navy Cross, DSC, 2 Silver Stars and Croix de Guerre, with Silver Star. Then occupation duty in Germany until July 1919. Duty in the Virgin Islands 1919–1922. Instructor with MCS, 1925–1927 and 1930–1932. CoS of 1st Marine Brig in Haiti 1932–1934. Assistant commandant of MCS 1937–1939. Bn commander in 5th Marines 1940–1941, Brigadier general in August 1940. Director of the plans and policy division at HQMC in 1941. CoS of 3d MarDiv 1942–1943. CoS and Deputy Commander of the IMAC during the Treasury Islands occupation, Choiseul Island landing and beachhead at Empress Augustas Bay, Bougainville. CoS of IMAC 1943–1944. ADC 3d MarDiv January 1944. CG of Training Command at Camp Lejeune 1945–1946. Pearl Harbor as CG of the Marine Garrison Forces, 14th Naval District. Tientsin, China, in August, 1946, as ADC of the 1st MarDiv, returned to the United States to take command of the Troop Training Unit, Amphibious Forces, Pacific Fleet, at Coronado, CA. His post-war

Alfred Houston Noble

assignments were varied and extensive. CG, Marine Corps Recruit Depot, Parris Island. CG of the MB at Camp Pendleton, CA and CG of the Dept of the Pacific; CG, FMF, Atlantic. Retired a lieutenant general in November 1956. Other decorations included two Legions of Merit, two Silver Stars and the Commendation Ribbon. Died on 27 September 1983 at La Jolla, CA.

Charles Frederick Berthold Price

Price, Charles Frederick Berthold. Lieutenant General. 2d MarDiv. Born on 18 September 1881, in Hamburg, Germany of American parents living abroad. Earned a Civil Engineering degree from Pennsylvania Military College in 1902. Commissioned a 2dLt of Marines in 1906 followed by education at the School of Application, Annapolis, MD. Expeditionary duty in Cuba September 1906–December 1908, Nicaragua and Panama Canal Zone 1909–1910 and the occupation of Vera Cruz in 1914. Bn commander in the 11th Marines, 5th Marine Brig, AEF in 1918. Instructor at MCS in 1923. Overseas duty with the American Legation in Peking 1925–1927, the American Electoral Mission in Nicaragua 1928 and 1930–1932, and with the Fourth Marines at Shanghai, China April 1935–November 1938. Especially noted and awarded a DSM for his superb handling of a delicate situation as the Japanese and Chinese struggled about Shanghai. Assigned to the Naval Examining Board at HQMC, 1938–February 1941. Brigadier general on 1 August 1940 while serving as a member of the Naval Examining Board at HQMC. CG of the Dept of the Pacific February–November 1941 then 2d MarDiv between November 1941 and April 1942. Major general in February 1942. Commanded the Defense Force, Samoan Group April 1942–May 1944. Commander of San Diego Area and Marine Training and Replacement Command May 1944–1948. Lieutenant general upon retirement on 25 October 1948. Decorations included the DSM and Legion of Merit, plus numerous campaign medals. Died in January 1954.

Puller, Lewis Burwell. Lieutenant General. Born in West Point, Virginian on 26 June 1898. Educated at Virginia Military Institute until enlisting as a Marine private in August 1918. Reduction in Corps after World War I reduced him to civilian. On 30 June 1919 he reenlisted and

Lewis Burwell Puller

served in Haiti, with the *Garde d'Haiti* as a officer. Commissioned a 2dLt of Marines in March 1924 and served at various posts in the US and at Pearl Harbor. In December 1928 he joined the *Garida Nacional,* Nicaragua where he was to earn plaudits and a Navy Cross. Infantry School at Benning, then back to Nicaragua and another Navy Cross. His next major assignment was with the MD, Peiping, China where he would command the "Horse Marines." Then sea duty, instructor at Basic School, and back to sea. With the 4th Marines in Shanghai and to the USS in August 1941. CO of 1/7; assigned to the 3d Brig, then in September 1942 joined the 1st MarDiv at Guadalcanal. Third Navy Cross for defense of Henderson Field. ExO of the 7th Marines at Cape Gloucester and another Navy Cross. Col Puller became CO of the 1st Marines and led it to Peleliu where it was shattered. Back to the US at Camp Lejeune and CO of the Trng Regt. Postwar he served in Korea as CO of the 1st Marines; BG and ADC of the 1st MarDiv. MG in September 1953 and illness forced retirement as a LG 1 Nov 1955. His awards were numerous. Five Navy Crosses plus many decorations, foreign and domestic. He died at his home in Virginia on 11 October 1971.

William Edward Riley

Riley, William Edward. Lieutenant General. 3d Mar-Div. Born in Minneapolis, Minnesota, 2 February 1897. He attended the College of St. Thomas at St. Paul and in June, 1917, reported for active duty at Winthrop, MD as a 2dLt in the Marine Corps. To France three months later as the "skipper" of the 74th Co, 1/6. At Verdun and Belleau Wood where he earned a Silver Star and Oak Leaf cluster in lieu of a second, Croix de Guerre with Gilt star. Twice wounded in action at Belleau Wood and Soissons, requiring evacuation to the United States in December 1918. Between wars his duties included service in Haiti, Puerto Rico, Santo Domingo, and Cuba. He was graduated from the Army Infantry School, and C&GS School, and the NWC. In 1940, he went to sea as FMO, Atlantic Fleet, remaining until 1942, when he joined the War Plans Division of Admiral King's staff at Washington. A year later, he entered a series of important assignments in the Pacific which culminated in being CG of the 3d MarDiv. Then Director, Division of Public Information and Division of Recruiting at HQMC, June 1946 to 31 May at which time he was detached to the 2d MarDiv, Camp Lejeune, NC. Held important post-war positions with the UN in Palestine and with State Dept. Retired from active duty, 31 May 1951. In addition to the World War I medals, he also earned a DSM, Legion of Merit and Letter of Commendation with Ribbon, plus numerous campaign medals from both wars and expeditionary services. He died 28 April 1970, at the US Naval Hospital, Annapolis, Maryland.

Robinson, Ray Albert. General. 3d MarDiv, 5th MarDiv. Born on 1 June 1896, in Los Angeles, California. Attended the University of Southern California before enlisting in the Marine Corps on 21 May 1917. Commissioned on 9 Oct 1917. Served with the 13th Marine Regt in France September 1918 to July 1919 partly as Aide-de-Camp to Brigadier General Smedley D. Butler. Duty at MB, Pearl Harbor September 1921-December 1923 then on the staff of the CG Third Marine Brig, Shanghai January 1927-March 1929, also Brigadier General Smedley D. Butler. Quantico, as CO, MD, President Hoover's summer camp. September 1929, MCS then sea duty in October 1930, then MB at the Puget Sound Navy Yard, Bremerton, WA. At Quantico, as Post Maintenance Officer and Safety Engineer, then Senior Course MCS in August 1938. Commander of Marine Forces North China and the embassy detachment at Peking May 1939-June 1941. Officer in Charge of the personnel section, headquarters Marine Corps June 1941-January 1944. Brigadier general in April 1943. CoS of 3d Marine Division January–October 1944 then 5th Division October 1944-June 1945. ADC of 5th Marine Division June 1945-March 1946. Numerous post-war assignments included CG, 2nd Marine Division

Ray Albert Robinson

June 1950-December 1951 and CG of FMF, Atlantic General on retirement in November 1957. His awards included a Legion of Merit with Combat V," a Gold star in lieu of a second Legion of Merit and the Bronze Star Medal, the Presidential Unit Citation Ribbon with one bronze star; the Navy Unit Commendation Ribbon with one bronze star; various expeditionary and campaign medals from World War I and World War II. He died in Seattle, Washington, on 26 March 1976.

Rockey, Keller Emrick. Lieutenant General. 2d MarDiv, 5th MarDiv. Born on 27 September 1888, in Columbia City, Indiana. Earned a B.S. from Gettysburg College in 1909. Attended Yale University Forestry School 1910–1911. Commissioned a 2dLt of Marines on 18 Nov 1913. Served with various MD's at sea. Major in 1918, and served as Adjutant, 1st Bn, 5th Marines, 2d Division in the AEF during World War I. Earned a DSC, Navy Cross, and Silver Star at Belleau Wood, June 1918. Assigned as major in the *Garde d'Haiti* 1919–1922. Then to HQMC, and at MCS and then graduated from C&GS School in 1926. Instructor at MCS 1926–1928. CO of 1st Bn, 11th Marines in Nicaragua 1928–1929. Staff officer with the Battle Force 1937–1939. Duty in the O, CNO 1939–1941. CoS of 2d MarDiv, 1941–1942. Brigadier general in August 1942, major general in August 1943. Director of Plans and Policy division at headquarters US Marine Corps 1943–1944. CG of 5th MarDiv at Iwo Jima, 1944–1945 and VAC 1945–1946, then IIIMAC in North

Keller Emrick Rockey

China. Assignments after the war included CG of FMF, Atlantic 1947–1949 and Dept of the Pacific 1949–1950. Retired as lieutenant general in September 1950. Additional decorations included a Gold Star in lieu of a second Navy Cross in Nicaragua and two DSMs, North China and Iwo Jima. He died on 6 June 1970 in Harwich Port, MA at age 81. Following services he was buried at Arlington National Cemetery.

Rogers, William Walter. Major General. 4th MarDiv. Born on 25 December 1893, in Thorntown, Indiana. Earned a B.S. from Miami University of Ohio in 1914. Enlisted service as a Cpl of Marines 1917–1918 in the AEF. Commissioned on 15 August 1918. Seriously wounded in the Blanc Mont battle on 7 Oct 1918. Resigned as a 1stLt on 15 Aug 1919. Reentered on 2 Apr 1921 as a captain. Recruiting at Pittsburgh, PA then QM Dept on 20 Mar 1924, at MB, Quantico, then Parris Island. Then to Nicaragua with the *Gardia Nacional* in December 1927 and with the 2d Brig in August 1929. MB, Quantico then Washington Navy Yard in 1930, now listed as an interpreter in French and Spanish. During this period he was awarded a Purple Heart and two Silver Stars for work in France. Serving with 7th Marines in November 1932. Major on 29 May 1934. Attended and graduated from Army Industrial College and MCS Field Officer's Course. Graduated NWC then DMO, Battleship 2 in June 1938. Then LtCol and at Quantico in 1939. Assigned to the plans and policies division at HQMC 1940–1943. CoS of the 4th MarDiv between August 1943 and August 1944. Duty with VAC 1946. Brigadier general in January 1945, major general upon retirement in December 1946. Decorations included the Distinguished Service Medal, two Silver Stars and the Purple Heart. Died on 15 October 1976.

William Henry Rupertus

Rupertus, William Henry. Major General. 1stMarDiv. Born in Washington, D.C., on 14 November 1889. Enlisted service in the District of Columbia National Guard 1907–1910. Graduated from the United States Revenue Cutter Service School in 1913 and commissioned in the Marine Corps. MOS at Norfolk then served with the MD aboard the USS *Florida* in December 1915. August 1916 1stLt and captain 26 Mar 1917 still on *Florida*. Major in July 1918 and at MB, Quantico. Served in Haiti 1920–1924. Graduated from C&GS School, in 1926. Duty with the American Legation in Peking 1929–1933 then the Fourth Marines in Shanghai 1937–1938. Commanded the MB in Washington, D.C. 1938–1940. ADC of the 1st MarDiv 1941–1943. Brigadier general in January 1942, major general in July 1943. CG of the 1st MarDiv July 1943-November 1944. Commandant of MCS until his death on 25 March 1945. Decorations included the Navy Cross earned at Guadalcanal.

Schmidt, Harry, General. 4th MarDiv. Born on 25 September 1886, in Holdrege, Nebraska. Attended Nebraska State Normal College. Commissioned a 2dLt of Marines on 17 Aug 1909. MOS then stationed at MB, Guam January

1911- September 1912. Duty with the expeditionary force in China November–December 1911. Served in the Philippines October 1912-April 1913. Instructor at MCS 1923–1926. Duty with the Sixth Regt in China April- September 1927 then the Second Brig in Nicaragua February 1928-June 1929. Graduated from Command and General Staff School in June 1932. Regt pay officer with the Expeditionary Force, Shanghai September 1934-April 1936. CoS of Second Marine Brig, Shanghai June 1937-June 1938. Executive and personnel officer at headquarters, Marine Corps July 193 8-January 1942 then assistant to the commandant of the Marine Corps January 1942-August 1943. Brigadier general in October 1941, major general in September 1942. CG of 4th Marine Division August 1943-July 1944 then V Amphibious Corps July 1944-February 1946. Assignments after the war included CG of Marine Training and Replace-

Harry Schmidt

ment Command February 1946-July 1948. General upon retirement in July 1948. Decorations included the Navy Cross, three DSMs, the Legion of Merit and Bronze Star. Died on 10 February 1968.

Shapley, Alan. Lieutenant General. 6th MarDiv. Born 9 February 1903, in New York City. US Naval Academy, graduating on 2 Jun 1927, commissioned as a 2dLt of Marines. He coached and played on the All-Marine Corps football teams of 1927 and 1928 among other sports. Basic School, Philadelphia Navy Yard. MB, Pearl Harbor January 1929. San Diego, CA; CO, MD, the USS *San Francisco*, detached in June 1936; Quantico aide to the CG of the MB. Captain in July 1936, MCS at Quantico until May 1938. Operations, Training and Intelligence Officer of the Dept of the Pacific until May 1940. CO, MD. USS *Arizona*. Awarded Silver Star Medal for heroism on 7 Dec 1941. Personnel officer to the Amphibious Corps, Pacific Fleet; IMAC in October 1942; CO, 2d Raider Bn from March to September 1943. CO, Second Marine Raider Regt at Bougainville, earning the Legion of Merit with Combat "V." LtCol Shapley given command of the First and Second Marine Raider Regt's from which he organized the Fourth Marines, which he commanded at Emirau, Guam, and Okinawa. Besides the Navy

Alan Shapley

Cross for heroism on Guam, awarded a second Legion of Merit with Combat "V" for outstanding service at Okinawa from April to June 1945. Col Shapley returned to the United States in July 1945 to become Assistant Inspector in the Inspection Division at HQMC. Accompanied Adm William F. Halsey on an official goodwill tour of Central and South America from June to August 1946. His post-war services were extensive. Schooling and later in Korea, with several appointments with the 1st MarDiv until his retirement on 1 July 1962. His other medals Shapley died 13 May 1973 at the National Naval Medical Center, Bethesda, Maryland.

Shepherd, Lemuel C. General and 20th Commandant. 6th MarDiv. Born at Norfolk, VA on 10 February 1896. Graduated from Virginia Military Academy and selected the USMC for his commission as 2dLt on 11 Apr 1917. After Basic School, assigned to the 5th Marine Regt. 4th Platoon leader in the 55th Company. WiA several times at Belleau Wood and fought at St. Mihiel, and WiA at Blanc Mont. Occupation of Germany. Earned DSC with Oak Leaf Cluster, and Navy Cross, a Silver Star, Purple Heart with two clusters, several French and other foreign decorations. Aide to the Commandant. Shepherd had a variety of post-war assignments including the Brazilian Exposition; sea duty; expeditionary duty in China; MCS; the *Garde d'Haiti*; Marine Corps Institute; NWC in 1936–37. As LtCol at Quantico. Col Shepherd on 16 Mar 1942, CO, 9th Marines. BG & ADC to the 1st MarDiv in

Lemuel C. Shepherd

which he served at the Cape Gloucester operation and awarded a Legion of Merit. In May 1944, CG, 1st Prov Marine Brig, which included the 4th and 22d Marines. Assault on Guam at southern beaches, and awarded a DSM. When the 29th Marines arrived on Guadalcanal 7 Sep 1944, and with the 1st Prov Brig, he was authorized to form what became the 6th MarDiv. The division became part of the IIIMAC to land on Okinawa on 1 April 45. The victory was eventually completed and later, in North China, MG Shepherd accepted the surrender of the Japanese at Tsingtao, China. In post-World War II he eventually became a general and 20th Commandant of the Marine Corps. He retired 1 January 1956. Other awards included two Gold Stars in lieu of DSM's, Oak Leaf Cluster in Lieu of Legion of Merit, Silver Star Oak Leaf Clusters, Bronze Star plus numerous campaign medals. He died at age 94 in 1990.

Shoup, David Monroe. General and 22d Commandant. 2d MarDiv. Born 30 December 1904 in Battle Ground, Indiana. DePauw University, BA, 1926, commissioned a Marine 2dLt on 20 Jul 1926. Services included with 6th Marines in Tientsin, China. Pensacola, FL; and San Diego, CA, June 1929 to September 1931. Sea duty; MB, San Diego; Puget Sound Navy Yard, Bremerton, WA; Civilian Conservation Corps in Idaho and New Jersey June 1933 to May 1934. 4th Marines in Shanghai and at the American Legation in Peiping in

1934. Junior Course, MCS, Quantico, in July 1937. Instructor for two years. 6th Marines in San Diego. Major and ordered to Iceland with the 6th Marines in May 1941. Regt Ops Officer, then in October 1st Marine Brig Ops Officer. CO, 2/6 February 1942. With 2/6 to San Diego. In July 1942, Asst Ops & Trng Officer of the 2d MarDiv. Observer with the 1st MarDiv on Guadalcanal in October 1942 and observer with the 43d Army Division on Rendova, New Georgia, in the summer of 1943, earning a Purple Heart in the latter operation. Colonel on 9 Nov 1943. G-3, Ops & Trng Officer of the 2d MarDiv, planned assault on Tarawa, while commanding all ground troops ashore earned him Medal of Honor and his first Legion of Merit with Combat "V" and a second Purple Heart between 20–22 November 1943. He was also awarded the British DSO for this action. In

David Monroe Shoup

December 1943, CoS of the 2d MarDiv. For the battles for Saipan and Tinian, he was awarded second Legion of Merit with Combat 'V." Returned to the United States in October 1944. Logistics Officer, Division of P & P, HQMC. Following the end of the war he held various posts inside and outside the US. On 2 Nov 1959, now lieutenant general and assigned duties as CoS, HQMC. Shoup was nominated by President Eisenhower on 12 Aug 1959 to be the 22d Commandant of the Marine Corps, promoted to 4 star rank. On 21 Jan 1964, shortly after his retirement, Gen Shoup was awarded the DSM by President Lyndon B. Johnson for exceptionally meritorious service as Commandant of the Marine Corps. General Shoup retired to Arlington, Virginia, in 1963. He died on 13 January 1983 after a long illness and was buried in Arlington National Cemetery.

Silverthorn, Merwin Hancock. Lieutenant General. Born on 22 September 1896, in Minneapolis, Minnesota. Attended the University of Minnesota 1914–1917. Enlisted service 1917–1918. Commissioned in 1918. Served in the AEF 1918–1919. Served at DC, Mare Island, and Quantico, after the war. Duty with the 1st Brig Marines and the *Garde d'Haiti* 1923–1926. Then to MB, Guam as Assistant QM in 1930. Detached in January 1932, and for the next several years served at various posts and stations in this country and completed various courses at USA and USMC schools. Instructor at MCS 1936–1937. Graduated from the NWC in 1938. Force Marine

Merwin Hancock Silverthorn

officer with the Scouting Force 1939–1941. Brigadier general in June 1942. Member of the Joint US Strategic Committee, JCS 1942–1943. Major general in April 1943. CoS of IIIMAC 1944–1945 then FMF, Pacific 1945–1946. Assignments after the war included assistant commandant of the Marine Corps 1950–1952. Retired as lieutenant general in July 1954 a veteran of more than 37 years in the Marine Corps Decorations from service in World War I included the Navy Cross, DSC, and two Silver Stars. In World War II, the DSM, Legion of Merit, Commendation Ribbon and Purple Heart. General Silverthorn died 14 August 1985 at Bethesda Naval Hospital and was buried with full military honors in Arlington National Cemetery in August of 1985.

Smith, Holland McTyeire. General. Born on April 20, 1882, in Seale, Alabama. Graduated from Alabama Polytechnic Institute in1901. Earned an LL.D. from the University of Alabama in 1903. Smith practiced law two years in Montgomery but decided that law was not for him. He accepted a commission as a 2dLt of Marines in 1905. Completed the School of Application (Basic School) in Annapolis and went for duty in the Philippines 1906–1908 and again between 1912 and 1914, Panama 1909–1910, and in the Dominican Republic 1916–1917, during which he earned the nickname "Howlin' Mad" Smith. Went to France as CO of the 8th Machine Gun Co, 5th Marine Regt. Saw combat in France with the 4th Brigade and 2d Division campaigns in World War I. Also served with the I Corps, 1st US Army in July 1918 as Assistant Operations Officer. Graduated from the NWC in 1921. In Washington in War Plans

Holland McTyeire Smith

Section, Office of Naval Operations and served on the Joint Army & Navy Planning Committee. Leaving DC in May 1923 he served as FMO aboard both the USS *Wyoming* and *Arkansas*. At HQMC where he was involved with planning joint Army and Navy maneuvers. Expeditionary duty in Haiti as CoS. Student at MCS, Quantico and then CO MB, Washington Navy Yard until January 1935. Then CoS Dept of the Pacific, followed by Assistant to the Commandant at HQMC, April-September 1939. Brigadier general in August 1939. CO of the 1st Marine Brig September 1939-August 1942. Major general in February 1941. CG of Amphibious Force, Atlantic Fleet, then Pacific Fleet September 1942-July 1944. Lieutenant general in February 1944. CG of FMF, Pacific July 1944-July 1945 then Camp Pendleton July 1945 until retirement as general in August 1946. Author of *Coral and Brass,* 1949. Decorations included the Purple Heart. Died on 12 January 1967.

Smith, Julian Constable. Lieutenant General. Born on 11 September 1885. Earned a B.A. from the University of Delaware in 1907. Accepted a commission as a 2dLt of Marines in 1909. Basic training at the MB, Port Royal, SC. Then to the MB, Philadelphia Navy Yard. Served at Camp Elliott in the Canal Zone 1912–1914, then at Vera Cruz in April 1914 and to Haiti in 1915 followed by Santo Domingo 1915–1916. NWC, Newport, RI and then instructor at MCS 1918–1919. CO of 2d Machine Gun Bn, 6th Marines in Cuba in 1919. Returned to HQMC. At MB, Quantico in August 1920. Sea-duty with the Scouting Fleet; then back to HQMC. Course at C&GS School, Ft. Leavenworth followed by again instructor at MCS 1928–1930. CoS of the Nicaraguan National Guard detachment 1930–1933 at which time he earned a Navy Cross. Operations officer with 7th Marines 1933–1934. Member, then director of operations and training division at HQMC, 1935–1938. CoS of the 1st Brig of Marines, 1938–1940. CoS to CG of the MB at Quantico 1940–1941. Brigadier general in March 1941, major general in October 1942. CG of FMF Training Schools, October 1942-May 1943, 2d MarDiv, 1943–1944 and then CG of expeditionary troops of the Third Fleet April-December 1944, which

Julian Constable Smith

captured the Palau Islands. Commander of the Dept of the Pacific then Marine Corps Recruit Depot at Parris Island 1944–1946. Lieutenant general upon retirement in December 1946. Decorations also included two DSM's. Died on 5 November 1975.

Smith, Oliver Prince. General. 1st MarDiv. Smith was born on 26 October 1893, in Menard, Texas. Graduated from the University of California at Berkeley in 1916. Accepted a commission as a 2dLt of Marines in May 1917. First service was at the MB, Guam then at the MB, Mare Island; with the MD aboard the USS *Texas*, followed by duty at HQMC for duty with the personnel section. He joined the *Garde d'Haiti* in 1928 then returned in June 1931. Field Officer's course at Fort Benning, and instructor at MCS, Quantico 1932–1933 and again 1936–1939. Staff officer with FMF, Pacific, 1939–1940. In between he served with the 7th Marines; the Embassy at Paris, France, and between November 1934 and July 1936 attended the *Ecole Superieure de Guerre*. At Quantico, instructor at MCS, then in 1939 to the west coast as operations officer with FMF, at San Diego. Commanded 1/6 between 1940–1942. At HQMC, 1942–1943. Became CO of the 5th Marines then assistant CG in of the division January-November 1944. Brigadier general in April 1944. Deputy CoS of Tenth Army November 1944-June 1945 in which he served on Okinawa. Commandant of MCS June 1945-April 1948. Primary post-war position was as CG, 1st MarDiv; in June 1950, he led the division in Korea, at its most difficult period. Retired as general in September 1955. Decorations included the DSC, two DSM's Silver Star, two Legions of Merit and the Bronze Star. Died on 25 December 1977.

Thomas, Gerald Carthrae. General. 1st MarDiv. Thomas was born on 29 October 1894, at Slater, Missouri, attended Illinois Wesleyan University, 1915–1917, then enlisted in the Marine Corps on 28 May 1917. Sergeant Thomas saw action with the 6th Marines at Verdun, Belleau Wood, Soissons, and at Blanc Mont. Commissioned a 2dLt in September 1918, after occupation of Germany, to the United States in July 1919. Post-war services included:

1st Marine Brig in Haiti; MB, Quantico, various courses, USMC and USA including the Infantry Officers School, Benning, and C&GS School at Fort Leavenworth. Instructor, Basic

School, Philadelphia Navy Yard; MCS, Quantico. To China in July 1935, MD at the American Embassy in Peiping. In May 1941, Thomas to Cairo, Egypt, as a naval observer with the British. Asst then Ops Officer of the 1st MarDiv in March 1942. Colonel Thomas was appointed CoS of the division in September 1942, at Guadalcanal. July 1943, CoS of IMAC. Promoted to BG in December 1943 and after participating in operation at Bougainville, he returned to HQMC where he was made Director of P & P in January 1944. His post war services were many and varied including CG of the 1st MarDiv in Korea in April 1951. Promoted to the rank of LG and designated by the President as Asst Commandant of the Marine Corps serving in that billet until June 1954. Thomas retired from the Marine Corps and was promoted to his ultimate rank on 1 January 1956. He was awarded the DSC and DSM plus Silver Star, Purple Heart in World War I. The DSM, two Legions of Merit, for World War II, then an Army DSC and DSM for Korea. Plus many campaign medals. Thomas died 7 April 1984 at his home in Washington, D.C.

Gerald Carthrae Thomas

Turnage, Allen Hal. General. 3d MarDiv. Born on 3 January 1891, in Farmville, North Carolina and attended the University of North Carolina. Commissioned as a 2dLt of Marines, 17 Nov 1913. Joined the First Brig in Haiti in 1915. Major Turnage was sent to France where he served as the CO, Machine Gun Bn, 5th Marine Brig. Post-war services included: Instruc-

tor at the MCS, Quantico; Haiti from 1922 to 1925; Field Officers' Course at Quantico. Later, between two tours of duty at HQMC, assigned sea duty; back to HQMC on 10 May 1932, appointed Director of the Basic School in 1935 at the Philadelphia Navy Yard. With 1st Bn, 5th Marines, as CO and Regt ExO, respectively. Colonel 29 Jun 1938 and in 1939 became CO of Marine Forces in North China, and CO of the MD, American Embassy, Peiping. HQMC in April 1941, serving as Director of the Division of P & P. BG Turnage, to Camp Lejeune, NC, CG of Base and Training Center. Major general in September 1942 and ADC of 3rd MarDiv October 1942-September 1943 then CG on Guadalcanal September 1943. He led the Division in the landing at Bougainville, 1943, and in the recapture of Guam, 1944. In September 1944 Turnage at HQMC as Director of Personnel, and,

Allen Hal Turnage

later, Asst Commandant of the Marine Corps. His final assignment was as CG, FMF, Pacific. Turnage retired from active duty on 1 Jan 1948, and was advanced to four-star rank on retirement by reason of having been specially commended for heroism in combat. Turnage earned the Navy Cross and the Distinguished Service Medal while leading the 3d MarDiv on Bougainville and Guam in World War II. He also earned a DSM, Legion of Merit and numerous other campaign medals. General Turnage died on 22 October 1971.

Underhill, James Latham. Lieutenant General. 4th MarDiv. Underhill was born on 12 June 1891, in San Francisco, California. Awarded a B.S. from the University of California in 1913 and accepted a commission as a 2dLt of Marines in November 1913. CO, MD aboard the USS *Arkansas, Minnesota,* and *Connecticut* between 1917 and 1918. CO of the Eighth Separate Bn in France in October 1918. Managua, Nicaragua with the embassy guard at the American Legation. Instructor at MCS, October 1921-June 1922. Judge advocate, then post QM at Cavite, Philippine Islands 1925–1926; to Shanghai, China, as plans and training officer in 1927, then as CO of the Third Bn, 4th Marines in 1928. MB, Quantico; CO of MD at the Naval Prison on Mare Island. DMO, Battleship, Division 3 on 18 Feb 1934. San Diego to become the ExO, then commander of the Sixth Marines 1937–1938 during much of their stay in China. MB, Portsmouth, NH between 1938–39 as ExO. ExO to the adjutant and inspector, HQMC, 1939–1942. Promoted to BG on 28 Mar 1942 and to MG retroactive to September 1942. CG of Marine Corps Base, San Diego April 1 942-March 1943. Camp Lejeune in April 1943 as CG, East Coast Echelon, 4th MarDiv April-August 1943. ADC of 4th MarDiv from August 1943-August 1944. Island commander of Tinian August-November 1944. Deputy commander, then IG of FMF, Pacific 1944–1945. Lieutenant general upon retirement on 1 November 1946, having been especially commended for performance of duty in actual combat. General Underhill's decorations include the Legion of Merit, and Bronze Star Medal plus numerous expeditionary and campaign medals. General Underhill died at age 100 on 7 October 1991.

Vandegrift, Alexander Archer. General and 18th Commandant. 1st MarDiv. He was born on 13 March 1887, in Charlottesville, Virginia. Attended the University of Virginia 1906–1908. Enlisted in the Marine Corps in 1908 and accepted a commission as a 2dLt of Marines in 1909. MB, Portsmouth, NH. Overseas duty in Cuba and Nicaragua in 1912; Canal Zone in 1913, at Vera Cruz, Mexico, April 1914; Haiti 1915, 1916–1918, 1919–1923, *Garde d'Haiti.* With the Marine Expeditionary Force in China 1927–1929. Legation Guard in Peking as ExO in 1934, again between 1935–1937. Secretary, then as assistant to MG Thomas Holcomb, commandant of the Marine Corps 1937–1941. Brigadier general in April 1940, then MG in March 1942. ADC then CG of 1st MarDiv 1942–1943. Vandegrift led division to New Zealand then in the landing and occupation of Guadalcanal. He and

Alexander Archer Vandegrift

his 1st MarDiv was relieved by MG Patch, USA and the US Army in December 1942. To Australia and a bit of rest. Performance at Guadalcanal earned him a Medal of Honor. He was promoted to LG in July 1943 and became CG of IMAC July-November 1943. Because of unfortunate circumstances, he served briefly again as CG IMAC. To Washington, D.C. to become Commandant of the Marine Corps, January 1944-January 1948. Promoted to general in March 1945, he became the first active duty four-star general in the Marine Corps. He retired in March 1949. Other decorations included a DSM for his service as commandant. He amassed other medals including; Presidential Unit Citation with Bronze Star; Navy Unit Commendation with Bronze Star; numerous expeditionary medals plus varied World War II campaign medals with four Bronze Stars. Gen Vandegrift died on 8 May 1973 at the USN hospital at Bethesda, MD and was buried at Arlington National Cemetery.

Vogel, Clayton Barney. Major General. 2d MarDiv. Born on 18 September 1882, in Philadelphia. Graduated from Rutgers University in 1904. Accepted a commission as a 2dLt of Marines in 1904. Foreign duty with the American Legation in Peking 1906–1909, then the Second Regt of the Expeditionary Brig in the Canal Zone in 1910 and in Cuba in 1911. Special White House Aide 1911–1912. Inspector with the Haitian Constabulary 1916–1918. CoS to the Commandant, Nicaraguan National Guard May 1929-June 1930 then the Commandant, *Garde d'Haiti*, November 1930-August 1934. Brigadier General in March 1937. Then adjutant and inspector of the Marine Corps March 1937-September 1939, CG of the Second Marine Brig, September 1939-February 1941. Major general in May 1941. CG of 2d MarDiv, February-November 1941 then CG Amphibious Corps, Pacific Fleet November 1941-October 1942. CG of IMAC October 1942-August 1943 then CG FMF, San Diego Area, August 1943-May 1944. CG of MB, Parris Island, May 1944-January 1946. Retired in January 1946. Died on 26 November 1964.

Walker, John Thaddeus. Lieutenant General. 2d MarDiv. Born on 15 September 1893, in Azle, Texas. Earned a B.S. from Texas Agricultural and Mechanical College. Commissioned a 2dLt of Marines in 1917. Served as a platoon leader with the 51st Co, 2/5, in France 1917–1918. Duty in the Dominican Republic 1920–1922. Aide to the Naval Commandant of the Norfolk Navy Yard 1922–1925. Instructor at MCS 1928–1932. Duty in Haiti July 1932-September 1934. Again instructor at MCS 1938–1940. Chief of the plans section at Marine Corps Base, San Diego 1940–1941. Selected as a naval observer with the British in Cairo July-December 1941. Operations officer with 2nd MarDiv January-June 1942. Commander of 22d Marines 1942–1944. Brigadier general retroactive to October 1942. CoS of First Prov Brig between March and December 1944. Assistant Director of Personnel at HQMC, December 1944-May 1945. ADC of the 2d MarDiv 1945–1946. Retired as a lieutenant general in July 1954. Decorations included the Navy Cross, Eniwetok Atoll, February 1944, Legion of Merit and Bronze Star. Died on 27 February 1955.

Watson, Thomas Eugene. Lieutenant General. 2d MarDiv. Watson was born on 18 January 1892, in Oskaloosa, Louisiana. He attended Penn College in that town between 1911 and 1912. On 11 November 1912 he enlisted in the Marine Corps. After four years enlisted service he accepted a commission as a 2dLt of Marines on 20 Oct 1916. Served in the Dominican Republic 1916–1919 with the Second Prov Brig and again between 1919 and 1924. During the next few years he was the CO of the Recruit Depot detachment at San Diego. Then service with the Third Marine Brig in Tientsin 1927–1928, and once again in the Dominican Republic

1930–1931 and in Nicaragua 1931- 1933. He graduated from the AWC in 1938. Had duty in the war plans division at headquarters US Marine Corps 1938–1942. Served in Western Samoa as commander of the 3d Marine Brig 1942–1943 and Tactical Group One 1943–1944. Brigadier general in August 1942, major general in January 1944. CG of 2d MarDiv from April 1944 to July 1945, leading it in the battles for Saipan and Tinian. Held several important posts post-war including CG, FMF, Pacific. He retired as a lieutenant general after 38 years service in July 1950. Decorations included two DSMs. He died in a hospital at the Panama Canal Zone on 6 March 1966.

Thomas Eugene Watson

Worton, William Arthur. Major General. 3d MarDiv. Born on 4 January 1897, in Boston, Massachusetts. Attended Harvard University and Boston University Law School. He was commission in the Massachusetts Naval Militia in 1917. Appointed a 2dLt of Marines on 6 Sep 1917 and served as a platoon leader with the 79th Co, 2/6 in the AEF in 1918, including the Belleau Wood battles where he was seriously wounded on 6 Jun 1918. A Chinese linguist, he saw extensive duty in China 1922–1926, 1927–1929 and 1931–1937. He was acting as a business man (spy) during part of that period, but undercover he was still a Marine officer. He became a brigadier general in October 1942. And ADC of the 3d MarDiv 1942–1945. Then CoS of IIIMAC June 1945-September 1946. Promoted to major general upon retirement in June 1949. General Worton died on 26 Jul 1973.

1st Marine Division

On 1 February 1941, the 1st Marine Brigade, then located at Guantánamo Bay, Cuba, was officially activated as the 1st Marine Division. At San Diego, on that same date, the 2d Brigade became the 2d Marine Division. The 1st Brig had a lineage that went back to 23 December 1913, when the 1st Advanced Base Brig was activated at Philadelphia, PA. It participated in various training activities in the eastern Caribbean in 1914, was re-designated the 1st Brig on 1 April 1914, and landed its force and occupied Vera Cruz between April and November 1914. In December 1914 the brigade was back at Philadelphia.

Next came the landing and occupation of Haiti by the 1st Marine Brig, between August 1915 and August 1934; they also were in Santo Domingo, between June and December 1916. The 1st Marine Brig wasn't deactivated until 15 August 1934, upon its return from Haiti. However, it was re-activated as the 1st Brigade at Quantico on 1 September 1935 and assigned duty with the Fleet Marine Force (FMF). Fifteen days later, 16 September 1936, it was re-designated the 1st Marine Brig. It would retain that designation and as such would be deployed to Guantánamo Bay, Cuba, in October 1940. BG Holland McT. Smith brought the brigade up to snuff in maneuvers around Culebra, Puerto Rico, and the Potomac River area. Upon designation as the 1st Marine Division it was removed to Quantico, VA, and Parris Island, SC, in May 1941.

The 1st MarDiv's first commanding general was MG Holland McT. Smith, 1 February 41 to 13 June 41. He was followed by MG Philip H. Torrey, 14 June 1941 to 22 March 1942. MG Alexander A. Vandegrift then assumed command beginning on 23 March 1942 and brought the division to Wellington, New Zealand, between June and July 1942.

The 1st Division was assigned three regiments of infantry; 1st, 5th, and 7th Marines (three bn's each), one regiment of artillery; 11th Marines (four bn's), plus a Raider Bn (formerly 1/5 from January 1942). The missing rifle battalion, 1/5, was replaced by taking men from 2/5 and 3/5 in February 1942. Later additions to the division would include the 1st Parachute Bn.

The First Marines (1st), as such, was actually formed at Guantánamo Bay, Cuba, on 1 March 1941 under the command of Col David L.S. Brewster. However, the numeric had been around almost as long as the Corps itself. As a designation, *1st Regiment, Marines* it began on 1 January 1900 under the command of a future Commandant, George F. Elliott, and fought in the Philippines, then in China and back to the Philippines. But as the regiment for the 1st MarDiv, the first date above is correct. LtCol James F. Moriarity, a hero of the 6th Machine Gun Bn, 4th Marine Brigade in France, relieved Brewster on 2 April and the change over was semi-permanent. Actually Moriarity commanded several times but eventually, in May 1942, Col Clifton B. Cates led the regiment at Guadalcanal and retained command until 9 February 1943.

The Fifth Marine Regiment has had almost as long an existence. Its formation can be dated from April 1914 when the regiment was among the units selected for the intervention into Mexico at Vera Cruz. Col Charles A. Doyen was the first CO, and would assume that role in 1917 when he led the regiment to France. Although the regiment was disbanded in August 1919, it was organized once again in 1920 with Col Frederic L. Bradman in command. It was disbanded once again, this time in Nicaragua, on 2 January 1933. Nonetheless, it was up and running again on 1 September 1934, and LtCol Charles F.B. Price commanded for a year. The regiment continued in existence from that date forward. It was brought to Guadalcanal by Col LeRoy P. Hunt, another hero of the regiment in France. His successor was Col Merritt A. Edson.

The 7th Marines was activated at Philadelphia, PA, on 14 August 1917 with Col Melville J. Shaw as CO. The 7th served in Cuba for two years protecting the island sugar supply, a wartime necessity. It was deactivated on 6 September 1919 and remained so until reactivated on 6 September 1933 at Quantico under the command of Col Richard P. Williams, another veteran of service in France. It was once again deactivated on 17 January 1934.

Its resurrection for World War II had to wait until 1 January 1941 when Col Earl H. Jenkins assumed command for a few months. His replacement, Col James W. Webb, brought the 7th to Samoa in April 1942. LtCol Armor LeR. Sims, another hero of the 4th Brigade, took the regiment overseas and into the Guadalcanal battle.

The 11th Marines, the artillery regiment, initially led by Col Pedro del Valle, had been born at Quantico on 3 January 1918 as an infantry regiment led by Col George Van Orden. It, with the 13th Marines and the 5th Machine Gun Battalion, formed the 5th Marine Brigade and was shipped to France in September 1918. To its sorrow it never entered combat as a unit. Most of the officers and men served during the occupation of Germany and returned to the US with the remnants of the 4th Brigade in July–August 1919. It was effectively deactivated on 11 August 1919.

Its next rebirth was during the Nicaraguan Campaign on 9 May 1927. During that period, as an infantry regiment, it was commanded by LtCol Arthur J. O'Leary, Col Randolph C. Berkeley, and O'Leary again, followed by Col Robert H. Dunlap who was in command when it was deactivated once again on 31 August 1929. Much of the active service during that campaign was performed by the 11th Marines.

The 11th was reactivated a third time on 1 March 1941 at Guantánamo Bay, Cuba, and assigned as an artillery regiment to the 1st MarDiv. Its first commanding officer was the famous del Valle who led it until 29 March 1943, fighting it in the Guadalcanal Campaign onwards through Eastern New Guinea, and Cape Gloucester.

The first units to be sent overseas, in March 1942, were the 7th Marines (Col James W. Webb); 1st Bn, 11th Marines (LtCol Joseph R. Knowland); and the 8th Defense Bn, which were detached and sent to Upolu, Samoan Islands, as the 3d Brig (BG Charles D. Barrett). They were to defend the Samoa and Wallis Islands under the overall command of BG Gen Henry L. Larsen. At the time the Japanese were running wild over the Pacific and it was expected that Samoa would soon see their troops. The first assault landings in August 1942, at Guadalcanal, Gavutu, and Tulagi, would sorely miss the 7th Marines (rein) until it arrived at Guadalcanal on 18 September 1942.

Meanwhile, the 1st MarDiv would send Marine and Navy officers to their predesignated port of Wellington, NZ, to arrange for housing, food supplies, and other necessities of life for the division upon its arrival. The 1st Division's advance echelon reached Wellington on 14 June 1942 and by 11 July, the balance of the division had arrived. Vandegrift and his subordinates expected to have at least six months to train their division. But,

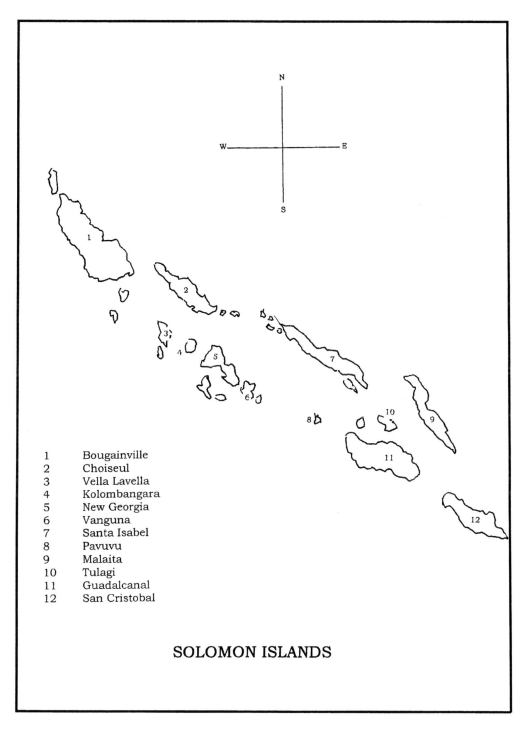

1	Bougainville
2	Choiseul
3	Vella Lavella
4	Kolombangara
5	New Georgia
6	Vanguna
7	Santa Isabel
8	Pavuvu
9	Malaita
10	Tulagi
11	Guadalcanal
12	San Cristobal

SOLOMON ISLANDS

Solomon Islands

on 26 June, Vandegrift received orders for the division's first operation, WATCHTOWER. Because of the inadequacy of support, among the inner circle the code name was unofficially modified to "Operation Shoestring." The procedure was to retake several of the British Solomon Islands, namely Guadalcanal, where the enemy was busy constructing an airfield. Northeastward across the Sealark Channel, off Florida Island, lay Tulagi and Gavutu. The division and support were at less than two-thirds of their regular strength (less than 20,000 men) and would lack necessary air support. There were only a total of 290 aircraft (few if any were Marine air, and all were beyond striking range of the target area). No carriers would get close enough for the Japanese to sink them.

The 1st MarDiv was under the overall command of Adm Chester W. Nimitz, who was Commander in Chief of the Pacific Ocean Area (CinCPOA), and who also continued to hold the title Commander in Chief Pacific Fleet (CinCPac). His subordinate commander, VA Robert L. Ghormley, commanded all Allied naval forces in the South Pacific (Com-SoPac), and was in direct command of WATCHTOWER. His subordinate commander was RA Frank J. Fletcher, who was to command the entire operation with Task Force 61, while his subordinates were RA Richmond K. Turner (TF 62) and MG A.A. Vandegrift (1st Mar-Div, rein). Turner was assigned the role of command of the amphibious operation and Vandegrift the ground operation. There were several disputes relative to where one command terminated and the other began. The admirals believed they continued in command forever, while the Marines believed their role ended when the troops were onshore. It was not settled to anyone's satisfaction for some time to come.

After a minimum training period mainly devoted to exercises in amphibious land-ings, the 1st MarDiv packed up and Fletcher's fleet began its approach toward the first Amer-ican amphibious target of the war, the Solomon Islands. Strongly communist stevedore unions in New Zealand had refused to load ships, so the Marines, working around the clock, had the obligation to do so. Interestingly enough, though New Zealand and Aus-tralia were expecting attack and possibly invasion by the enemy, the unions would not lift their hands to help the Marines. In fact, they raised hell and called Marines "scabs." That roadblock was not forgotten by members of the division.

GUADALCANAL

On 7 August 1942, after a preliminary bombardment, Task Groups Yoke (Tulagi area) and X-Ray (Guadalcanal) of the 1st MarDiv landed. Yoke was under the direct command of BG William H. Rupertus, Assistant Division Commander (ADC), and included 1st Raider Bn (LtCol Merritt A. Edson); 1st Parachute Bn (Maj Robert H. Williams); and 2/5 (LtCol Harold E. Rosecrans); all with reinforcing units attached. Edson commanded on Tulagi, and Williams the Gavutu–Tanambogo landing. Across Sealark Channel, the 1st Marines (Col Clifton B. Cates) and the 5th Marines (Col Leroy P. Hunt), less 2/5 (LtCol Harold E. Rosecrans), landed on Guadalcanal near Lunga Point. The 2d Marines (2d MarDiv), under the command of Col John M. Arthur, had been included in the task force and waited aboard ships as landing force reserve.

The Marines on Tulagi, Gavutu, and Tanambogo got their bellies full of fighting, for that was where most of the enemy soldiers were located. Meanwhile, Marines of the 1st and 3d Bn's, 5th Marines, landed unopposed on Guadalcanal. They, and the 1st Marines that followed them ashore, quickly moved inland and by the end of the day had taken posses-sion of an incomplete air field. The enemy on the island was estimated as being composed of about 1,000 laboring Koreans and another 1,000 Japanese soldiers. MG Vandegrift ordered the occupation of the air field and a defensive line along the Lunga River.

In the meantime, Edson and his 1st Raider Bn, plus 2/5, had met no opposition and

Transports unloading 5th Marines aboard Higgin's boats off Guadalcanal, 7 August 1942.

deployed from shore to shore, then pushed southeast, parallel to the ridge that runs the length of the island. That night they halted at a heavily fortified ravine where the spine ends. The Raiders bivouacked the first night. They would soon learn what that meant to the enemy. Shortly after darkness settled in, the enemy came filtering through the Marines' lines, penetrating deep, and were soon killing sleeping Marines. The Raiders, however, fought back and soon had the Japanese on the run. The next morning, 8 August, the Marines outflanked the enemy around the ravine and by mid-afternoon the island was secured.

Major Williams and his Para Bn had a difficult time landing because of damage caused by the naval bombardment. They managed to land the first wave without encountering enemy fire, but the second was clobbered as they crossed the damaged jetties. They were even catching it from Tanambogo, five hundred yards away. Those Japanese on Gavutu were mainly in caves so the Marines had to go up and dig them out, and dig them out they did. Though suffering high casualties they managed, using explosive charges, to blast the Japanese out of their caves. The Para Bn fought all night. Next morning they got support from 3/2 (LtCol Robert G. Hunt), who helped to mop up. That unit had been scheduled to take Tanambogo on 7 August but had been unsuccessful.

On 8 August 3/2 had gone back in but this time supported by two tanks from the 2d Tank Bn (Maj Alexander B. Swenceski) and managed to successfully take most of Tanambogo. But first they absorbed a nighttime assault with knives and bayonets, the same treatment as given to Williams' men. However, the Japanese were unable to drive off the Marines. They had come to stay.

The Marines were successful, but the U.S. Navy was badly hurt the night of 8–9 August when five cruisers, four American and one Australian, plus several destroyers, fell victim to an Imperial Japanese Navy (IJN) fleet off Savo Island. These were the U.S. warships set to protect the land forces from an enemy naval bombardment. Whereupon RA Turner withdrew the mostly unloaded transports, effectively leaving the 1st MarDiv with but 4 units of fire and 37 days' supply of food. Because RA Fletcher had already withdrawn the carriers, there was also no air support. The 1st MarDiv and its supporting units were effectively all alone. On 12 August the Marines were reduced to two meals a day. Although the enlisted men had no idea of the USN's defeat at Savo they soon wondered why IJN submarines were able to stroll into the area and shell the ground positions, seemingly at ease. Enemy planes also worked their will and Marine defenses were just deep foxholes. It was a very unpleasant period for the men of the 1st MarDiv.

On Guadalcanal, MG Vandegrift had established a defensive arc. The east flank was on the Ilu River, the west on what later became known as Edson's Ridge, about two miles from the coast. In between were periodic strong points in ridges and ravines. This was the best that could be arranged under the circumstances, what with the lack of personnel and matériel. This same perimeter was what the Marines defended until American naval superiority was established in November. The enemy would launch four major assaults against these lines, one each month.

The first, on 21 August, erroneously called the Battle of the Tenaru, was really against the Ilu River line. The Japanese had reason to want to retain Guadalcanal and very soon after the initial landing of the Marines began moving troop reinforcements there. Marine patrols soon discovered a large party ashore on 19 August and defenses were strengthened along the Tenaru River and between it and the Ilu River. It was also learned that the enemy, about 1,000 strong, were located east of the Tenaru. The west bank of the Ilu was held by 2/1 (LtCol Edwin A. Pollack) and the enemy commander decided to take the Marines out. On the evening of 20 August flares went up and firing began against the Marines' defenses. At 0310 the enemy started across the sand bar in a tightly packed formation and they were slaughtered. Some survived and got into the Marines' positions but a reserve company counterattacked and drove them out. Then artillery and mortars began exchanging fire and by morning when 1/1 crossed the Ilu and flanked the Japanese the end was in sight. At 1700 the fight was over. More than 900 of the enemy lay scattered about the river and the other 100 or so managed to escape. It was a perfect example of a soldier's stupidity and there would be many more examples before the war terminated.

The next, a more famous account than all the others, was fought between 12 and 14 September when the Japanese attempted to retake the important ridge just south of the all-important airfield, now known as Henderson Field. The high ground was defended by Edson and his Raiders and the remnants of the Para Bn. Fighting had been going on all day with air attacks on the ridge as well as shelling from Japanese destroyers. It wasn't until 1830, however, that the ground attack began. The enemy launched an attack straight against the main part of the defensive line, driving a hole 250 yards wide. The Para's retaliated, filling that gap and losing 40 percent of their manpower in so doing. Edson was forced to withdraw a short distance in order to keep his lines intact.

The lines held, but the next night 2,000 enemy tried once again. As they came forward near his lines, they yelled "Gas Attack" in hopes that the 300 Marines would fold up. They didn't, but during the fighting Edson was down to but sixty men to hold one section of the

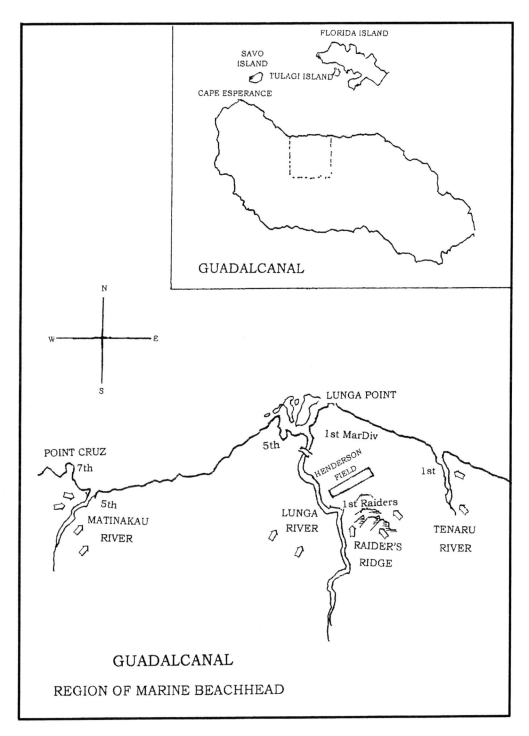

Guadalcanal

ridge. Yet, they held. All the while enemy ships were firing into the ridge indiscriminately, causing heavy casualties. Maj Kenneth D. Bailey, born in Pawnee, OK, now CO of Company C, 1st Raider Battalion, had managed to reorganize his men from the previous night's attack. Taking their place as a reserve battalion between the line and Henderson Field, they were severely threatened on the right flank where the Japanese had managed to penetrate

Marine patrols probing the jungle near the Matanikau River.

the front line. He and his men repulsed this attack and while the line of Marines was withdrawing managed to cover their pullback. Despite a severe head wound, Bailey managed to continue fighting hand-to-hand for over ten hours and his skill and indomitable courage and fighting spirit held his men together. He was a posthumous recipient of a Medal of Honor. His "boss," Col Merritt A. "Red Mike" Edson, in command of the Raider Bn and attached Para Bn, was also awarded a Medal of Honor for his defense of the ridge that now bears his name.

Pressure continued most of that night until about 0500 the following morning, 14 September, when it began to cease. The ridge had held; it was to be known thereafter as "Edson's Ridge" for the stalwart leader who did so much to defend it.

On the night of 12–13 September the enemy tried once again to take the Marines at the Ilu, the eastern flank, but 3/1 (LtCol William N. McKelvy, Jr.), with bayonets fixed, drove them off. The following day, 14 September, the Japanese also tried the defenses on the west flank, but 3/5 (LtCol Frederick C. Biebush) managed to repulse that attack with minimal trouble. The Japanese were getting a bit frustrated. Up until Midway they had been victorious in almost every engagement against the Allied Forces. Now things were different, so they continued doing what they had been doing all along. They sent in a few troops, rather than a large force. LG Haruyoshi Hyakutake, who was at Rabaul, was also sent to command on Guadalcanal.

Finally, on 18 September, the orphan 7th Marines (Col James W. Webb) arrived and was immediately pressed into service. Webb remained behind and LtCol Amor LeR. Sims was now in command. Another welcome arrival, earlier in the month, was BG Roy S. Geiger with the command echelon of his 1st MAW. However, the badly shot-up 1st Para Bn departed for Espiritu Santo. Between 23 and 27 September a Marine effort to cross the Matanikau

The 7th Marines heading toward Point Cruz, October 1942.

upstream was repulsed by the enemy. The defeat was shared by 1/7 (LtCol Lewis B. Puller), 2/5 (LtCol Walker A. Reaves), and the 1st Raider Bn (LtCol Samuel B. Griffith, II). Puller's battalion had landed in a shore-to-shore operation, was quickly isolated behind the enemy's lines, and forced to withdraw. This would be the only defeat suffered by the 1st MarDiv during their Guadalcanal engagement.

In the meantime the newly arrived Marine flyers were busy. By the end of September they had dropped 171 Japanese planes. Capt Joe Foss, Maj's Bob Galer and John Smith, were awarded the Medal of Honor for their part. Another MoH was awarded posthumously to Coast Guard coxswain Douglas Munro for his part in retrieving Puller's Marines from their isolation at the Matanikau.

The Marines, who for weeks had been mainly on the defensive, were now bringing the war to the enemy. Between 7 and 9 Oct the 5th Marines (Col Merritt A. Edson) went after the Japanese at the mouth of the Matanikau. While they were so engaged, the 7th Marines under Sims, supported by 3/2, crossed the river inland and attacked the Matanikau village and the Point Cruz area. They managed to take the east bank of the river from which the Marines would not be dislodged. This was now their east flank. LG Hyakutake had planned on using that position for a forthcoming drive, and the loss further complicated his life. The Japanese drive had been predicated upon an upcoming combined land-sea-and air attack upon the Marines.

That primary attack came on the night of 12 October when an IJN fleet consisting of two battleships, a cruiser, and eight destroyers made it through into Sealark Channel. The Marines paid heavily for this success. For over one hour the IJN pounded the shore positions of the 1st MarDiv, the worst bombardment the Marines suffered during the entire war. Not only the men but the irreplaceable planes were very badly hurt. The following night, one remaining plane spotted a fleet of enemy transports bound for Guadalcanal. Two nights later, a few repaired Marine planes managed to get at the transports, sinking three ships, but only after most of the troops had been disgorged ashore.

On the 13th, transports arrived with the very welcome reinforcements from the U.S. Army Americal Division's 164th Infantry, led by LtCol (later Col) Bryant E. Moore, USA. They were at once blended into the defensive perimeter, now increased to five sectors. The Matanikau River sector was the most likely entry for Japanese forces and consequently was the place of greatest manpower strength. The night of the 14th witnessed a huge and successful raid by enemy air against the "Cactus Air Force" with the ultimate destruction or damaging of 42, or about half, of the 90-plane air force available. On the 15th, Cactus aircraft battered an IJN transport landing at Tassafaronga, forcing the ships to scatter up Sealark Channel, but not until 80% of the troops and supplies were safely ashore. These would provide about 20,000 men of the IJA for future operations.

General Hyakutake had planned to attack and recover Henderson Field and, as part of this program, had sent a large force inland through the jungles. He decided not to await their positioning before making a poorly coordinated attack upon a Marine position on the Matanikau bridgehead. At about 1700 on 23 October, Japanese troops, supported by ten medium tanks and preparatory mortar and artillery fire, moved rapidly across the river and attacked positions held by 3/1 and 3/7 (LtCol Edwin J. Farrell). The supporting 11th Marines (Col Pedro del Valle), with ten batteries of 105mm guns, sent death and destruction into the narrowly packed IJA, wiping out an estimated two battalions. Those few enemy soldiers that got into the Marines' defensive positions were eliminated by Marine rifle, mortar and machine gun fire.

Those 5,600 IJA men of the 2d Division (LG Masao Maruyama) moving through the jungle were well equipped with artillery and supporting troops. Their addition to those Japanese already on line against the 1st MarDiv was going to create serious problems for Vandegrift. Vandegrift now had four defensive sectors around Henderson Field. They included (clockwise from Kukum) the 3d Defense Bn (Col Robert H. Pepper) holding 7,100 yards that straddled the Lunga River, in the 1st sector; the 164th Infantry holding 6,600 yards from the beach inland along the Ilu River to a point near the east slope of Bloody Ridge; in Sector Three two battalions, 1/7 and 2/7 (LtCol Herman H. Hanneken), on a 2,500 yard front from Bloody Ridge west to the Lunga River; next the First Marines (Cates), less 3/1, holding 3,500 yards west from Lunga to the inland flank of the 1st Sector. Hyakutake had his work cut out for him, even with reinforcements. On 23 October another attack was launched against the Matanikau with several tanks leading. It was repelled with the loss of one tank and the following day another attempt was made with the same results.

On 24 October repeated IJA assaults against the southern defensive positions, defended by 1/7 (Puller) and by 2/164 (LtCol Arthur C. Timboe) and 3/164 (LtCol Robert K. Hall), were repelled each time. The following day, during an IJN shelling of the 3d Defense Bn's positions, enemy bombers attacked Henderson Field. Sgt John Basilone, commanding two sections of heavy machine guns, managed to keep his guns firing even when one of his sections was knocked out and only two men were able to continue. Basilone moved a spare gun into position, repaired another and then personally manned it. He unwaveringly returned to the rear for ammo and supplies, thereby contributing greatly to the ultimate defeat of the attacking enemy. He was awarded a Medal of Honor. Later, he landed at Iwo Jima and on 19 February was killed on the beach, but earned a Navy Cross.

Meanwhile, an attack against 1/164 (LtCol Frank Richards) on the south flank of the Lunga River was repulsed, as was another attack upon 2/7 south of Hill 67. That attack was partially successful and elements of the 5th Marines helped 2/7 drive the IJA out of their positions. Platoon Sgt Mitchell Paige of 2/7, and of Charleroi, PA, was cited for conspicuous gallantry on 26 October for holding together his machine gun section even after every member, except him, had been put down, killed or wounded. Moving from gun to gun, Paige blasted the entire line of approaching Japanese even though subjected to enemy artillery and machine gun fire. Reinforcements arrived and Paige put together a new line and led a bayonet charge, driving the enemy back, and preventing a breakthrough of the Marine's lines. Paige was awarded a Medal of Honor and eventually retired as a colonel of Marines in 1959.

The IJA had enough exercise for the moment and withdrew into the jungle. Marine patrol activity was continual as was sea action in the general area.

The next action by Marines against the enemy was at the pocket established by the IJA west of Point Cruz. A Brooklyn-born Marine, Cpl Anthony Casamento, of Company D, 1/5, while serving as a leader of a machine gun section, positioned his section to provide covering fire for two flanking units and his company. During the course of this action every man in his section was either killed or wounded. He himself suffered severe multiple wounds but continued providing critical supporting fire in defense of his position and in cover for an attack. He destroyed one enemy gun just before him and repulsed repeated enemy attacks upon him. He continued this until relieved by the main body of his unit, when he could then accept medical attention. He was rightfully awarded, though very late, in 1980, a Medal of Honor.

The 5th Marines, with 1/5 (Maj William K. Enright) and 3/5 (Maj Robert O. Bowen) leading, advanced and overcame enemy resistance over the 2d and 3d of November. On 4 November the 164th Infantry moved to aid the 7th Marines around Koli Point. Meanwhile, more troops landed, including the 8th Marines (Col Richard H. Jeschke), 1st Bn, 147th Infantry (attached to the Americal Div), a provisional battalion of the 246th FA (LtCol Alexander R. Sewall), Americal Div, Carlson's Raiders and Seabees to build another airfield. Upon landing, the 2d Raider Bn (LtCol Evans Carlson) was ordered by Vandegrift to march overland toward Koli Point and intercept any enemy forces escaping eastward from the envelopment of the 7th Marines and 164th Infantry. The 7th Marines, attacking eastward on 6 November, crossed the Nalimbiu River and moved along the coast, pushing back IJA forces. Next day BG Louis E. Woods replaced BG Roy S. Geiger in command of Guadalcanal air operations.

Moving eastward on 8 November, 1/7 and 2/7, plus the 164th Infantry, planned to surround IJA forces on Koli Point. Over the following four or five days both American units would attack Japanese troops at Gavaga Creek, but by the 12th of November the enemy had managed to escape the entrapment. On the 10th and 11th Col Arthur's 2d Marines (less 3/2), supported by the 8th Marines and the 164th Infantry (less 2/164), pushed west from Point Cruz toward Kokumbona. However, the attack was called off by Vandegrift. He had information that Hyakutake and Adm Yamamoto were planning a severe strike against him and he wanted all available hands under his direct control and near the airport.

For the next few days the action was mainly naval. On 12 November an IJN force intent on destroying Henderson Field was driven back by Adm Halsey's force. Losses for the USN were heavier than for the enemy but air support from Cactus was the factor that led to the "victory." On the 12th the 182d Infantry (Col Daniel W. Hogan) less 3/182 (Maj Charles L. Marshall), the 245th FA Bn (LtCol Elisha K. Kane), and assorted engineer and medical units arrived at Guadalcanal and unloaded. On 14 Nov the USN scored a victory when they defeated a transport force with the IJA 38th Division headed for Guadalcanal. Seven of the eleven transports went down, eliminating most of the division's strength. The following day, the remaining transports went aground on Tassafaronga. They and their troops were literally destroyed by the 3d Defense Bn, the 244th Coast Artillery Bn, USA, plus assistance from the air and a USN destroyer. The few Japanese that escaped would join the others already starving on Guadalcanal.

There were no more serious encounters while the 1st MarDiv remained on the island. Brigadier General Edmund B. Sebree, USA, was taking over more responsibility for the operations on Guadalcanal, and the Army units, supported by the 8th Marines, were relieving the exhausted 1st MarDiv. On 9 December 1942 command passed from MG Vandegrift to MG Alexander M. Patch, USA, and the 1st MarDiv began loading up, bound for Australia. The 2d MarDiv would remain, and we will pick up the balance of the story on Guadalcanal in their history. Meanwhile, MG Vandegrift was awarded a Medal of Honor for the entire period he successfully commanded on Guadalcanal.

The 1st Marine Division earned the Presidential Unit Citation, five men earned the Medal of Honor, well over 115 were awarded the Navy Cross and numerous more the Silver Star. In so doing they paid heavily in men and materiel. They had over 2,100 casualties plus 5,600 cases of malaria. By November 1942 the division was literally "out of business." The U.S. Navy's losses were extensive in ships and manpower. It was a difficult campaign, but in the Pacific the United States was now on the road to complete victory.

Order of Battle
Guadalcanal
(7 August 1942 to 8 December 1942)

Headquarters

MG Alexander A. Vandegrift	CG
BG William A. Rupertus	ADC
Col William Capers James	CoS (To 24 Sep)
Col Gerald C. Thomas	CoS
Col Robert C. Kilmartin, Jr.	D-1
LtCol Frank B. Goettge	D-2 (KIA 12 Aug)
LtCol Edmund J. Buckley	D-2
LtCol Gerald C. Thomas	D-3 (To 24 Sep)
LtCol Merrill B. Twining	D-3
LtCol Randolph McC. Pate	D-4

First Marines

Col Clifton B. Cates	CO
LtCol Julian N. Frisbie	ExO (To 23 Sept)
LtCol Edwin A. Pollack	ExO
Capt Elmer W. Myers	R-1

2dLt George P. Hunt	R-2
LtCol William W. Stickney	R-3 (To 23 Sept)
Maj Walker A. Reaves	R-3
Capt Charles A. Cogswell	R-4
Capt Francis W. Eagan	R-4

1/1

LtCol Lenard B. Cresswell	CO
Maj Marion A. Fawcett	ExO
2dLt Donald K. Dayton	B-3

2/1

LtCol Edwin A. Pollack	CO (To 23 Sept)
LtCol William W. Stickney	CO
LtCol William W. Stickney	ExO (To 23 Sept)
Maj William Chalfant, III	ExO (To 2 Oct)
Maj Charles L. Cogswell	ExO
2dLt Arthur W. Larson	B-3

3/1

LtCol William N. McKelvy, Jr.	CO
Maj Walker A. Reaves	ExO (To 23 Sep)
Capt Alexander R. Benson	B-3

Fifth Marines

Col Leroy P. Hunt	CO (To 21 Sep)
Col Merritt A. Edson	CO
Col William J. Whaling	ExO (To 25 Sep)
LtCol Walker A. Reaves	ExO (To 12 Oct)
LtCol William S. Fellers	ExO
Capt Donald L. Dickson	R-1 (To 22 Nov)
Capt Robert D. Shine	R-1
Capt Wilfred H. Ringer, Jr.	R-2 (To 12 Aug)
Capt Henry J. Adams	R-2
Maj William I. Phipps	R-3 (To 24 Sep)
Maj Lewis W. Walt	R-3 (To 12 Oct)
LtCol Walker A. Reaves	R-3
2dLt William L. Williams	R-4

1/5

LtCol William E. Maxwell	CO (To 30 Aug)
Maj Donald W. Fuller	CO (To 13 Oct)
Maj William K. Enright	CO
Maj Milton V. Ó Connell	ExO (To 30 Aug)
Maj William F. Thyson, Jr.	ExO (To 19 Sep)
Capt Gordon D. Gayle	B-3

2/5

LtCol Harold E. Rosecrans	CO (To 11 Sep)
Capt Joseph J. Dudkowski	CO (To 17 Sep)
LtCol Walker A. Reaves	CO (To 24 Sep)
Capt Joseph J. Dudkowski	CO (To 30 Sep)
Maj David S. McDougal	CO (To 8 Oct)
Maj William J. Piper	CO (To 11 Oct)
Maj Lewis W. Walt	CO
Maj Donald W. Fuller	ExO (To 30 Aug)
Maj George T. Skinner	ExO (To 11 Sep)
Maj William J. Piper, Jr.	ExO (From 1 Oct)
Capt Joseph J. Dudkowski	B-3 (To 14 Oct)
Capt Harry S. Conner	B-3

3/5

LtCol Frederick C. Biebush	CO (To 22 Sep)
Maj Robert O. Bowen	CO
Maj Robert O. Bowen	ExO (To 22 Sep)
Maj William H. Barba	ExO (From 25 Sep)
Capt William F. Thyson, Jr.	B-3 (To 18 Sep)
Capt Lyman D. Spurlock	B-3

Seventh Marines

Col James W. Webb	CO (To 20 Sep)
Col Amor LeR. Sims	CO
Col Amor LeR. Sims	ExO (To 20 Sep)
LtCol Julian Frisbie	ExO
Maj Harold G. Walker	R-1 (To 24 Sep)
Capt Theodore G. Bateman, Jr.	R-1 (To 3 Nov)
Capt John S. Day	R-1
Capt Carl L. Peed	R-2 (To 1 Oct)
Capt Claude B. Cross	R-2
LtCol William R. Williams	R-3 (To 25 Sep)

Capt William J. King	R-3
Maj Frederick L. Wieseman	R-4

1/7

LtCol Lewis B. Puller	CO
Maj Otho L. Rogers	ExO (To 27 Sep)
Maj John E. Weber	ExO
Capt Charles J. Beasley	B-3

2/7

LtCol Herman H. Hanneken	CO
Maj Odell M. Conoley	ExO
Capt Arthur B. Sherwood	B-3

3/7

LtCol Edwin J. Farrell	CO (To 24 Sep)
LtCol William R. Williams	CO
Maj Burdette Hagerman	ExO (To 24 Sep)
Maj Harold G. Walker	ExO
Capt Jacob Joseph	B-3 (To 14 Oct)
Capt Victor H. Streit	B-3

Eleventh Marines

Col Pedro del Valle	CO
BG Pedro del Valle	CO (From 9 Oct)
LtCol John A. Bemis	ExO (To 17 Oct)
LtCol Robert B. Luckey	ExO (To 28 Nov)
LtCol Thomas B. Hughes	ExO
1stLt Thomas H. Tatsch	R-1 (To 1 Sep)
MarGun Charles E. Stuart	R-1
1stLt Maurice L. Appleton, Jr.	R-2
Maj Thomas B. Hughes	R-3 (To 28 Nov)
Maj Charles M. Nees	R-3
Maj James M. Clark	R-4

1/11

LtCol Joseph R. Knowlan	CO (To 19 Oct)
LtCol Manley L. Curry	CO (To 28 Nov)
LtCol Donovan D. Sult	CO (To 2 Dec)
Maj Harry K. Zimmer	ExO
Capt Samuel S. Wooster	B-3

2/11

LtCol Edward G. Hagen	CO (To 14 Sep)
Maj Forest C. Thompson	CO
Maj Forest C. Thompson	ExO (To 14 Sep)
Maj Louis A. Ennis	ExO
Capt Louis A. Ennis	B-3 (To 14 Sep)
Maj Ernest P. Foley	B-3

3/11

LtCol James J. Keating	CO
Maj Lewis J. Fields	ExO
Maj George B. Wilson, Jr.	B-3

4/11

LtCol Melvin E. Fuller	CO (To 28 Oct)
Maj Carl G. F. Korn	CO (To 31 Oct)
Capt Albert H. Potter	CO (To 6 Dec)
LtCol Melvin E. Fuller	CO
Maj Carl G. F. Korn	ExO (To 28 Oct)
Maj Charles M. Nees	B-3 (To 27 Aug)

<table>
<tr><td colspan="2" align="center">5/11</td></tr>
</table>

LtCol E. Hayden Price	CO (To 18 Oct)	
Maj Noah P. Wood, Jr.	CO	
LtCol Edmund J. Buckley	ExO (To 12 Aug)	
Maj Noah P. Wood, Jr.	B-3 (To 18 Oct)	

1st Raider Battalion

Col Merritt A. Edson	CO (To 21 Sep)
LtCol Samuel B. Griffith, II	CO (To 27 Sep)
Capt Ira J. Irwin	CO

LtCol Samuel B. Griffith, II	ExO (To 21 Sep)
Capt Robert H. Thomas	ExO (27 Sep to 19 Nov)
Maj Robert S. Brown	B-3 (To 14 Sep)

First Aviation Engineer Battalion

Maj Thomas F. Riley	CO
Maj James M. McQueen	ExO
Capt Douglas P. Devendorf	B-3

AUSTRALIA

After departing the "canal" the Division was sent to Brisbane, Australia, to recover. In so doing, they came under the general command of LG Douglas MacArthur. The division was selected to defend the island continent against any enemy invasion attempt while U.S. Army and Australian forces were busy defending New Guinea, a huge island located just to the north of Australia. In the meantime the men of the Division began to assimilate with the locals as they sashayed around Brisbane. However, the camp in which they had been installed was, in many ways, worse than the "canal." Many more men came down with, or had a recurrence of, malaria.

Their next move was to Melbourne and a much better climate for recovering their depleted health. Generally speaking, the men of the Division were given a hearty welcome by the Aussies, and after a few skirmishes with ANZACs on leave, they managed to make many friends. Plenty of rest and absorption of replacements filled the next few months. On 8 July 1943 General Vandegrift was promoted to LG and called away to command the IMAC (I Marine Amphibious Corps), and the Assistant Division Commander, MG William H. Rupertus, assumed command of the 1st MarDiv.

That month MacArthur's headquarters sent initial orders to Rupertus to prepare to aid the Sixth Army in his campaigns. The Japanese airfield at Cape Gloucester on New Britain was to be their target. In late August 1943 the division engineers departed first to prepare camps, and in late September the rest of the division sailed for different locations in New Guinea. It was the army's plan, not the Marines'. This was followed by several reconnaissance efforts by the Alamo Scouts, a conglomerate organization of soldiers, Marines and even a few sailors. After some rather haphazard plans were put forward and objections stated, the 1st MarDiv received Sixth Army Field Order No. 5, which permitted the entire 1st MarDiv to land at Cape Gloucester, which is located on the western end of the island of New Britain.

CAPE GLOUCESTER

By the evening of 24 December 1943 the invasion flotilla was loaded and had rendezvoused at Buna Harbor. Probably it isn't necessary to add that the men were quite solemn at this time. They had, after all, been out of action for over a year and this long period of inactivity had sapped all desires for more jungle warfare. The weather conditions would actually be worse than on Guadalcanal. The Marines would suffer incessant rain, pounding them the entire period they were at Cape Gloucester. This operation,

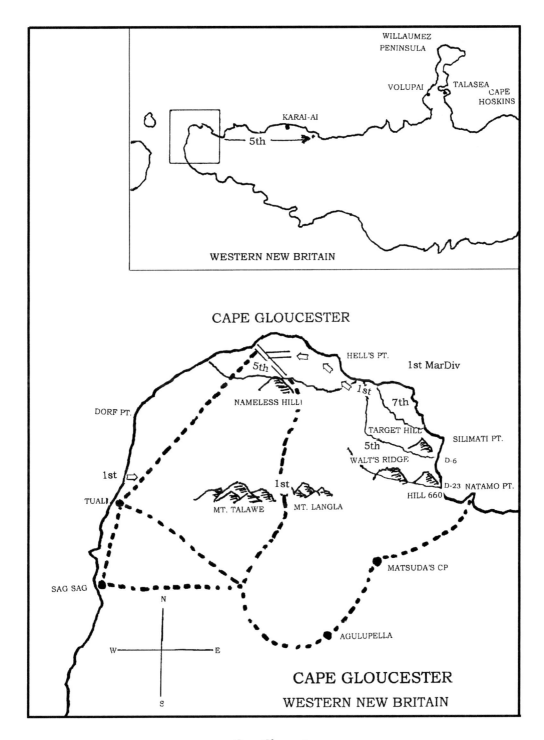

Cape Gloucester

coded BACKHANDER, would take all the resilience and fortitude the Marines could muster.

A naval bombardment, and attacks by the Fifth Army Air Force and Marine Fighter Squadrons 214, 216, 222, 223, and 321, aided in the landing by the 7th Marines, also known as "Combat Team C" (Col Julian N. Frisbie), of the 1st MarDiv on the morning of 26

December 1943. Soon, the Yellow beachhead, located on the north side of the cape, was secured, and the 7th Marines and two battalions of the 1st Marines, a.k.a. Combat Team B (Col William J. Whaling), had taken up positions which ensured that situation would continue. At the southern side of the cape, 2/1 (LtCol James M. Masters, Sr.) landed at Green beach, their part of the operation known as STONEFACE. Their task was mainly defensive: to block a trail and hold it against elements of the 53d Japanese Infantry.

Temporarily, the enemy reaction was mainly an aerial counterattack which badly damaged some of the USN ships offshore, but their own losses precluded any further raids in strength. On the eastern end of New Britain, MG Iwao Matsuda ordered his 141st Infantry and 51st Reconnaissance Regiment to join their colleagues at Cape Gloucester to defend the airfield.

The first moves made by the 1st MarDiv was southeast toward Hill 660, an important feature of the southern defense perimeter, and westward toward the airfield. The Japanese weren't just sitting on their hands while the Marines were busy. They reacted with numerous small attacks upon the perimeter while the 1st Marines' assault forces, supported by the 5th Marines, Combat Team A (Col John T. Selden), beginning on 29 December, were soon attacking the defenders at the airfield. The attack was led by LtCol Walker A. Reaves, CO of 1/1, and LtCol Lewis W. Walt, CO of 2/5. Airfields No 1 and No 2 were both secured on 31 December 1943. In the meantime, the 7th Marines defended the beachhead from continual attacks by the IJA's 2/53, which the Marines effectively put out of action. With that success, the Marines began preparing for an eastward shift toward Borgen Bay.

Thrusting eastward on 2 January 1944 were 2/7 (LtCol Odell M. Conoley) and 3/7 (LtCol William R. Williams) supported by 3/5 (LtCol David S. McDougal), all led by BG Lemuel C. Shepherd. In the meantime, on 3 January, 1/7 (LtCol John E. Weber) repulsed an enemy attack upon Target Hill within the Yellow Beach defensive perimeter. The following day, 3/5 and 3/7 took out 2/53 defending Suicide Creek, thereby moving their lines another half mile outward. On 11 January 3/5, now led by LtCol Lewis W. Walt (replacing two CO's WIA and the temporary replacement Col Lewis B. Puller), with support by Marine artillery, assaulted and took Aogiri Ridge (later known as "Walt's Ridge"), which had been tenaciously defended by 2/53 and 2/141.

During this second phase, through 16 January, the Marines suffered their heaviest casualties. The taking of Hill 660 by 3/7 (LtCol Henry W. Buse) on the 16th was what shattered that IJA defensive line. The hill dominated all else at the western end of Borgen Bay. The Marine tanks, which were in the advance of the infantry, were soon bogged down in the mud and had to be left behind. It was a tough climb up the steep hill, with weapons slung, and the enemy contesting every foot. The hill was taken but the IJA tried a massive counterattack to retake what was now Marine property. That failed, and with it the entire Japanese defense of that part of New Britain. Essentially, since the Marines had taken the airfields and Borgen Bay, they had won. During the next few months all action would be in other areas of the island. On 10 February operations in western New Britain were declared ended. Army and Marine patrols met at Gilnit on the Itni River, effectively ending any aggressive enemy action in western New Britain.

It became evident, however, that the only route that could be used by escaping IJA forces heading eastward would be along the northern part of the island. Therefore, several landings by Marines were made along that line to intercept and defeat any groups found. This went on for many weeks. On 23 February LG Yashushi Sakai received orders to get

Top: Mortars of the 1st Marines pounding Japanese positions near Hell's Point, Cape Gloucester, on 28 December 1943. *Bottom:* Navajo Indian Code Talkers, resting during the Cape Gloucester Campaign.

his 17th Division back to Rabaul. Most of his men began making tracks to join him at his headquarters but were still two weeks from Talasea on the Willaumez Peninsula.

The Marines had already formulated a plan to upset any effort to save the remnants. On 6 March the 5th Marines (Col Oliver P. Smith), reinforced, landed at the Volupai Plantation on the west side of the Willaumez Peninsula. This was the narrowest part of the peninsula, only 2 1/2 miles, wide and in a few days they crossed the neck and had taken Garua Harbor, Talesea town and the Garua Island and plantation. Company K of 1/5 was down to the village of Garili by 11 March. The advance continued, and besides cleaning up stragglers, the 5th Marines continued their move southward along the eastern side of the peninsula. They were at Kilu on 16 March and, after a fight with a contesting company from the IJA, continued their advance. Weeks of fighting by patrols ended on 9 April when Marines caught Maj Shinjuro Komori and three of his men in an ambush, killing three and wounding one. That effectively ended the 1st MarDiv's part in the New Britain campaign. On 11 April, after being relieved by units of the 185th Infantry, 40th Division, the Marines began their withdrawal from what was perceived as essentially a U.S. Army type of action, ill-suited for the amphibious-trained Marines. Marine losses have been calculated at 1,400 killed and wounded and estimated at least 3,900 Japanese killed and wounded.

Order of Battle
Cape Gloucester
(26 December 1943 to 11 April 1944)

Headquarters

MG William H. Rupertus	CG
BG Lemuel C. Shepherd, Jr.	ADC (To 11 Apr)
BG Oliver P. Smith	ADC
Col Amor L. Sims	CoS (To 3 Feb)
Col Oliver P. Smith	CoS (To 29 Feb)
Col John T. Selden	CoS
Maj Elmer W. Myers	D-1
LtCol Edmund J. Buckley	D-2 (To 23 Feb)
LtCol Harold D. Harris	D-2
Col Edwin A. Pollack	D-3 (To 30 Jan)
LtCol William K. Enright	D-3
Col William S. Fellers	D-4

Headquarters Battalion

LtCol Frank R. Worthington	CO
LtCol Asa J. Smith	ExO

First Marines (CT B)[1]

Col William J. Whaling	CO (To 28 Feb)
Col Oliver P. Smith	CO
Col Lewis B. Puller	CO
LtCol Harold D. Harris	ExO (To 23 Feb)
LtCol John E. Weber	ExO (To 20 Mar)
LtCol Walker A. Reaves	ExO (From 8 Apr)
1stLt James K. Young	R-1 (To 22 Jan)
1stLt James D. Currie	R-1 (To 6 Mar)

1stLt Frank C. Shephard	R-1
Capt George P. Hunt	R-2 (To 6 Jan)
Capt James W. Horton	R-2
Maj Martin F. Rockmore	R-3 (To 6 Jan)
Capt John N. Rentz	R-3 (To 20 Jan)
Capt Arthur W. Larson	R-3 (To 13 Apr)
Maj Bernard T. Kelly	R-3
Maj Francis T. Eagan	R-4

1/1 (BLT 11)[2]

LtCol Walker A. Reaves	CO (To 7 Apr)
Maj Raymond G. Davis	CO
Maj Louis E. Huggins, Jr.	ExO
Capt Robert K. McClelland	B-3 (To 21 Feb)
Capt James M. Rogers	B-3

2/1 (BLT 21)

LtCol James M. Masters, Sr.	CO (To 9 Feb)
Maj Charles H. Brush, Jr.	CO (To 11 Apr)
LtCol William W. Stickney	CO
Maj Charles H. Brush, Jr.	ExO (To 9 Feb)
Capt Roy W. Wallace, Jr.	ExO (To 11 Apr)
Maj Charles H. Brush, Jr.	ExO
Capt Arthur W. Larson	B-3 (To 20 Jan)
Capt John J. Jachym	B-3

3/1 (BLT 31)

LtCol Joseph F. Hankins	CO
Maj William McNulty	ExO

[1]Combat Team B
[2]Battalion Landing Team 11.

Capt George B. Gierhart	B-3 (To 21 Feb)
1stLt James A. Junkin	B-3

5th Marines (CT A)

Col John T. Selden	CO (To 29 Feb)
Col Oliver P. Smith	CO (To 11 Apr)
LtCol Henry W. Buse, Jr.	CO
LtCol William K. Enright	ExO (To 5 Jan)
LtCol Lewis W. Walt	ExO (To 8 Jan)
Maj Harry S. Connor	ExO (To 12 Jan)
LtCol Lewis W. Walt	ExO (To 31 Jan)
LtCol Odell M. Conoley	ExO (From 9 Feb to 20 Feb)
LtCol Henry W. Buse, Jr.	ExO (To 11 Apr)
LtCol Harry S. Connor	ExO
Capt Alan F. Dill	R-1
Capt Henry J. Adams, Jr.	R-2 (To 31 Mar)
Maj Walter S. McIlhenny	R-2 (To 10 Apr)
Capt Levi T. Burcham	R-2
Maj Gordon D. Gayle	R-3 (To 5 Jan)
Maj Harry S. Connor	R-3
Capt William L. Williams	R-4

1/5 (BLT 15)

Maj William H. Barba	CO
Maj Harry S. Connor	ExO (To 5 Jan)
Maj Harold T. A. Richmond	ExO
Capt Walter S. McIlhenny	B-3 (To 17 Jan)
Capt Maurice Raphael	B-3

2/5 (BLT 25)

LtCol Lewis W. Walt	CO (To 5 Jan)
Maj Gordon D. Gayle	CO
Maj Charles R. Baker	ExO
Capt Walter H. Cuein	B-3 (To 31 Jan)
Capt Edward W. Bryan	B-3

3/5 (BLT 35)

LtCol David S. McDougal[3]	CO (To 7 Jan)
Maj Joseph S. Skoczylas	CO (7 Jan)
Col Lewis B. Puller	CO (To 8 Jan)
LtCol Lewis W. Walt	CO (To 12 Jan)
LtCol Harold O. Deakin	CO (To 10 Apr)
Maj Walter S. McIlhenny	CO
Maj Joseph S. Skoczylas	ExO (To 7 Jan)
Maj Robert H. Dillard	ExO (To 31 Mar)
Maj Clyde A. Brooks	ExO (From 11 Apr)
Capt George W. Smith	B-3 (To 22 Jan)
Capt Erskine W. Wells	B-3

Seventh Marines (CT C)

Col Julian N. Frisbie	CO (To 20 Feb)
Col Herman H. Hanneken	CO
LtCol Lewis B. Puller	ExO (To 23 Feb)
LtCol John E. Weber	ExO (From 21 Mar)
1stLt Frank C. Sheppard	R-1 (To 6 Mar)
CWO Frank R. Shaw	R-1 (To 31 Mar)
Capt Robert A. Scherr	R-1
1stLt Francis T. Farrell	R-2

Maj Victor H. Streit	R-3
Capt Marion S. Reed	R-4

1/7 (BLT 17)

LtCol John E. Weber	CO (To 6 Mar)
Maj Waite W. Worden	CO (To 11 Apr)
LtCol Harold O. Deakin	CO
Maj Waite W. Worden	ExO (To 6 Mar)
Maj Lloyd W. Martin	ExO (To 11 Apr)
Maj Waite W. Worden	ExO
Capt Preston S. Parish	B-3

2/7 (BLT 27)

LtCol Odell M. Conoley	CO (To 7 Feb)
Maj Charles S. Nichols, Jr.	CO (To 14 Feb)
LtCol John W. Scott, Jr.	CO
Maj Charles S. Nichols, Jr.	ExO (To 7 Feb; from 15 Feb to 17 Mar)
Maj Claude B. Cross	ExO (From 17 Mar)
Capt Louis G. Ditta	B-3 (To 31 Jan)
Capt William T. Watkins	B-3 (To 23 Feb)
Capt George E. Sexton	B-3

3/7 (BLT 37)

LtCol William R. Williams	CO (To 3 Jan)
LtCol Lewis B. Puller	CO (To 8 Jan)
LtCol Henry W. Buse, Jr.	CO (To 20 Feb)
Maj William J. Piper, Jr.	CO
Maj William J. Piper Jr.	ExO (To 20 Feb)
Maj Hierome L. Opies, Jr.	ExO
Capt William J. King	B-3 (To 3 Jan)
1stLt Robert B. Morton	B-3 (To 31 Mar)
1stLt Hugh S. Tremaine	B-3

Eleventh Marines

Col Robert H. Pepper	CO (To 31 Jan)
Col William H. Harrison	CO
LtCol Robert B. Luckey	ExO (To 14 Feb)
LtCol Thomas B. Hughes	ExO
Capt Floyd C. Maner	R-1
Maj Daniel S. Pregnall	R-2 (To 21 Mar)
Capt Richard W. Payne	R-2
Maj Louis A. Ennis	R-3 (To 16 Feb)
Maj Elliott Wilson	R-3 (From 22 Feb)
1stLt Gordon R. Dalglish	R-4

1/11

LtCol Lewis J. Fields	CO
Maj Hoyt U. Bookhart, Jr.	ExO
Maj Elliott Wilson	B-3 (To 21 Feb)
Maj John R. Chaisson	B-3

2/11

Maj Noah P. Wood, Jr.	CO
Maj Fred T. Bishop	ExO
Maj Archie D. Swift, Jr.	B-3

3/11

Maj Ernest P. Foley	CO (To 2 Feb)

[3]*McDougal and Skoczylas were WIA on the same day and Puller assumed command of the regiment plus 3/7, pending Walt's arrival.*

LtCol Forest C. Thompson	CO (To 25 Mar)
LtCol Richard A. Evans	CO
Maj Henry M. Wellman, Jr.	ExO (To 2 Feb)
Maj Ernest P. Foley	ExO (To 12 Mar)
LtCol Richard A. Evans	ExO (To 25 Mar)
Maj Henry M. Wellman, Jr.	ExO
Capt Searle W. Gillespie	B-3 (To 2 Feb)
Maj Henry M. Wellman, Jr.	B-3 (To 12 Mar)
Capt Searle W. Gillespie	B-3 (To 21 Mar)
Maj Daniel S. Pregnall	B-3

4/11

LtCol Thomas B. Hughes	CO (To 16 Feb)
LtCol Louis A. Ennis	CO
Maj Dale H. Heely	ExO (To 16 Mar)
Maj George E. Bowdoin	ExO
Capt Ivan L. Smith	B-3 (To 10 Jan)
Maj George E. Bowdoin	B-3 (To 16 Mar)
Capt Marshall Smith	B-3

5/11

LtCol Charles M. Nees	CO
Maj James H. Moffatt, Jr.	ExO
Maj Samuel S. Wooster	B-3 (To 9 Feb)
Maj William M. Miller	B-3 (To 13 Mar)
Capt William J. Hannan	B-3

Seventeenth Marines (Engineers)

Col Harold E. Rosecrans	CO (To 18 Feb)
Col Francis I. Fenton	CO
LtCol Robert G. Ballance	ExO (From 22 Feb)
Capt William I. Kent	R-1 (To 31 Jan)
Capt Francis L. Cooper	R-1 (To 30 Mar)
WO Paul Adams	R-1 (To 19 Apr)
Capt Francis L. Cooper	R-1
Capt Albert N. Lange	R-2 (To 21 Feb)
Capt Warren S. Sivertsen	R-2
Maj John P. McGuinness	R-3 (To 21 Feb)
Maj Levi W. Smith, Jr.	R-3
Maj William A. Stiles	R-4

1/17

Maj Henry H. Crockett	CO (To 4 Mar)
Maj John P. McGuinness	CO
Maj Austin S. Igleheart, Jr.	ExO (To 21 Feb)
Maj John P. McGuinness	ExO (To 4 Mar)
Maj John H. Goodwin	ExO (To 17 Apr)
Capt Sidney Schulder	ExO
Capt Sidney Schulder	B-3 (To 21 Mar)
Capt Jim M. Joyner	B-3 (To 8 Apr)
Capt Sidney Schulder	B-3 (To 17 Apr)
Capt Eugene T. Schoenfelder	B-3

2/17 (Pioneers)

LtCol Robert G. Ballance	CO (To 21 Feb)
Maj Austin S. Igleheart, Jr.	CO
Maj Levi W. Smith, Jr.	ExO (To 21 Feb)
Capt Nathaniel Morgenthal	ExO
Capt Nathaniel Morgenthal	B-3 (To 21 Feb)

Capt Franklin P. Walton	B-3 (To 31 Mar)
1stLt John H. Heussner	B-3

3/17 (Seabees)

Cmdr Thomas A. Woods	CO (To 31 Jan)
LtCmdr James T. Redd	CO
LtCmdr James T. Redd	ExO (To 31 Jan)
Lt William W. Wickes	B-3 (To 31 Mar)
Lt C. B. Farrell	B-3

1st Amphibian Tractor Battalion

Maj Francis H. Cooper	CO
Capt Albert E. Reutlinger	ExO
Capt Albert E. Reutlinger	B-3 (To 1 Mar)
Capt John I. Fitzgerald, Jr.	B-3

1st Medical Battalion

Cmdr Everett B. Keck	CO (To 27 Feb)
Cmdr Stanley P. Wallin	CO (To 18 Apr)
Cmdr Emil E. Napp	CO

1st Motor Transport Battalion

Maj Kimber H. Boyer	CO
Capt James E. Delaney, Jr.	ExO (To 3 Apr)
Capt Joseph L. Harrington	ExO
Capt Joseph L. Harrington	B-3 (To 16 Jan)
Capt Howard E. Wertman	B-3 (To 8 Apr)
1stLt Walter M. Greenspan	B-3

1st Service Battalion

LtCol Edward F. Doyle	CO
Capt James G. Triebel	ExO

1st Special Weapons Battalion

Maj Raymond G. Davis	CO (To 5 Apr)
Maj John P. Leonard, Jr.	CO
Maj John P. Leonard, Jr.	ExO
Capt Frederick H. Scantling	B-3 (To 13 Feb)
Capt Joe P. Beattty	B-3 (To 1 Apr)
Capt Edward J. Cunningham	B-3 (To 9 Apr)
1stLt Robert G. Main	B-3

1st Tank Battalion

LtCol Charles G. Meints	CO (To 15 Apr)
Maj Donald J. Robinson	CO
Maj Roland L. Hall	ExO (To 14 Jan)
Maj Donald J. Robinson	ExO (To 14 Apr)
Capt Michael J. DeSandis	ExO
Maj Rowland L. Hall	B-3 (15 Jan to 19 Mar)
Capt Michael J. DeSandis	B-3

12th Defense Battalion

Col William H. Harrison	CO (To 31 Jan)
LtCol Merlyn D. Holmes	CO
LtCol Merlyn D. Holmes	ExO (To 31 Jan)
LtCol Louis C. Reinberg	ExO
Maj Robert C. McGlashan	B-3 (To 21 Jan)
Maj Harry F. Noyes, Jr.	B-3 (To 31 Jan)
Maj Joseph K Jacyno	B-3

PAVAVU

The Division was on its way to Melbourne, Australia, or at least that was the rumor going about. Some Marines believed that MG Rupertus had promised that was their destination.

Wrong! They were instead on their way to the island of Pavavu in the Russell Island chain. This was considered by members of the Division to be a kind of punishment for something imagined, but no one knew quite what. Mainly, the veterans later remembered rain, mud, insects, malaria, warmed-over C and K rations, and it went on for four months. The hospital was continually full, the ponchos rotted away, and the tents and cots did much the same.

Sickness was not limited to malaria; there were several other diseases readily available, like ringworm and jungle rot. It was generally decided that Pavavu was all wrong and somebody was to blame for the mess. The Division was supposed to be being prepared for another amphibious assault but suffering so much illness and accompanying morale loss was not the way to do it.

PELELIU

Originally known as STALEMATE, the operation changed to STALEMATE II on 7 July 1944 when revised orders were issued to all commands taking part in the assault in the Palaus Island group. The need to take the Palaus group was to protect LG MacArthur's left flank as he and his army proceeded to retake Leyte in the Philippine Island chain. Taking Peleliu, the largest and most heavily fortified of that group, proved to be expensive protection. MacArthur was going to land on 20 October 1944 and the Marines were required to take Peleliu beforehand. The whole operation was expected to be short. Rupertus even went so far as to tell his division officers: "We're going to have some casualties, but let me assure you this is going to be a short one, a quickie. Rough but fast. We'll be through in three days. It might only take two." More like months rather than days. But optimism reigned, at least among the Joint Chiefs of Staff.

Task Force 32 arrived off Peleliu and began an intensive naval bombardment on 12 September 1944. On D Day, 15 September, there were three beach assignments: White, 1 and 2, upon which the 1st Marines (Col Lewis B. Puller) were to land; Orange 1, 2, and 3, upon which 2 Bn's of the 5th (Col Harold D. Harris) and on that right flank, the 7th (Col Herman H. Hanneken). On the opposite side of the island was Beach Purple, which in a period of about ten days would become a hospital/rest home for a badly battered 1st Marine Regiment.

After a preliminary bombardment of the beaches by RA Jesse B. Oldendorf's fire support ships, Marines in their landing craft headed for the beaches at 0800 on 15 September. The LCI's and LVT's began landing on the beaches at 0832 with armored amphibians leading, troops following. The blanket of fire laid down on that island by warships, naval aviators and LCI/LVT's equipped with 4.5 rocket launchers and 4.2 mortars seemed, at the time, to be adequate. But it didn't really make a dent on the left flank, where the enemy had created caves with armored doors for protection. That was where Puller's 1st Marines landed and they took a shellacking, especially 3/1 (LtCol Stephen V. Sabol) on White Beach

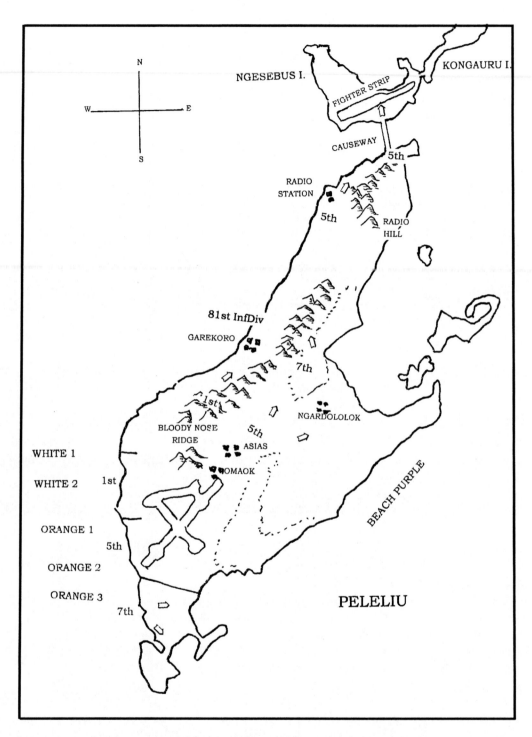

Peleliu

1, and most especially Co K (Capt George P. Hunt) on the extreme left flank. Their story in the next two days was the story of the 1st MarDiv during the coming weeks. Marine casualties were enormous; the wounded and survivors suffered greatly from the 105-degree heat. The entire landing was a disaster which ultimately proved to be completely unnecessary, and, like Blanc Mont in World War I, almost forgotten (purposely?) by nearly everyone.

The 5th Marines supporting the 1st Tank Battalion on D-Day, 15 September 1944.

Lieutenant Colonel Robert W. Boyd and his command, 1/5, landed on Orange 1 with two rifle companies abreast while LtCol Austin C. Shofner and 3/5 landed on Orange 2, in the same formation. Maj Gordon D. Gayle commanded 2/5, regimental reserve, which landed at 1015 on Orange 2. Gayle's command immediately got off the beach and headed inward. Boyd's Marines landed and went directly to the western edge of the airfield, arriving at 0900. There they and three tanks from LtCol Arthur J. Stuart's 1st Tank Bn dug in and awaited an anticipated tank attack. Shofner and 3/5 came over the beach to Boyd's left and proceeded inland, making the Phase One line within an hour of landing. Heavy enemy fire at landing craft coming in forced those carrying 3/7 (Maj Edward H. Hurst) to veer to their left and land Marines in Orange Beach Two, causing some confusion. It was soon righted and 3/7 managed to move to their right and begin their phase of the assault.

Late in the afternoon, enemy light tanks, with soldiers aboard, rumbled toward the lines of Marines, the latter picking off the riders and the tanks swerving out of the line of fire. Marine Shermans moved up and shelled them and completely broke up the attack. As they were heading back they were followed closely by Gayle's 2/5 which reached nearly the center of the airfield. During this fighting, an officer of 1/5, 1stLt Carleton R. Rouh, from Lindewood, NJ, was wounded. While he was being escorted to the rear an enemy grenade dropped among him and two Marines helping him. Dropping on the grenade he absorbed the blast and saved the lives of the two other Marines. Somehow he survived and earned a

Medal of Honor. Another Marine member of 1/5, Cpl Lewis K. Bausell, of Washington, D.C., while engaged in attacking a pillbox, saw a grenade drop within his group, and he too dropped upon it to save his buddies' lives. However, he lost his own, and a posthumous award of a Medal of Honor was presented to his next of kin.

By dusk, the 5th and 7th Marines had crossed the island and the latter had pushed south to close off that portion of the island to the enemy. However, the 1st Marines were still having great difficulties and were unable to get anywhere near their Phase One line, thus forestalling the 5th and 7th Marines from their trip north. Within an hour of landing all assault platoon leaders, and their platoon sergeants, were casualties. Command was now down to sergeants, when they were still available.

The next morning, Captain Hunt (Navy Cross for Peleliu), skipper of K Co, was only able to muster 78 Marines for duty, including the walking wounded. Regardless of that, the 1st Marines were still working over, as best they could, the worst position on the island. Their leader, Col Puller, was constantly pressuring the regiment to "do more." Eventually, the regiment was near and even onto what became known as "Bloody Nose Ridge." The name was given for obvious reasons. There was lots of blood all about it.

The other two regiments, 5th and 7th, were very busy but had less imposing obstacles to overcome and were able to manage the enemy much better. The 7th cleaned up the southern portion during the next few days and by the 18th were the victors. They had two Marines that earned the ultimate decoration. PFC Arthur J. Jackson, 3/7's own hero, from Cleveland, OH, boldly took the initiative when his platoon's left flank was being held up by Japanese in heavily fortified positions. Charging one, he poured fire from his BAR into the aperture and then tossed in phosphorus grenades, then satchel charges. He demolished the pillbox and killed off at least thirty-five of the enemy. He proceeded to destroy two more pillboxes and then charged other enemy positions, killing everything in his path. He eventually succeeded in demolishing twelve pillboxes and killing at least fifty Japanese soldiers. This one-man Marine Corps was appropriately awarded the nation's highest honor, a Medal of Honor.

While Jackson was killing and surviving, 2/7's PFC Charles H. Roan of Claude, TX, dropped on a grenade and saved the life of other Marines of his squad. His posthumous award was a Medal of Honor. That same day 2/1 (LtCol Russell E. Honsowetz) and 2/7 (LtCol Spencer S. Berger) took Hill 210, and Company B, 1/1, managed to take Hill 205. The 5th's obligations were a bit heavier and required the best they could provide, which was most satisfactory. They continued to press the IJA backward, taking most of the planned phase lines within their assignment. The hard-luck 1st Marines had the worst terrain to cover, the rugged high ground in which the enemy was well dug in, but they continued their efforts. They even managed to reach the "Five Sisters," the southern face of the final pocket of resistance on 19 September. Another hero, the skipper of Company C, 1/1, Capt Everett P. Pope of Milton, MA, witnessed his company's disorganization and destruction and decided to do something about it. Rallying his men, he and they once again attempted to assault the rock face which had defeated them so often. The machine guns, mortar, and rifle fire had reduced his command so badly it was a wonder that they could hold their place in line, let alone attack anyone. However, the remaining few made it and Pope decided to remain on this height all night with his one wounded officer and twelve men. All night they beat back attacks, resorting to hand-to-hand combat as their ammo was depleted. When daylight finally arrived he and his remaining eight Marines still held. Finally, he was ordered

Headquarters, 1st Marines establishing a Command Post.

to withdraw, but his leadership and determination to stand against overwhelming odds earned him a Medal of Honor.

The well-worn 1st Marines were so wasted that eventually, on 21 September, the regiment was replaced by the fresh, untried 321st (Col Robert F. Dark, USA) Infantry of the 81st InfDiv. Most Marines in a position to know were not surprised and many wondered why it took so long. General Rupertus and Col Puller were two notable dissenters but MG Roy S. Geiger, IIIAC Commander, ordered it done.

The 321st would have their hands full but the worst was over. The 5th Marines concluded their mission by taking the tiny island north of Ngabad on 23 September. It was now up to the infantry to take most of the burden on the west side of the island. A group titled the Neal Task Force, USA, landed in mid-island on 25 September, and headed north. Another man from 2/7, PFC John D. New, of Mobile, AL, threw himself upon a grenade and gave his life for his country, earning a posthumous Medal of Honor for his courage.

On 26 September, LtCol Boyd and 1/5 attacked toward the Amiangal, the northernmost hills on the island, and reached the northern tip, sealing it off. The infantry continued the fight to compress the Umurbrogal Pocket until relieved by the 7th Marines on 29 September. Ngesebus Island, off the northern tip of Peleliu, was taken by 3/5 (Maj John H. Gustafson).

The island, or most of it, was, for all intents and purposes, taken by 30 September. All except the "Pocket," which was in the middle of the island, occupying an area 900 by 400 yards. That was so heavily developed and defended that the Marines and soldiers were subjected to costly attrition at its deadliest. It was mainly the 5th Marines' action but the others assisted, as did recently landed Marine fighters from MAG 11. Sincere efforts were made to convince the very reluctant IJA to surrender, even to using captured Japanese soldiers to entice them with gifts of food, cigarettes and even candy bars. None of it was very successful. Heat prostration with accompanying near-lack of water caused more agony. As October came in the rains also came, the seas became more turbulent, and providing water and supplies from ships became even more difficult. One more member of 3/7, Pvt Wesley Phelps of Neafus, KY, threw himself on a grenade on 4 October, and though losing his life was posthumously awarded a Medal of Honor. The next day, 5 October, a member of the 8th Amphibious Tractor Bn, PFC Richard E. Kraus, born in Chicago, IL, threw himself upon a grenade to save his fellow Marines as they were trying to save wounded men. He too was posthumously awarded a Medal of Honor.

On 6 October the 5th Marines relieved the now exhausted 7th as the assault team. The 5th Marines continued doing what the 7th had been doing, but even though they were wearing the IJA down, they in turn were being worn down. On 14 October the 321st Infantry relieved the 5th Marines and on 15 Oct the 81st InfDiv (MG Paul J. Mueller, USA) officially relieved the 1stMarDiv. The Marine casualties numbered nearly 6,800 of which 1,300 died, plus 300 attached navy personnel. There were nearly 2,000 casualties on D-Day alone. The 1st MarDiv had many heroes, possibly the entire personnel, but the seven Marines that earned the Medal of Honor are the standouts.

Order of Battle
Peleliu
(15 September to 15 October 1944)

Headquarters

MG William H. Rupertus	CG
BG Oliver P. Smith	ADC
Col John T. Selden	CoS
Maj William E. Benedict	D-1 (To 23 Sept)
LtCol Harold O. Deakin	D-1
LtCol John W. Scott, Jr.	D-2
LtCol Lewis J. Fields	D-3
LtCol Harvey C. Tschirgi	D-4

Headquarters Bn

Col Joseph F. Hankins	CO (KIA 3 Oct)
LtCol Austin C. Shofner	CO

First Marines

Col Lewis B. Puller	CO
LtCol Richard P. Ross, Jr.	ExO
1stLt Frank C. Sheppard	R-1
Capt James W. Horton	R-2
Maj Bernard T. Kelly	R-3
Maj Francis T. Eagan	R-4

1/1

Maj Raymond C. Davis	CO
Maj Nikolai S. Stevenson	ExO
Capt James M. Rogers	B-3

2/1

LtCol Russell E. Honsowetz	CO
Maj Charles H. Brush, Jr.	ExO
Capt Robert W. Burnette	B-3 (To 18 Sept)
1stLt Bernard J. Baker	B-3

3/1

LtCol Stephen V. Sabol	CO
Maj William McNulty	ExO
Maj Jonas M. Platt	B-3

Fifth Marines

Col Harold D. Harris	CO
LtCol Lewis W. Walt	ExO
Capt Alan F. Dill	R-1 (To 16 Sept)
Capt Paul H. Douglas	R-1
Capt Levi T. Burcham	R-2
Maj Walter S. McIlhenny	R-3 (To 16 Sept)
Capt Donald A. Peppard	R-3
Maj Joseph S. Skoczylas	R-4 (To 30 Sept)

1/5

LtCol Robert W. Boyd	CO
Maj Harold T. A. Richmond	ExO
Maj Hierome L. Opie, Jr.	B-3 (To 15 Sept)
Capt Edwin B. Glass	B-3

Marine firing a bazooka into enemy caves.

2/5

Maj Gordon D. Gayle	CO
Maj John H. Gustafson	ExO (To 15 Sept)
Maj Richard T. Washburn	ExO
Maj Richard T. Washburn	B-3 (To 15 Sept)
Capt James H. Flagg	B-3

3/5

LtCol Austin C. Shofner	CO (To 15 Sept)
LtCol Lewis W. Walt	CO (Night 15/16)
Maj John H. Gustafson	CO (from 16 Sept)
Maj Robert M. Ash	ExO (To 15 Sept)
Maj Hierome L. Opie, Jr.	ExO
Maj Clyde A. Brooks	B-3

Seventh Marines

Col Herman H. Hanneken	CO
LtCol Norman Hussa	ExO
2dLt Richard F. Spindler	R-1
Capt Francis T. Farrell	R-2
Maj Walter Holomon	R-3
Maj Hector R. Migneault	R-4

1/7

LtCol John J. Gormely	CO
Maj Waite W. Worden	ExO
Maj Lloyd W. Martin	B-3

2/7

LtCol Spencer S. Berger	CO
Maj Elbert D. Graves	ExO (To 20 Sept)
Maj John F. Weber	ExO
Maj John F. Weber	B-3 (To 20 Sept)
Capt Lee W. Langham	B-3

3/7

Maj Edward Hunter Hurst	CO
Maj Victor H. Streit	ExO
Maj William J. King	B-3

Eleventh Marines

Col William H. Harrison	CO
LtCol Edson L. Lyman	ExO
1stLt Robert M. Alderson	R-1
Capt Richard W. Payne	R-2 (To 24 Sept)
2d Lt. Ralph W. Smith	R-2
LtCol Leonard F. Chapman, Jr.	R-3
Capt Lewis F. Treleaven	R-4

1/11

LtCol Richard W. Wallace	CO

Maj James H. Moffatt, Jr.	ExO	
Maj John R. Chaisson	B-3	

2/11

LtCol Noah P. Wood, Jr.	CO
Maj Floyd C. Maner	ExO (To 15 Sept)
Maj John P. McAlinn	ExO
Capt David R. Griffin	B-3

3/11

LtCol Charles M. Nees	CO
Maj William J. Hannan	ExO
Capt William R. Miller	B-3

4/11

LtCol Louis C. Reinberg	CO
Maj George E. Bowdoin	ExO
Maj Elliott Wilson	B-3

1st Tank Bn

LtCol Arthur J. Stuart	CO
Maj Donald J. Robinson	ExO
1stLt Ernest A. Hayden, Jr.	B-3

1st Service Bn

Col John Kaluf	CO
Maj Charles F. Rider	ExO

1st Motor Transport Bn

Capt Robert B. McBroom	CO
Capt George O. DeBell	ExO
1stLt Walter M. Greenspan	B-3

1st Pioneer Bn

LtCol Robert C. Ballance	CO
Maj Nathaniel Morgenthal	ExO
Capt Warren S. Sivertsen	B-3

1st Engineer Bn

LtCol Levi W. Smith, Jr.	CO
Maj Theodore E. Drummond	ExO
Maj Eugene T. Schoenfelder	B-3

1st Medical Bn

Comdr Emil E. Napp	CO

PAVAVU

Essentially, that was all for the Marines on Peleliu. It had taken one month since D-Day, and the infantry had a piece of work before the island was entirely secured. By 7 November the remaining members of the much smaller division was back on Pavavu. But it was a much different and better island than the one they had left in September. Their new CG, MG Pedro del Valle, had seen to that. Now they had tents, screened mess halls with better food, movie equipment that actually worked, plus movies, and beer, and even rest. But, as with Marines in every time and place, training for the next mission was soon the regular activity. Rumors, sometimes (usually) called scuttlebutt, had it as a landing on Formosa (Taiwan). They were all wrong. It was rather to be on the large island of Okinawa in the Ryukyu chain, bigger than any they had been on previously, and, they believed, free of assaulting caves. They soon learned that Okinawa was basically just that: caves and better prepared positions even than Peleliu, though with more square feet to maneuver around on. Okinawa was considered, by the Japanese, to be a part of the home islands, and it was only 600-odd miles from the southernmost tip of Kyushu, mainland Japan. This was close enough for one-way flights of war planes with shrinking available gasoline supplies. Planning included the problems inherent with a civilian population of about 300,000, including numerous native Japanese. Previous experiences on Saipan had made the specter of even more civilian deaths, especially suicides, a likely reality. Troop numbers in the chain were calculated at nearly 90,000 with approximately 83,000 in the southern part of Okinawa. This chain of islands was considered to be Japan proper and could be expected to be defended to the death, and it was.

OKINAWA

ICEBERG was the operational title given this final amphibious assault in the Pacific war. Three divisions of Marines were to participate, the 1st (MG Pedro del Valle), and the newly created 6thMarDiv (MG Lemuel C. Shepherd, Jr.), which, as a division, would be going into its premier landing. They would be part of the Marine IIIAC (LG Roy S. Geiger). The 2d MarDiv (MG Thomas E. Watson) was part of the initial overall plan, but was not brought ashore to solve a severe problem in the southern portion of the island. Elements of that division would, however, be engaged in a feint on L-Day and suffer the first casualties of the operation.

This was a joint effort and the IIIAC was part of the Tenth Army. Twenty-fourth Corps (MG John R. Hodge, USA) was the second half of the Tenth Army (LG Simon B. Buckner, Jr., USA) and also included the 7th InfDiv (MG Archibald V. Arnold, USA) and the 96th Inf Div (MG James L. Bradley, USA). Two other divisions plus the 2d MarDiv (Landing Force Reserve) were part of the XXIV Corps, the 27th (MG George W. Griner, Jr., USA) and 77th InfDiv (MG Andrew D. Bruce, USA). The latter had been actively cleaning out small pockets of Japanese troops on various islands in the Ryukyu chain while the former had served on Saipan with the 2d and 4th MarDivs. Planners were well aware that the most trouble would be encountered in the southern portion of the island, and, presumably, took that into account. It seldom appeared that way to the infantry, who would bear most of the burden for the first weeks.

Tenth Army landed four divisions on L-Day, 1 April 1945, and, much to their collective surprise, against token resistance. Both MarDivs landed north of the Bishi Gawa (River) and the 7th and 96th Divs, USA, south of that line. In order from north to south they were the 6th MarDiv (beaches Green 1 and 2, Red 1, 2, and 3), the 1st MarDiv (Blue 1 and 2, Yellow 1, 2, and 3); 7th InfDiv (beaches Purple 1 and 2, Orange 1 and 2) and lastly, the 96th InfDiv (White 1, 2, and 3; and Brown 1, 2, 3, and 4). Shortly after landing, the 1st MarDiv was able to drive across the island south of the Yonton Air Field and reach the opposite shore, without too much difficulty. The 6th MarDiv swung northeast and, eventually, it also found little resistance. The USA divisions would be severely tested as they headed southeast, for that is where the IJA had decided to defend Okinawa.

The 1st MarDiv reached the easternmost coast by 3 April with minimal resistance. Actually, the 1st MarDiv's Recon Co made the east coast on 2 April. Del Valle and his staff were perplexed. This was totally unexpected, yet highly welcomed by everyone in the division. By the 4th they held all of that mid-portion of the island. This state of affairs went on for two weeks, during which time souvenir-happy Marines collected anything not nailed down. This included livestock, including goats and even horses. Here, in their fourth major landing, the division was living the life of Riley. During this early period the division usually lacked immediate artillery support. Prime gun movers were not available ashore to move the guns for several days. Fortunately, the guns were seldom required. All that would change. During this period, the 6th MarDiv went northeast and managed, after a big fight on Motobu Peninsula, to take the entire northern portion of Okinawa. (See the entry for the 6th Division).

But what of the enemy? Where was he, why had he not defended the beaches or at least this central part of the island? The IJA had made their defensive plans and didn't share them with the American command. It was their decision to select their ground and it was found to be formidable as the XXIV Corps made their way southeast. The ground south of the airfields became rough and that continued down to Shuri, about 10 miles below the Kadena Air Field. There are two horrific ridges in between and, in getting through, the XXIV Corps had their work cut out for them. They ran into the Machinato Line on 4 April and, temporarily, were effectively stopped "dead in the water."

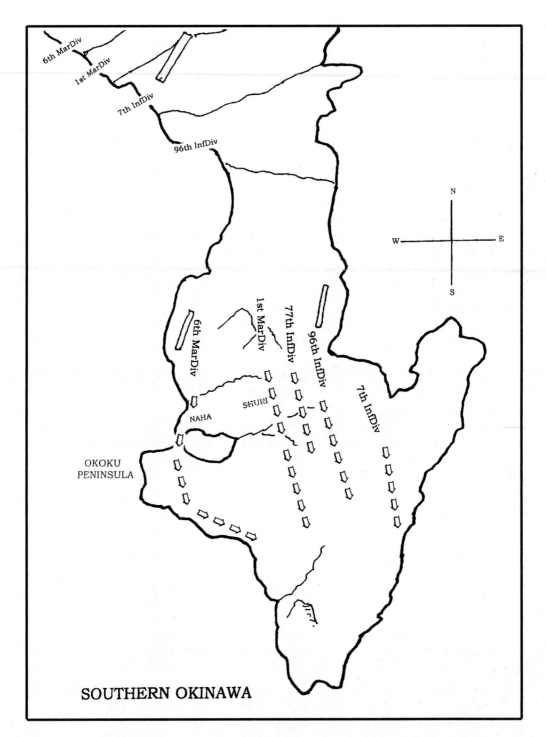

Okinawa

On 6 April the IJN launched a suicide mission led by the super battleship *Yamato* (largest warship on earth) with just enough fuel to get to where the invasion fleet was anchored. RA Raymond Spruance was informed and prepared to receive the monster before it reached its target. On 7 April USN fleet aircraft destroyed *Yamato* and its accompanying light cruiser. Also on 7 April came the first of the "Divine Wind" (*Kamikaze*) suicide aerial attacks against allied shipping. They were horrendous to the sailors aboard anchored ships and each attack created havoc, even though their ultimate value has historically been minimized. Meanwhile ashore, the XXIV Corps was running into violent opposition and the casualties mounted precipitously.

Buckner called in the un-engaged 27th InfDiv on 9 April to assist the badly used 96th and 7th Inf Divs. He also took the 11th Marines from the 1st MarDiv and placed them in line with the 7th and 96th Artillery Regiments. The Tenth Army's new formation had the 27th on the western flank, the 96th in the center and the 7th still on the far eastern flank. The slugfest went on. Gen Buckner decided to utilize the 1st MarDiv by incorporating it into the XXIV Corps, but in small units, not as a division. The Army didn't want too many Marines involved. On 27 April he decided to parcel out the balance of the 1st MarDiv, leaving MG Geiger with a one-division (6th MarDiv) corps.

However, the advance of the under-strength 27th InfDiv soon stalled, and on 1 May Buckner placed them in the rear areas as garrison troops. He substituted the 1st MarDiv in its place in line on the western flank and they continued the battle from there. Giving up lives was immediate for the 1st MarDiv. On 2 May a Marine from Cleveland, OH, 3/1's PFC William A. Foster, with a comrade, was engaged in tossing grenades at the enemy. When one landed in their hole he quickly absorbed it, gave his grenades to his buddy and yelled "Make 'em count." This brought a posthumous Medal of Honor. This was followed on 4 May by a Greenville, TN, Marine, Sgt Elbert L. Kinser of Company I, 3/1, who also absorbed a live grenade and "gallantly gave his life for his country." His award for a courageous action was a Medal of Honor.

After a week of slugging it out, Gen Geiger was ordered to assume command of the 1st MarDiv zone and to bring the 6th MarDiv into line on their right along the coast. With that the IIIAC was brought into action and assumed positions on the western flank of the Tenth Army. U.S. Army XXIV Corps remained on the eastern flank, and both corps pressed southeastward.

Meanwhile, much pressure was being exerted upon Buckner to bring in the 2d MarDiv to deploy at the tip end of the island and take the IJA in the rear. For some reason he refused everyone, including RA Richmond K. Turner, who wanted rapid movement on the ground in order to move his ships away from their targeted positions just offshore. One correspondent wrote complaining that "Our tactics were ultra-conservative. Instead of an end-run, we persisted in frontal attacks." The enemy air attacks had been creating havoc, especially upon the smaller vessels. Instead of Buckner using 2d MarDiv as recommended, the two corps continued pounding the defense lines, straight forward, much like World War I. On 3 May the IJA made an amphibious landing in substantial force behind the 1st MarDiv but was defeated and literally destroyed by 5 May. In the meantime, the unused 2d MarDiv was shipped back to Saipan. Management had decided that two Marine divisions ashore were enough.

Three Medals of Honor were awarded for actions by Marines on 7 May 1945. Chicago's Cpl John P. Fardy, of 1/1, tossed himself onto a grenade, thereby giving up his own life that his comrades might live. Over in 2/1, Wisner, NE's own Pvt Dale M. Hansen took the initiative when he took a rocket launcher and attacked several hostile pillboxes. When his weapon was destroyed by enemy fire he then grabbed an M-1 and continued his one-man assault. Jumping into a hole with six Japanese he killed four with his rifle, and when it jammed, beat the other two off with his rifle butt. Falling back to his comrades, he grabbed

Heavy rains in May and June caused the 1st MarDiv great problems.

more grenades and another rifle, then ventured forth once more. Hansen destroyed a mortar position and annihilated eight more of the enemy. He was heavily responsible for the success of the division on that front that day. His reward was a Medal of Honor, which he richly deserved. The third went to a member of 1/5, a flamethrower man from Oklahoma named PFC Albert E. Schwab. Schwab, seemingly without fear, advanced straight at the enemy under a hail of bullets, and quickly demolished a machine gun. Suddenly another machine gun opened up, killing and wounding several Marines. Schwab went forward and, though low on fuel and severely wounded by the gun, attacked and destroyed the second gun. This enabled his company to advance, and his reward was a Medal of Honor. On 11 May Tenth Army opened an all-out attack upon Shuri's inner defenses and 2/5 eliminated the last enemy resistance in the Awache Pocket. The following day, it was the turn of the 7th Marines (Col Edward W. Snedeker) to lead the 1st MarDiv, and for about a week they suffered heavy casualties while taking Dakeshi Ridge and trying to take Wana Ridge. A week passed and Snedeker and his regiment were relieved on line by the 1st Marines (Col Arthur T. Mason). In nine days the regiment had suffered 1,250 casualties. At the same time, on the coast, the 6th MarDiv was also pressing forward in the region of Sugar Loaf Hill, which they took on 18 May. The entire IIIAC had run into stiffening resistance on 14 May and it became apparent that they had struck the IJA's main line of resistance. Unlike up north, this was truly a slugging match and the conquest of the island was not coming easy. The 1st MarDiv was still trying to take the Wana Ridge and its draw. It would take most of May to accomplish that one objective.

On the 14th, a leader of a machine gun squad attached to Company C, 1/1, Cpl Louis J. Hauge, Jr., from Ada, MN, boldly took the initiative when his company's left flank was

Tanks evacuate the wounded as men of the 1st Marines press the fight to capture Sugar Loaf.

pinned down by a heavy machine gun and mortar attack, suffering severe casualties. While his guns concentrated on pinning down the enemy guns, Hauge launched a personal attack with grenades. Though suffering from several wounds he single-handedly knocked out one gun, then went for the second. With grenades he managed to wipe out the second gun before falling to a severe density of enemy fire upon himself. His enterprise and courage enabled his company to advance and successfully attain their objective. However, he suffered the ultimate, and the reward was a posthumous Medal of Honor.

On 29 May, 1/5 (LtCol Charles W. Shelburne) was finally able to take Shuri Ridge, and soon after captured Shuri Castle. This forced the 32d Japanese Army to vacate the Shuri Line, which had been holding up the Americans for most of the month. The enemy fell back to the Kiyamu Peninsula at the southernmost edge of the island, thereby escaping the flanking drives of both the IIIAC and the XXIV Corps. In a combined operation, the 1st MarDiv and the 77th InfDiv took the entire Shuri Line on 31 May.

On 1 June the IIIAC launched a coordinated drive by both Marine Divisions and secured the high ground overlooking the new enemy defensive positions in the Kokuba Gawa Valley. The XXIV Corps changed its direction to attack the main enemy defensive positions in the southern sector of the island. The IIIAC boundary was narrowed as it shifted to the west and the 1st MarDiv was made responsible for cutting off the Oroku Peninsula and for the capture of the most southerly portion of the island. The 6th MarDiv eventually fought the peninsula, capturing it on or about 13 Jun.

The 2d Bn, 7th Marines (LtCol Spencer S. Berger), continuing southward, captured Itoman, a large town on the coast. Meanwhile 1/7 (LtCol John J. Gormley) took Tera, lying about 1,000 yards to the east; both were taken over the night of 11–12 June. Continuing forward, the 7th Marines encountered another strongly held position on Kunishi Ridge. Not only was the enemy well-ensconced on that coral outgrowth but the ground leading to it was a broad valley containing rice paddies and providing little cover. The initial assault was costly and ineffective, and Col Snedeker called it off on the afternoon of 11 June. He made an aerial reconnaissance and, concluding the ridge was too strong to attack in daylight hours, decided to instead attack it at night. During the 13th the entire division was engaged in preparation for the assault upon Kunishi, planned for the early morning of the 14th.

The assault went off and included the 1st Marines as well as the 7th Marines. The fighting was intense and it was nearly a full week before the Marines had taken the last strong point leading south on Okinawa. Among other innovations during this battle, tanks were commonly utilized to bring the many wounded back off the ridge. The 1st MarDiv casualties for the period were 1,150 and there was still more fighting to the south. In the meantime, the 8th Marines, 2d MarDiv (Col Clarence R. Wallace) arrived and were attached to the 1st MarDiv.

On 18 June LG Simon B. Buckner was killed while observing the progress of the 8th Marines' first attack on the island. MG Roy S. Geiger, CG IIIAC, assumed command of and directed the final combat operations of the Tenth Army. On 21 June the 1st MarDiv captured Hill 81 while the 29th Marines, 6th MarDiv took the southernmost part of the islands. The following day, 22 June, was proclaimed as the formal termination of the Okinawan campaign.

However, the two Marine divisions and the 7th and 97th Inf Div's were ordered to mop up the northern parts of the island of any holdouts, allowing ten days for the completion of that action. Their sweep began on 25 Jun. On 23 June LG Joseph W. Stilwell, USA, arrived from the United States and formally relieved MG Roy S. Geiger in command of the Tenth Army.

Order of Battle
Okinawa
(1 April to 22 June 1945)

Headquarters

MG Pedro A. del Valle	CG
BG Louis R. Jones	ADC
Col Robert O. Bare	CoS
LtCol Harold O. Deakin	G-1
LtCol John W. Scott, Jr.	G-2
LtCol Russell E. Honsowetz	G-3
LtCol Harvey C. Tschirgi	G-4

Headquarters Bn

LtCol James S. Monahan	CO (To 20 May)
Col Kenneth B. Chappell	CO (To 31 May)
Maj Lewis M. Andrews	ExO
2dLt William G. Porter	S-3
Capt John E. Williams	CO Hdqs Co
1stLt Lawrence E. Kindred	CO 1st MP Co
1stLt Robert J. Powell, Jr.	CO Reconn Co
Capt Thomas J. Flynn, Jr.	CO 1st Sig Co
LtCol John E. Morris	CO 1st ASCO
Capt Grammer G. Edwards	CO 3d Amph Trk Co

First Marines

Col Kenneth B. Chappell	CO (To 5 May
Col Arthur T. Mason	CO
LtCol Richard P. Ross, Jr.	ExO (To 20 May)
LtCol James S. Monahan	ExO
Maj Bernard T. Kelly	S-3 (WIA 5 Apr)
Maj Jonas M. Platt	S-3 1st
Lt Walton M. Rock	CO H&S Co (To 21 Apr)
1stLt Eustace C. M. Waller	CO H&S Co (To 1 Jun)
Capt Wayne B. Davis	CO H&S Co
Capt Lawrence K. Hennessy	CO Wpns Co (To 21 Apr)
Maj Robert W. Burnette	CO Wpns Co (WIA 3 Jun)
Capt Francis D. Rineer	CO Wpns Co

1/1

LtCol James C. Murray, Jr.	CO (WIA 9 May)
LtCol Richard P. Ross, Jr.	CO (To 12 May)
LtCol Austin C. Shofner	CO

Maj Jonas M. Platt	ExO (To 22 Apr)
Maj Henry G. Baron	ExO (To 14 May)
Capt Thomas K. Greer	ExO (To 10 Jun)
Maj Franklin B. Nihart	ExO
1stLt Fendall W. Yerxa	S-3 (To 18 Jun)
Maj Leon Goldberg	S-3
Maj William F. Belcher	CO Hdqs Co (To 14 May)
1stLt Richard M. Highsmith Jr.	CO Hdqs Co (To 20 May)
1stLt Marion G. Truesdale	CO Hdqs Co
1stLt Paul E. Burke	CO A Co (WIA 6 Jun)
1stLt James R. Currler	CO A Co
Capt Francis D. Rineer	CO B Co (WIA 30 April, * to 29 May)
Capt Richard A. Poe	CO B Co (To 6 Jun)
Capt Francis D. Rineer	CO B Co (To 18 Jun)
1stLt Fendall W. Yerxa	CO B Co
1stLt Weldon M. Longbotham	CO C Co (WIA 14 May)
Capt Richard A. Poe	CO C Co (WIA 24 May, * to 28 May)
1stLt Francis T. Burke	CO C Co (To 3 Jun)
Capt Richard A. Poe	CO C Co (From 7 June, WIA 11 Jun)
Capt Thomas K. Greer	CO C Co (From 11 Jun)

1/2

LtCol James C. Magee, Jr.	CO
Maj Raymond C. Portillo	ExO (To 21 Apr)
Maj Bernard T. Kelly	ExO
Maj Robert W. Burnette	S-3 (To 21 Apr)
Maj Raymond C. Portilo	S-3
Capt George L. Dacy	CO Hdqs Co (To 14 May)
1stLt William K. Hunt	CO Hdqs Co
1stLt Robert W. Schmitt	CO E Co (WIA 7 May)
1stLt Richard B. Watkins	CO E Co (WIA 13 May)
Capt Edward R. Tiscornia	CO F Co (KIA 2 May)
1stLt Walter E. Burke	CO F Co
1stLt Fay K. Koiner, Jr.	CO G Co (WIA 14 May)
1stLt Jim "J" Paulos	CO G Co (To 17 May)
1stLt John J. Cavanaugh	CO G Co (To 1 Jun)
1stLt Marcus H. Jaffe	CO G Co

1/3

LtCol Stephen V. Sabol	CO (To 20 May)
LtCol Richard P. Ross, Jr.	CO
Maj Frederick W. Lindlaw	ExO (To 18 May)
Capt Wayne B. Davis	ExO (To 25 May)
Maj Leon Goldberg	ExO (To 6 Jun)
Maj John V. Kelsey	ExO (To 18 Jun)
Maj Frederick W. Lindlaw	ExO
Capt Wayne B. Davis	S-3 (To 21 Apr)
Capt James M. Marshall	S-3 (To 18 Jun)
Maj John V. Kelsey	S-3
1stLt Eustace C. M. Waller	CO Hdqs Co (To 21 Apr)
Capt Wayne B. Davis	CO Hdqs Co (To 1 Jun)
1stLt James D. Currie	CO Hdqs Co (To 18 Jun)
1stLt Charles J. Kohler, Jr.	CO Hdqs Co
1stLt William A. Young, Jr.	CO I Co (To 21 Apr)
Capt Lawrence K. Hennessy	CO I Co (KIA 21May)
1stLt Elmer L. Cochran	CO I Co (To 1 Jun)
1stLt William A. Young, Jr.	CO I Co
1stLt William O. Sellers	CO K Co
Capt Alton C. Bennett	CO L Co (To 13 May)
1stLt James J. Haggerty	CO L Co (To 15 May)
1stLt Harry L. Ziegler	CO L Co (WIA 4 Jun)
1stLt Eustace C. M. Waller	CO L Co

Fifth Marines

Col John H. Griebel	CO
LtCol John D. Muncie	ExO
Maj James H. Flagg	S-3
Capt Nicholas R. Goche	CO H&S Co
Capt Carl H. Lockard	CO Wpns Co

1/5

LtCol Charles W. Shelburne	CO
Maj Frank W. Poland, Jr.	ExO (To 16 May)
Maj Reed F. Taylor	ExO
Capt Lloyd E. Howell	S-3
2dLt Lewis J. Schott	CO Hdqs Co (To 30 Apr)
Capt Julian D. Dusenbury	CO A Co (WIA 10 May * to 18 Jun)
1stLt Walter R. Wilson	CO B Co
1stLt Walter E. Lange	CO C Co

2/5

LtCol William B. Benedict	CO (To 20 Jun)
Maj Richard T. Washburn	CO
Maj Richard T. Washburn	ExO (To 20 Jun)
1stLt Martin F. Fritz	ExO
Maj John R. Hogan	S-3 (WIA 4 May)
1stLt Ward M. Wilcox	S-3

2dLt Richard F. Simpson	CO Hdqs Co (To 30 Apr)
1stLt Martin F. Fritz	CO Hdqs Co
1stLt Michael D. Benda	CO E Co (WIA 29 May)
Capt Franklin D. Sills	CO E Co (WIA 13 June *)
1stLt William A. Taylor	CO F Co (WIA 3 May)
1stLt Joseph H. Bowling	CO F Co (WIA 10 May)
1stLt Robert F. Fry	CO F Co (WIA 17 May)
1stLt William A. Brougher	CO F Co
1stLt Richard R. Breen	CO G Co (WIA 7 May *)

3/5

Maj John H. Gustafson	CO (WIA 1 Apr)
LtCol John C. Miller, Jr.	CO (4 April to 16 May)
Maj Frank W. Poland, Jr.	CO (To 8 Jun)
LtCol Robert B. Hill	CO
Maj Martin C. Roth	ExO
Capt George S. Sharp	S-3 (WIA 14 May)
Capt Edwin B. Glass	S-3
Capt William Flynn	CO Hdqs Co
Capt James P. Ó Laughlin	CO I Co (WIA 7 May * WIA 24 May)
1stLt John A. Fredenberger	CO I Co (WIA 28 May)
1stLt Carrol R. Wilson	CO I Co (KIA 2 Jun)
1stLt Richard H. Sengewald	CO I Co
1stLt Thomas J. Stanley	CO K Co (To 24 May)
1stLt George B. Loveday	CO K Co
Capt Robert P. Smith	CO L Co (To 8 Jun)
1stLt Robert D. Metzger	CO L Co

Seventh Marines

Col Edward W. Snedeker	CO
LtCol James M. Masters, Sr.	ExO
Maj Walter Holomon	S-3 (To 22 May)
LtCol Stephen V. Sabol	S-3 (To 19 Jun)
Maj John W. Arnold	CO H&S Co (To 4 Apr)
1stLt Maurice J. Cavanaugh, Jr.	CO H&S Co
Capt Welton H. Bunger, Jr.	CO Wpns Co

1/7

LtCol John J. Gormley	CO
Maj Hector R. Migneault	ExO (WIA 14 May)
Capt Don P. Wyckoff	ExO (To 17 May)
Maj Henry G. Baron, Jr.	ExO (To 9 Jun)
Maj Harold C. Howard	ExO
Capt Don P. Wyckoff	S-3

Capt Robert L. Gibson	CO Hdqs Co (To 31 May)
1stLt Russell R. Feazell	CO Hdqs Co
1stLt Robert Romo	CO A Co (KIA 14 May)
1stLt Ernest McCall	CO A Co
1stLt Roger A. Golden	CO B Co (To 18 May)
Capt Leonard R. Heller	CO B Co (To 11 Jun)
Capt Lee W. Langham	CO B Co
Capt Richard E. Rohrer	CO C Co (To 17 Jun)

2/7

LtCol Spencer S. Berger	CO
Maj Louis O. Ditta	ExO
1stLt Harry B. Wheeler	S-3 (To 18 Jun)
Maj James M. Robinson	S-3
Capt Lee W. Langham	CO Hdqs Co (To 10 May)
1stLt Joseph W. Kensik, Jr.	CO Hdqs Co
Capt Paul C. Beardslee, Jr.	CO E Co (KIA 1 Apr)
1stLt William G. Hudson, Jr.	CO E Co (To 15 Apr)
Capt Robert J. Noonan	CO E Co (WIA 2 Jun)
1stLt William G. Hudson, Jr.	CO E Co (WIA 11 Jun)
1stLt Franklin W. Myers	CO E Co
Capt Harold E. Grasse	CO F Co (DOW 12 May)
Capt Lee W. Langham	CO F Co (To 11 Jun)
1stLt John W. Huff	CO F Co
Capt Kirt W. Norton	CO G Co

3/7

LtCol Edward H. Hurst	CO (WIA 19 Jun)
LtCol Stephen V. Sabol	CO
Maj John F. Corbett	ExO (To 18 May)
Maj William F. Belcher	ExO (To 22 May)
Maj Walter Holomon	ExO
Maj James B. Kirk, Jr.	S-3 (To 15 May)
Capt Henry J. Guinivan. Jr.	S-3
Capt James G. Triebel	CO Hdqs Co (To 28 Apr)
Capt Henry J. Guinivan, Jr.	CO Hdqs Co (From 30 Apr to 15 May)
1stLt Arlus C. Henderson	CO Hdqs Co (To 17 May)
Maj William F. Belcher	CO Hdqs Co (KIA 14 Jun)
Maj Alexander W. Chilton	CO Hdqs Co
Capt Robert I. Owen	CO I Co (To 30 Apr)
1stLt Peter I. McDonnell	CO I Co (KIA 18 May)

Maj John F. Corbett	CO I Co (WIA 19 May)
2dLt Emory A. Baner	CO I Co (TO 19 May)
1stLt Charles B. Crow	CO I Co (To 20 Jun)
Capt Robert I. Owen	CO I Co
1stLt Robert B. Morton	CO K Co (To 18 Apr)
1stLt Charles R. Hickox	CO K Co (To 20 Apr)
1stLt Robert B. Morton	CO K Co (To 23 Apr)
1stLt Robert W. Dalryrmple	CO K Co (WIA 16 May)
Maj James B. Kirk. Jr.	CO K Co
Capt Roland H. Collins	CO L Co (WIA 9 May *)
Capt Henry J. Guinivan, Jr.	CO L Co (To 18 May)
Capt Roland H. Collins	CO L Co

Eleventh Marines

Col Wilburt S. Brown	CO
LtCol Edson L. Lyman	ExO
Maj Charles D. Harris	S-3
1stLt Joseph Ermenc	CO H&S Btry

1/11

LtCol Richard W. Wallace	CO
LtCol George M. Lhamon	ExO
Maj Ernest E. Schott	S-3
Capt Glenn E. Morris	CO H&S Btry
Capt Neal C. Newell	CO A Btry
Capt Maurice L. Cater	CO B Btry
Maj Lawrence A. Tomlinson Jr.	CO C Btry

2/11

LtCol James H. Moffatt, Jr.	CO
Maj John L. Donnell	ExO
Maj William C. Givens	S-3
1stLt Martin R. Bock. Jr.	CO H&S Btry
Capt James T. Pearce	CO D Btry
Capt Lorenzo G. Cutlip	CO E Btry (WIA 22 Jun)
Capt Fritz Stampeli	CO E Btry
Capt Robert S. Preston	CO F Btry

3/11

LtCol Thomas G. Roe	CO
LtCol Samuel S. Wooster	ExO
Capt Benjamin H. Brown	S-3 (To 6 Jun)
Maj Robert E. Collier	S-3
2dLt Charles E. Edwards	CO H&S Btry (WIA 12 Apr)
Maj Everett W. Smith	CO H&S Btry (To 26 Apr)
Capt Edward T. Haislip	CO H&S Btry
Capt Charles W. Fowler	CO G Btry
Capt William R. Miller	CO H Btry
1stLt John L. McDonald, Jr.	CO I Btry (WIA 4 April *)

4/11

LtCol Leonard F. Chapman, Jr.	CO
Maj Andre D. Gomez	ExO
Capt James A. Crotinger	S-3 (To 12 Jun)
Maj Lewis D. Baughman	S-3
Capt Randall L. Mitchell	CO H&S Btry (To 30 Apr)
Capt Thomas F. Moran	CO H&S Btry (To 31 May)
1stLt Gordon C. Petersen	CO H&S Btry
Maj Lewis F. Treleaven	CO K Btry (WIA 28 April *)
Capt Richard M. Moordale	CO L Btry
Capt George S. Nixon	CO M Btry

1st Engineer Bn

Maj Theodore E. Drummond	CO
Maj William A. Swinerton	ExO
Capt Robert C. Snyder	S-3
Capt William H. Owens, Jr.	CO H&S Co (To 2 May)
Capt John N. Rathwell	CO H&S Co
Capt Daniel J. McLellan	CO A Co
Capt Charles A. Hamilton	CO B Co
Capt John G. Aldworth	CO C Co

1st Medical Bn

LCmdr Francis Giuffrida	CO
Lt Roger Stevenson	CO H&S Co
Lt Charles E. Schoff	CO A Co (To 1 Jun)
Lt Lloyd F. Sherman	CO A Co
Lt Rupert B. Turnbull	CO B Co
Lt David S. Slossberg	CO C Co
LCmdr Joseph C. Fremont	CO D Co
LCmdr Edwin B. Murchison	CO E Co

1st Motor Transport Bn

LtCol Marion A. Fawcett	CO (To 15 Apr)
LtCol Calvin C. Gaines	CO
Maj Henry D. Shields	ExO
1stLt Walter M. Greenspan	S-3
1stLt Edwin J. Sehl	CO H&S Co
Capt Ben Sutts	CO A Co
Capt Francis I. Ford, Jr.	CO B Co
1stLt Wayne "W" Miller	CO C Co

1st Pioneer Bn

LtCol Robert G. Ballance	CO
Maj Warren S. Sivertsen	ExO
1stLt William J. Selfridge, Jr.	S-3
Capt Benjamin T. Cocke	CO H&S Co (To 1 Jun)
1stLt Darrell A. Watson	CO H&S Co
Capt Stanley W. Slowakiewicz	CO A Co
Capt John M. Kennedy	CO B Co
1stLt John H. Heussner	CO C Co

1st Service Bn

LtCol Calvin C. Gaines	CO (To 17 Apr)
Col John Kaluf	CO
Capt Edwin B. Glass	ExO (To 14 May)

Maj William F. Belcher	ExO (To 17 May)	1stLt Harold A. Ipson	CO B Co
Capt Alton C. Bennett	ExO (From 20 May)	Capt Wilfred S. LeFrancois	CO C Co (To 7 May)
1stLt Harry L. Tovani	CO Hdqs Co	1stLt Hillard "D" Thorpe	CO D Co
Capt Edward P. Faulkner	CO Ord Co		

1st Amph Trac Bn

1stLt Herbert R. Peterson	CO S&S Co

LtCol Maynard M. Nohrden	CO

1st Tank Bn

		Maj Victor J. Harwick	ExO
LtCol Arthur J. Stuart	CO (WIA 13 Jun)	1stLt Harold F. Harman	S-3
Capt Richard A. Munger	ExO (To 18 Jun)	Capt John A. Lockwood, Jr.	CO H&S Co
Maj Robert M. Neiman	ExO	1stLt Paul Phillips	CO A Co
1stLt Lester T. Chase	S-3	1stLt William H. Blatti	CO B Co
Capt John K. Gaieski	CO H&S Co	1stLt Harry O. Lee	CO C Co

1stLt Howard R. Taylor, Jr.	CO A Co
Capt Jack R. Munday	CO B Co

8th Amph Trac Bn

1stLt George E. Jerue	CO C Co

		LtCol Charles B. Nerren	CO (To 13 Apr)
		Maj Bedford Williams	CO (To 17 Apr)

3d Armored Amph Bn (Prov.)

		LtCol Charles B. Nerren	CO
LtCol John I. Williamson, Jr.	CO (To 7 May)	Maj Bedford Williams	ExO (To 13 Apr)
Maj Arthur M. Parker, Jr.	CO	Maj Bedford Williams	ExO (From 18 Apr)
Maj Arthur M. Parker, Jr.	ExO (To 7 May)		
Capt Wilfred S. LeFrancois	ExO	1stLt John R. Tull	S-3
Capt Marvin E. Mitchell	S-3 (To 19 Jun)	1stLt Robert W. Caveney	CO H&S Co
Capt Whitley A. Cummings, Jr.	CO H&S Co (From 22Apr)	Capt Robert P. Rapp	CO A Co
1stLt Norman C. Bray, Jr.	CO A Co	Capt William D. Evans	CO B Co

The 1st MarDiv had expected to be relieved and anticipated being sent to Hawaii for rehabilitation, but as always, the division was to be retained in the western reaches of the Pacific Ocean. It had not been in a "civilized" society since Australia, last seen in September 1943, nearly two years before. It had been in more operations than any of the other five divisions, and its casualty rate put it forward of all the rest. The division's total casualties reached nearly 20,000 during the war.

Its next move would be to Northern China, in September 1945. There they would perform services for the Chinese Nationalists and try to eliminate any power plays by the Communists. They would fail, not for their inadequacies, but for those of Chiang Kai-shek and his minions. While in China, the men would engage in processing surrendered Japanese soldiers out of China and back to Japan. They would also fight the Communists several times while engaged in protecting trainloads of coal and other valuables moving from the north to the south. The division would not return to the United States until 1 Sep 1948; however, Company C, 1st Battalion, 7th Marines would remain behind in China until 26 May 1949. It would serve nobly in several more wars to come: Korea, Vietnam, and the Gulf Wars in the 20th–21st Centuries.

2d Marine Division

The 2d MarDiv came into existence at Camp Elliott, near San Diego, on 1 February 1941. It was organized from the 2d Marine Brigade, which had its birthday on 1 July 1936. The brigade served with the 4th Marines in Shanghai, China, arriving on 19 Sep 1937, and was composed, principally, of the 6th Marines. It was redeployed back to California during early 1938. Major General Clayton B. Vogel became the first CG of the 2d MarDiv and by late spring, 1941, the division was composed of three regiments of infantry, the 2d, 6th, and 8th Marines; and the artillery regiment, the 10th Marines. It had the usual service units, medical, engineers, transport, tanks, signal, and antiaircraft battalions and companies. All three infantry and the artillery regiments had long and noble service.

On 1 January 1901 the first recognizable 2d Marine Regiment came into existence when it was formed at Cavite, Philippine Islands, under the command of LtCol Allen C. Kelton. With almost as many "seconds" or 2ds, as the 1st Marine Regiment in its history, the regiment has had its ups and downs for a century plus. The main body was also known, frequently, as the "First" between June 1913 and 1932.

The 2d Marines came back into existence on 1 January 1933 and went out again on 15 August 1934. On 1 February 1941 the Corps tried once more and brought into life, under Col Joseph C. Fegan, the 2d Marines as an integral part of the 2d MarDiv. During its earlier years the regiment served in Haiti and its neighbor, Santo Domingo.

Its first World War II engagement was when Company B, 1/2, landed on Florida Island to protect the left flank of the unit landing on Tulagi Island during the Guadalcanal Campaign. The other companies of 1/2 spread out on Florida nearer to Gavutu and Tanambogo, cleared their objectives, and re-embarked to await further orders.

The 6th Marines had been in France as part of the 4th Brigade, and served nobly. They assisted the 5th Marines and the 6th Machine Gun Battalion in "winning the war in France." During the 1920's the 6th Marines was deactivated numerous times. When activated it was more a skeleton than a bona fide live regiment. Its primary occupation between the wars was when, twice, it was sent to China, in 1927 to support BG Butler's 3d Marine Brigade, and again in 1937. The 6th Marines plus one battalion of the 10th Marines, accompanied by support units, sailed to Iceland in May–June, 1941, there to relieve British troops, as part of the president's policy to keep the Germans from occupying territory in the Atlantic Ocean.

The 8th Marines was originally activated on 9 October 1917 when it was deployed to the 3d Brigade at Galveston, TX, to observe the border with Mexico for possible anti-American activity. When World War I terminated, so did the necessity of watching the Mexicans. On 25 April 1919 the 8th Marines was deactivated.

Over the years following that, several times a separate battalion was, on occasion, reactivated and soon after deactivated like so many other Marine regiments. The unit that became part of the 2d MarDiv was activated on 1 April 1940 with a hero of the 4th

Brigade in command: Col Leo D. Hermle. The following 24 July, Col Henry L. Larsen, another in the long line of 4th Brigade heroes, assumed command. He was replaced by Col Richard H. Jeschke as the regiment was preparing, with the 2d MarDiv, to move into Guadalcanal.

In the meantime the regiment became part of the 2d Marine Brigade on 1 February 1941. After reinforcement, it was deployed to Samoa on 19 January 1942 where it was brought to strength by transfer of personnel from the 3d Marines. It was redeployed and attached to the 1st MarDiv at Guadalcanal from November 1942 to February 1943. Once again it would be attached to the 1st MarDiv, at Okinawa in June 1945. But for the balance of its World War II existence it served continually as a unit of the 2d MarDiv.

The 10th Marines was the only U.S. Marine unit to serve as an artillery regiment during its entire career, beginning on 15 April 1914 as a battalion with the 1st Brigade at Vera Cruz. Elements of that force served briefly in the islands but it did not become a regiment until 15 January 1918. Its two battalions were deactivated following World War I and though that numeric was often reactivated during the ensuing years, sent to China with Butler in 1927, and again in September 1937, it was once more deactivated.

On 1 November 1940, a new 1st Battalion was constructed from the activated reserve 22d Battalion and assigned to the 2d Brigade. The 10th Marine regiment was reactivated on 27 December 1940. The various battalions were combined and the regiment, as such, was assigned to the 2d MarDiv on 1 February 1941. One of its battalions, 2/10, served with the Iceland contingent from June 1941 until its return in March 1942. The 1st Bn went to Samoa with the 2d Marine Brigade. When the 2d MarDiv was finally formed with all its constituents, and landed on Guadalcanal, the 10th Marines was then composed of four battalions, the 5th was organized but soon became the 1st Bn, 12th Marines (3d MarDiv).

Other portions to be included as part of the 2d MarDiv acted as part of the defense of California from an anticipated enemy invasion. Gen Vogel was yet to have his entire division together as a command, and as of 7 December 1941 he was relieved in command by MG Charles F.B. Price. His lack of overall supervision, through no fault of his own, would continue until he too was relieved on 1 April 1942. MG John Marston was next and he remained so until 3 April 1943. It was his hard luck to rank Gen Patch, who came to command on Guadalcanal, and Marston consequently agreed to remain behind in New Zealand, for greater service harmony. His ADC, BG Alphonse DeCarre, a hero at Belleau Wood, assumed command of the division during the Guadalcanal exercise.

In the meantime, the 6th Marines had returned from Iceland and, after some training, left Camp Pendleton for New Zealand in mid-October 1942, and was soon followed by the rest of the division. The 8th Marines were still in Samoa and would remain there until called upon to serve on Guadalcanal.

With the arrival of two more regiments, the 2d MarDiv got into the fray in all seriousness. On 9 December 1942 the 2d Marines (Col John M. Arthur) relieved the 164th and 182d Infantry Regiments, of the Americal Division, near Point Cruz, and on 16 December the 8th Marines (LtCol Richard H. Jeschke) relieved the 132d Infantry.

In the original Guadalcanal landing, the 2d Marines, as we have seen, participated with the 1st MarDiv and would be relieved 31 January 1943 to return to New Zealand. Later, after the 1st MarDiv was relieved by the 8th Marines and assorted U.S. Army units in November 1942, then the arrival of the 6th Marines (Col Gilder D. Jackson) in January 1943, much of the 2d MarDiv was together, for the first time in its existence.

For the first few weeks, elements of the division, along with their army comrades, were engaged in patrolling. When the U.S. Army 25th Infantry Division arrived in January 1943, they assumed a far-reaching probe that ended at Cape Esperance. It began on 10 January, and they continued the advance while several army units combined with the 6th and 8th Marines in forming a hybrid division. The latter joined with the 25th InfDiv on 25 January at the high ground above Kokumbona. The Army-Marine division then attacked along the coast, meeting light resistance, and the enemy managed to escape entrapment when they completed their evacuation on the night of 7–8 February 1943.

On 9 February, MG Patch announced the "total and complete defeat of the Japanese forces on Guadalcanal." That night two battalions of the 8th Marines, 2/8 & 3/8, plus Hdqs, Weapons Co, and others, boarded transports and sailed for New Zealand. The 6th Marines, last to arrive, were last to leave, except for the 18th Marine engineers who helped to further develop Henderson Field. On 19 Feb the 6th Marines left, and a few weeks later, so did the engineers. The total losses during their six months' exposure were 263 killed and 932 wounded; however, most of the division, like the 1stMarDiv, suffered from various tropical diseases, mainly malaria. This caused many problems, not only for the sick but also for satisfactory operation of a combat division.

New Zealand

The weather was superb. It was cool, very cool for units recently exposed to tropical humidity and heat. But the 2d MarDiv men managed to survive that wondrous change, and even enjoyed it. And, in Wellington, there were females, lots of them. The 6th Marines had spent some time in the island before going to the "canal" so the people knew what to expect from "their division." They were mainly spendthrifts and hard drinkers. They began to fill their bellies with decent food for a change. Life was sweet.

However, first there was training. Replacements for the sick, lame and lazy had once again filled the units and the weather was still somewhat summery, it only being March or April (not yet fall in the Southern Hemisphere). Their next CG, from 1 May 1943 to 10 April 1944, was MG Julian C. Smith, who replaced MG Marston. Colonel Leo D. Hermle, another heroic veteran of the 4th Brigade (DSC with the 6th Marines in the Meuse River campaign), came up from Chief of Staff to BG and became division ADC. Another favorite, Col Merritt Edson, replaced him as CoS. This 2d MarDiv was on a fast-track with these officers.

The weather turned cold, but the training continued. When it became September the news of air attacks upon the Tarawa Atoll in the Gilbert Islands made the Marines in New Zealand wonder, "What's next?" The island of Betio had an airfield which the IJN was using to inflict pain upon the U.S. supply lines in the South Pacific. The Joint Chiefs made a decision: that had to stop. So, the 2d MarDiv's next stop: Tarawa Atoll.

Tarawa

Naval air attacks continued against various islands in the atoll, with Betio gaining the most attention. This went on for weeks and then literally months. The U.S. Navy planes from the Southern Carrier Group bombed Betio on 18 and on 19 November, and Cruiser

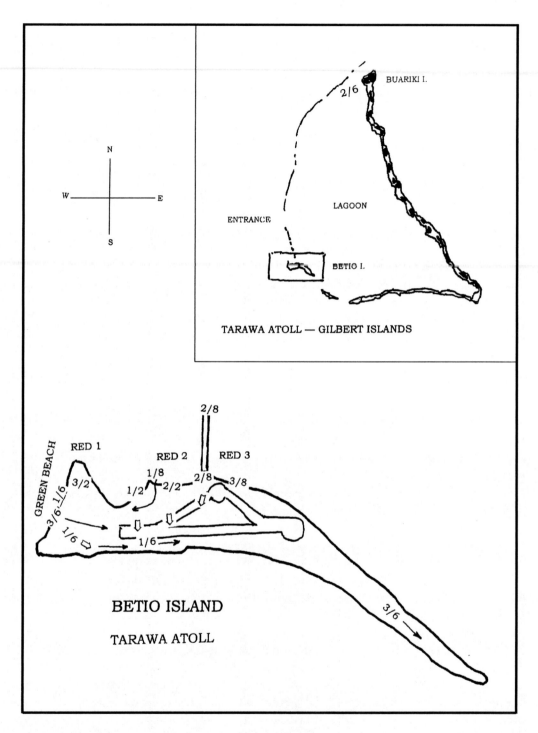

N

W —— E

S

BUARIKI I.

2/6

LAGOON

ENTRANCE

BETIO I.

TARAWA ATOLL — GILBERT ISLANDS

2/8

RED 1

GREEN BEACH

3/2

RED 2   RED 3

1/8

1/2   2/2   2/8   3/8

3/6 1/6

3/6

1/6

1/6

BETIO ISLAND

TARAWA ATOLL

3/6

Tarawa

Division 5 walloped the island with its main batteries. Another air and naval bombardment on 20 November silenced the main IJN batteries.

That day, 20 November, the 2d MarDiv (reinforced) landed on Red Beaches, 1, 2, and 3. Leading forces were 2/8 (Maj Henry P. Crowe), 2/2 (LtCol Herbert R. Amey, KiA that day), and 3/2 (Maj John F. Schoettel), supported by 1/2 (Maj Wood B. Kyle), and 3/8 (Maj

Robert H. Ruud) in reserve. Colonel David M. Shoup, CO of the 2d Marines, was designated assault commander. The 6th Marines (Col Maurice C. Holmes) constituted Corps Reserve. The Navy was convinced that they had literally "wiped out" the enemy on the island and the Marines would just "walk in and take it." Wrong; how very wrong they were. This landing would possibly be the most fouled-up and bloodiest of all the Pacific operations, but the 2d MarDiv, through its personnel, would overcome all the handicaps and win out over the most tenacious defense the Japanese would mount in the World War II island campaign. Bravery was not even extraordinary, in fact it was most common. From all reports, it appears that just about every Marine and Navy Corpsman on Tarawa was a hero.

Amey was in command of 2/2, and after the third wave moved out, he and his command group in their LCM's moved out. Upon reaching the reef Amey found that his LCM would not cross the reef and he secured the use of two LVTs. They headed in to Beach 2. About 200 yards out, barbed wire stopped them. Over the side they went and began treading water as they approached the beach. Machine gun fire from the right nailed several of them, including Amey, and the others swam to a protective lee of the abandoned boat. LtCol Jordan, the observer, assumed command until Maj Howard J. Rice could make contact.

A platoon of Scout Snipers (1stLt William D. Hawkins) from the 2d Marines was the advance party and the first Marines to land. Their job was to secure the long pier jutting out from the north side of Betio before the rest of the 2d MarDiv arrived on the scene. Their fight was fearsome but they successfully made it to the beach after destroying many of the enemy along the way. Hawkins was the first to disembark and unhesitatingly moved forward along the pier under intense fire. Leading his troops to support those Marines already ashore and desperately trying to establish a beachhead, he was in the forefront and dangerously exposed. He crawled to one pillbox position, fortified by five machine guns, and fired directly into its aperture, then completed its destruction with grenades. Though severely wounded in the chest, he refused to withdraw and continued his attacks, destroying three more pillboxes. Hawkins was mortally wounded when caught in a burst of enemy shell fire. For his outstanding spirit and leadership as well as courage he earned a Medal of Honor, one of three for the landing force.

In the meantime, as the main landing force was approaching the island, the personnel carriers were forced to go over coral reefs. Only the tracked vehicles could make it, and the other boats had to drop the Marines offshore, into the deep water, sometimes as much as 1,000 yards from the beach. Consequently, the enemy had an easy time of it, picking off those Marines who waded in with their weapons held overhead to keep them dry. After that abuse they came upon the barbed wire in the water which they had to climb over. It was a very bad time for the Marines and their losses were dreadful.

The first unit to reach shore was 3/2, when their tractors climbed up on Red Beach 1 at 0910. The first three waves were hit hard by machine gun fire and anti-boat guns which damaged most of the tractors. Company I leaped out of the LVT's and over the log seawall and began advancing inland. Between Beaches One and Two was a strong Japanese position which raked 3/2. Company K lost heavily before they could reach the log barricade. Both companies lost half their men in two hours. Company L (skipper then was Maj Ryan) and the mortar platoon came in as far as their boats would take them, about 500 yards from the beach. Then everyone got out and walked, or rather treaded water. They lost 35% of the company in the water.

Red Beach 2. Major Crowe's men of 2/8 attempting to advance on 20 November 1943.

The next battalion to reach the shore was 2/8 (Maj Henry P. Crowe, Navy Cross, Tarawa) at 0917 on Red 3, located just east of the troublesome pier. Companies E and F were first with a part of G following. Two of the tractors, with troops aboard, made it through the seawall and as far as the airfield main strip. The 500-plus men suffered but 25 casualties, a record low for the day, mainly because they were well-protected by their armored carriers. The losses to the officers were serious. Company F lost five of its six officers coming on the beach, its left flank along the pier. Company E landed to their right.

One of the reasons there was some success on D-day was the impact of individuals, like this man, "Jim" Crowe. Another would be "Mike" Ryan of 3/2 (see below). Despite the fiercest resistance, Crowe was the first battalion commander to reach shore. Braving intense machine gun and shell fire, constantly with his men at the most violent points of fighting, he organized the establishment of a beachhead and directed the elimination of hostile snipers and gun crews from along the seawall and inland of the beachhead. Without rest and at great personal risk, he maintained continuous aggressive pressure against heavily reinforced enemy emplacements. Major Crowe was personally largely responsible for winning and maintaining the beachhead at Tarawa. Most of the foregoing was taken from his Navy Cross citation, which notes his extraordinary heroism, the greatest of personal and unflinching valor, great military skill, inspirational and outstanding leadership, and ceaseless energy.

During the first day, all the news was bad. All the news that could be reported: the Marines' TBY radio sets were inefficient when running at full speed, but now most were waterlogged and wouldn't work at all. Schoettel, with the 4th wave, was in partial communication with Shoup. At 0959 Shoup received a message from Schoettel advising that he and his group were unable to land. "Issue in doubt." Eight minutes later he repeated approximately the same discouraging message. Shoup replied, "Land Beach Red 2 and work west." Schoettel replied, "We have nothing left to land."

Kyle's Combat Team Two was ordered by Shoup to provide support for 2/2 (now LtCol Walter A. Jordan, an observer from the 4th MarDiv), and when Ruud's 3/8 was released to Shoup he had them come ashore on Beach 3.

That night many Marines were scattered around behind the seawall or a few on the beaches, unattached to their units, having lost direction during the day. They would be lost to the effectiveness of organization until pulled together on D-day plus one, 21 November. They would also be in serious difficulties if the Japanese launched attacks that night.

Maj Michael P. Ryan (Navy Cross, Tarawa), of Company L, had assumed command of 3/2 when his battalion commander, Maj John F. Schoettel, failed to reach shore. As senior office, Major Ryan immediately began his task of collecting the badly disorganized and isolated survivors of three battalions. He organized and directed critical operations of these elements throughout the battle, leading assaults on enemy positions, retaining initiative in his sector, and clearing his isolated beachhead into which reinforcements could be moved. He would then be able to report to Shoup, at 1450, that several hundred of his Marines and two tanks had pushed 500 yards beyond Red Beach 1. That greatly pleased Shoup, it being one of the first positive messages he had received. There weren't many more that day.

Aside from a couple of tanks, Ryan's men had overrun many Japanese pillboxes with just infantry weapons. They had no flamethrowers nor demolitions, just grenades, and they would usually put the "hard places" out of action just temporarily. Ryan later acknowledged he expected the enemy still hidden in the bunkers to counterattack after dark. Fortunately for him they didn't. Ryan, like Crowe, was accorded recognition as another Marine that held the beachhead together those first few troublesome hours.

There were several other men who made a great impact on D-day and days following. From Atlanta, GA, came 1stLt Alexander Bonnyman, Jr., with 2/8, an older man who, when war came, had volunteered for service with the Marines. When he arrived ashore the Marines were pinned down at the end of Betio Pier by a heavy concentration of artillery and machine gun fire. Taking the initiative, Bonnyman organized and led the men along that long pier and then assumed command of several flamethrower and demolition men. He began directing the destruction of several installations before the end of D-day. The following day he, alone, crawled forward toward the entrance of a massive blockhouse where he placed demolitions. However, that proved to be not entirely successful, so he then organized an assault upon that same position, having munitions placed at both entrances while he took to the roof of it. The ensuing blast drove at least 100 Japanese out, who were instantly cut down by the waiting Marines. At least another fifty had already been killed inside the blockhouse by the explosion. Bonnyman was on the top of the structure when he was personally assaulted by a large body of the enemy who charged his position. He killed three more before succumbing to mortal wounds received as he made his last stand. Later, his daughter was given the Medal of Honor her father was awarded for his courage and leadership.

Another Marine, SSgt William J. Bordelon, a San Antonio, Texas native, with the 18th Marines, landed early on D-day with the assault waves. He and just three others in his boat survived the violent enemy fire. Once ashore, putting together demolition charges, Bordelon personally took out two pillboxes and while assaulting a third, was hit by machine gun fire, and the charge exploded in his hands. Though he was badly wounded he grabbed a rifle and began furnishing cover fire for men going over the seawall. When another demolitions man was hit, he, ignoring his own serious condition, rescued the man. Then, still refusing first aid for his own serious wounds, he made another demolitions charge and single-handedly charged another Japanese machine gun position. This time he had run his race. He was caught in a crossfire of several machine guns and killed instantly. For his courage and initiative he too was awarded a Medal of Honor.

The defenders had, for the most part, come through the offshore shelling with no more than temporary shell shock. The first day's fighting by the Japanese Special Naval Landing Force (Japanese Marines) proved that they could hand it out as well as take punishment.

Replacements for the U.S. Marines ashore were badly needed as were reinforcements. When night closed down the active assaults had ceased, but the shooting continued. However, a beachhead had been established against determined resistance, and even though it wasn't always apparent, the Americans were on Betio to stay. In fact, Shoup sent a positive message: "Casualties many; Percentage of dead not known; Combat efficiency: We are winning."

Colonel Elmer E. Hall, commanding the 8th Marines, finally received his orders to land 1/8 on 21 November, at about 0715. He and his men had been afloat at the line of departure throughout the previous night. Several times, in official histories, mention is made that the division CG, MG Julian Smith's communications "failed again." Those in command seemed to think that Hall had received orders to land late on 20 November, but he hadn't. Fog of War, as they say. Maj Lawrence C. Hays, Jr. and 1/8 came ashore at Red Beach 2 to reinforce the landing force. Division Hdqs had incorrectly assumed that 1/8 and 1/10, with pack howitzers, had been ashore on 20 November, but the units had spent twenty hours on the landing craft waiting for the word. Fog of War as they call it, and seasickness they didn't mention.

Hays and his men were subjected to much of the same as their buddies had received the day before. Regardless, by 1400, 1/8 was ashore and had established themselves. By the end of the day, though they had not advanced very far, 1/8 had destroyed numbers of the enemy located in numerous defensive positions. However, Jim Crowe and 2/8 were unable to move far the second day. Nonetheless, in the morning Mike Ryan brought his men from Red Beach 1 south to conquer Green Beach and the entire west end of the island.

In the meantime, at 1740, BG Hermle was sent orders, by Julian Smith, to assume command over all Marines ashore. However, Hermle never received those orders, and there followed some contention between him and Col Shoup, who was still in overall command. Hermle was senior and ADC, but Shoup maintained his previous orders. Shoup had with him LtCol Evans F. Carlson as an observer. Luckily, since the radios weren't working as well as they should, Carlson was Shoup's liaison officer with Division. Carlson had seen 1/8 (Hays) go into the beach and take heavy casualties and had been able to go out to the USS *Maryland* to talk with Julian Smith and staff.

Holland Smith released the 6th Marines to Julian Smith at 1525 that day, which was gratifying. They were badly needed ashore. Maj William K. Jones, Silver Star on Betio, then

Colonel David Shoup (map case) conferring with Major Thomas Culhane, 2d Marines R-3. Evans Carlson resting in foreground.

led 1/6 ashore on Green Beach, on the east side of Betio. They were to be followed by 2/6 (LtCol Raymond L. Murray, Silver Star, Betio) as support, but his orders were changed to instead land on Beach Blue 1 & 2 on Bairiki Island "immediately." Seems that some of the enemy were deserting to another island adjacent to Betio and 2/6 was to stop that flow and contain them at Betio. The atoll was nearly all connecting land to Buariki Village at the extreme northern end. Jones on Green Beach found the beach secured by Ryan and his crowd, therefore, upon arrival at 1855, he set up defensive positions for the night. Murray landed at 1655 on Bairiki with minimum resistance and by nightfall had secured that island.

At 0700 on 22 November, D-day + 2, 1/8 moved westward and met strong enemy fortifications. Three light tanks from the 2d Tank Bn (LtCol Alexander B. Swenceski, Silver Star) were unable to deliver the knockout punch required and withdrew. By evening Companies A, B, and C of 1/8 had so severely weakened those enemy positions that the enemy was completely cut off. The airfield was taken by 1/2 and 2/2, and they then moved to the south coast, splitting the enemy forces on the island. Major Kenneth F. McLeod, Silver Star, with 3/6 landed on Beach Green and headed eastward. Jones' 1/6 advanced along the south coast to secure that side of the island and then attacked east toward the airfield. Shoup was still commanding ashore until late on D-Day+2 when the CG MG Julian Smith came ashore and relieved him of the burden.

The night of 22–23 November, 1/6 repelled three enemy counterattacks, and on the 23d, 3/6, in four hours fighting, secured the southeast tip of Betio. Major General Julian C. Smith then declared that all organized resistance on Betio had ceased. However, some Japanese from the eastern tail were killed while counterattacking the 6th Marines during the night of 23–24 November. The next night, the 2d and 8th Marines were transported to their new base camp at Kamuela, Hawaii, while the 2d Defense Bn arrived from Samoa to defend Betio. Smith ordered the ADC, BG Leo D. Hermle, to send the 6th Marines around the atoll to wipe out any pockets of Japanese resistance, and by the 27th all was clear. On 4 December MG Smith turned over the island to Capt Jackson R. Tate, USN. The 2d MarDiv was finished with Tarawa and Tarawa nearly finished the 2d MarDiv.

Col David M. Shoup, though shocked when, upon landing, a blast landed nearby and seriously wounded his leg, a wound that became infected, survived the entire period. His fearlessness during the three days, including rallying his men and leading them when approaching the island, and his steadfastness ashore, were due for recognition. He was awarded a Medal of Honor for his brilliant leadership, daring tactics, and selfless devotion to duty. This Hoosier, who was credited with being responsible for the final decisive defeat of the enemy, was awarded numerous other Navy awards. In fact, he also was promoted over the heads of numerous other senior officers and made Commandant of the Marine Corps on 1 January 1960.

The total time for the invasion and final conquest of Tarawa has been calculated at 76 hours. During that period the 2d Division suffered 3,080 casualties of which 989 were killed and 2,091 wounded. Arguably, these were proportionately the most serious losses for the Marines during the entire war. Most of the casualties were created as they tried to make the shore. The landing craft, for the most part, were not capable of crossing the reef and left the Marines a long walk to get to the beach. The enemy were able to concentrate their fire, artillery, mortars, machine guns, and rifles, on the defenseless men as they made their way to shore. There was at least one instance where a USN coxswain of a landing craft lost his nerve on D-day + 1 and instead of bringing his Marines in as close as possible, dropped them off into 15 feet of water, then scrambled back for cover. Most of those Marines with packs and weapons drowned. There may have been more incidents of that nature; the going was rough and some men didn't have what it took to stay the route.

The Japanese were well prepared, and the pre-invasion pounding by the naval guns was terribly inadequate, as was the equipment to land the landing force. Later, after some discussion, it was perceived by the powers that be that Tarawa was totally unnecessary. Tell that to the Marines.

Order of Battle
Tarawa
(20 November to 23 November 1943)

Division Headquarters		*Second Marines*	
MG Julian C. Smith	CG	Col David M. Shoup	CO
BG Leo D. Hermle	ADC	LtCol Dixon Goen	ExO
Col Merritt A. Edson	CoS	Capt James E. Herbold	R-1
LtCol C. P. Van Ness	D-1	Capt John L. Schwabe	R-2
LtCol T. J. Colley	D-2	Maj Thomas A. Culhane, Jr.	R-3
LtCol J. P. Risely	D-3	Capt Vernon L. Bartram	R-4
LtCol Jesse S. Cook	D-4		

1/2

Maj Wood B. Kyle	CO
Maj William S. Vasconcellos	ExO
Capt Harold R. Thorpe	B-3

2/2

LtCol Herbert R. Amey	CO (KIA 20 Nov)
Maj Howard J. Rice	ExO
Capt Benjamin T. Owens	B-3

3/2

Maj John F. Schoettel	CO
Maj Samuel D. Mandeville	ExO
Capt Richard Phihippi	B-3

6th Marines

Col Maurice C. Holmes	CO
LtCol Russell Lloyd	ExO
1stLt P. J. Costello	R-1
Capt Donald Jackson	R-2
Maj Loren E. Haffner	R-3
Maj Cyril C. Sheehan	R-4

1/6

Maj William K. Jones	CO
Maj John E. Semmes, Jr.	ExO
Capt Charles H. Triplett	B-3

2/6

LtCol Raymond L. Murray	CO
Maj Richard C. Nutting	ExO
Capt Joseph E. Rowland	B-3

3/6

LtCol Kenneth F. McLeod	CO
Maj John E. Rentsch	ExO
Capt William W. McKinley	B-3

8th Marines

Col Elmer E. Hall	CO
LtCol Paul D. Sherman	ExO
Capt Cleland E. Early	R-1
Capt Wilmot J. Spires	R-2
Maj Hewitt D. Adams	R-3
Capt Alfred E. Holland	R-4

1/8

Maj Lawrence C. Hays, Jr.	CO
Maj Robert J. Oddy	ExO
Capt Daniel V. McWethy, Jr.	B-3

2/8

Maj Henry P. Crowe	CO
Maj William C. Chamberlin	ExO
1stLt K. C. Fagan	B-3

3/8

Maj Robert H. Ruud	CO
Maj Stanley E. Larsen	ExO
Capt Scott S. Corbett	B-3

10th Marines

BG Thomas E. Bourke	CG
LtCol Ralph E. Forsyth	ExO

Capt Ralph D. Pillsbury	R-1
1stLt David J. Lubin	R-2
LtCol Marvin H. Floom	R-3
Capt Marshall R. Breedlove	R-4

1/10

LtCol Presley M. Rixey	CO
Maj James E. Mills	ExO
Maj Wendell H. Best	B-3

2/10

LtCol George R. E. Shell	CO
Maj Richard B. Church	ExO
Maj Kenneth C. Houston	B-3

3/10

LtCol Manly L. Curry	CO
Maj Gene N. Schraeder	ExO
Maj Earl J. Rowse	B-3

4/10

LtCol Kenneth A. Jorgensen	CO
Maj Harry N. Shea	ExO
Maj James O. Appleyard	B-3

5/10

Maj Howard V. Hiett	CO
Maj William L. Crouch	ExO
Maj Wade H. Hitt	B-3

18th Marines (Engineers)

Col Cyril W. Martyr	CO
LtCol Ewart S. Laue	ExO
1stLt Haldon E. Lindfelt	R-1
Maj James F. Geary	R-2
LtCol Kenneth P. Corson	R-3
Capt Robert F. Ruan	R-4

1/18

Maj George L. H. Cooper	CO
Maj Joseph S. Reynaud	ExO

2/18 (Pioneers)

LtCol Chester J. Salazar	CO
Maj Robert L. Smith	ExO
Capt Jerome R. Walters	B-3

3/18 (Seabees)

Cmdr Lawrence E. Tull	CO
LtCmdr Edwin E. Gibson	ExO
Lt Robert Cleghorn	B-3

2d Amph Trac Bn

Maj Henry C. Drewes	CO (KIA 20 Nov)
Capt Henry G. Lawrence, Jr.	ExO
Capt William H. Housman	B-3

2d Tank Bn

LtCol Alexander B. Swenceski	CO (WIA 20 Nov)
Maj Charles W. McCoy	ExO
1stLt Edward C. Hennessey	B-3 (KIA 20 Nov)

HAWAII

The division was soon in their "rest" camp in Hawaii, but, of course, training began almost at once. In fact it was a seven-day-a-week experience, for the old-timers and the replacements. Something new was added, and it began with the 2d MarDiv. The formation of a squad was changed from twelve men plus a leader, to three fire teams of four men each and a leader. More firepower was added. Each FT had three riflemen and a Browning Automatic Rifleman (BAR).

There was stateside beer, but it was limited to two cans per day, per Marine. The USO entertained and the movies were reasonably modern. All-in-all, it was better than what other Marine divisions experienced when not in combat. One thing did bother the members of the division, though. The battle, because of the losses, wasn't "advertised" much in the States and that bothered many of the veterans. It, like the later Peleliu, would be ignored for many years after the fact. Both campaigns are, more or less, just coming into public exposure. Both were later admitted to be less than necessary and terribly bloody.

On 10 April 1944, MG Smith was detached and BG Thomas E. Watson assumed command of the 2d MarDiv. Watson, for various reasons, was a different kind of CG than was Smith, and it wasn't very long before he rearranged some of the staff and regimental positions. Soon to be BG, Edson was promoted to ADC from CoS, and Col Shoup replaced him as CoS. The latter two added much to the planning for the forthcoming campaign, now know to be in the Marianas. The island chain included the largest, Guam, formerly an American possession lost in December 1941; plus Saipan, the second largest, and its nearby sister, Tinian, among several others. The islands had once belonged to Spain, then briefly to Germany until Japan took them in 1914. Guam was the only one that became a U.S. possession, in 1898, and continued as such until taken by Japan in 1941.

SAIPAN

Saipan was selected to be the first target, Tinian second. In addition to the 2d Mar-Div (MG Thomas E. Watson), the 4th MarDiv (MG Harry Schmidt) and the U.S. Army's 27th Infantry Division (MG Ralph C. Smith) would tackle this large, well-populated island. In addition, the high command was well aware that things might be very punishing in this landing. So the 3d MarDiv (MG Allen H. Turnage), planned for a landing on Guam, waited off-shore for a stretch of days until it was obvious they wouldn't be needed on Saipan. This divisional group formed V Amphibious Corps (VAC) led by LG Holland McT. Smith. Saipan had numerous civilians, many of whom were Japanese, plus roads, schools, caves, mountains, and worst of all, a large defending force of close to 20,000 Japanese troops. It would not be as terrible as Tarawa but it would not be easy.

The slow LST's left Pearl Harbor on 25 May 1944, the transport group on 30 May, and all made for the recently captured Marshall island of Eniwetok, arriving by 9 June. On the 11th the entire TF 56, again led by VA Richmond Kelly Turner, would set sail for its target. It and VA Marc Mitscher's TF 58 would arrive at Saipan for the invasion on D-day, 15 June. On that date, at 0542, six battleships and cruisers of the fleet opened fire with their big guns. The firing continued until the first amtracs made the beaches at 0843. Both Marine Divisions went in on the western beaches, south of the large town of Garapan. The 2d Mar-

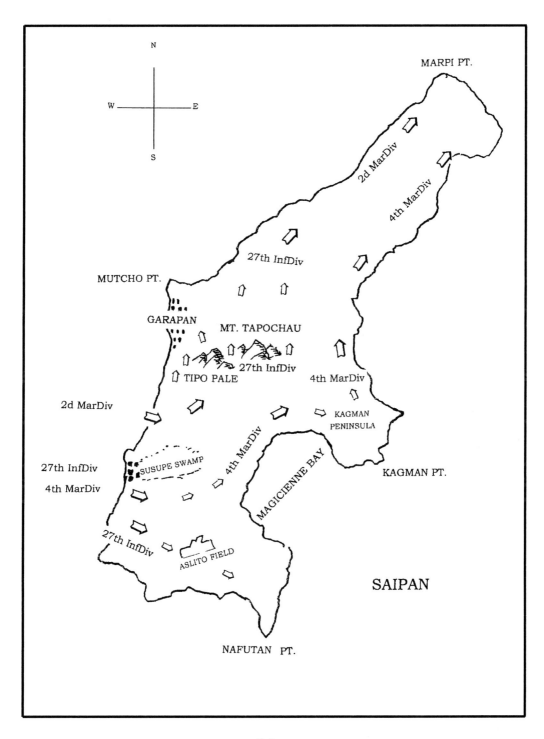

Saipan

Div landed in the north, on Beaches Red and Green, and the 4thMarDiv south of them on Beaches Blue and Yellow. Both were quickly engaged in heavy fighting. As usual, the operational plan had broken the advance up the island into daily objectives; O-1, 2, 3, and so forth. Anticipating the worst, Holland Smith made the decision to not wait long before committing his reserve, the 27th InfDiv (except for the 106th Infantry, which would remain

The 8th Marines preparing to advance off the beach at Saipan on D-Day, 15 June 1944.

aboard ships as reserve). It would be made available for immediate commitment if, as expected, it would be necessary.

The 2d MarDiv landed on the left, two regiments abreast; on the far left was 2/6 (LtCol Raymond L. Murray, Navy Cross, wounded that day), with 3/6 (LtCol John W. Easley, wounded that day) at their right, both on Red Beach. On their right on Green Beach 1 was 3/8 (LtCol John C. Miller, wounded that day) and then 2/8 (LtCol Henry P. Crowe, wounded that day). For some reason both battalions landed on the same beach. Officially it was caused because the currents were too strong and it was expected that the boats would move to the left as they went in. The enemy's anti-boat gun positions lining that beach plausibly helped make the decision for the navy coxswains. As can be seen from the above, the casualty rate for battalion commanders was quite heavy on 15 June.

The 8th (Col Clarence H. Wallace) had a tough fight securing their beach, as did the 6th Marines (Col James P. Riseley). In fact, as soon as they could organize ashore, 2/8 began a move southwards toward Afetna Point. They had a tough fight, and were not able to connect up with the 4th MarDiv as hoped for that day. The 2d Marines (Col Walter J. Stuart) landed later as support for the 6th. Earlier, the 2d Marines had made a diversionary movement off the northwest coast.

Holland Smith quickly recognized that this was going to be another long and costly battle. Therefore, on D-day + 1, 16 June, the 27th landed, still in Corps reserve, with the 165th Infantry landing on the right flank of the 4th MarDiv. This was so it would be in position to move southward on the 17th with the 4th MarDiv in order to clean up the enemy that were expected to retreat in that direction.

On the 16th slow progress was made, but mainly it was in the consolidation of all positions. By the end of the second day the beachhead was well controlled. The 2d and 4th Mar-

Divs had gained a depth of 1,500 yards at a frontage of 10,000 yards. It was tough going, but they were there to stay. That night, 16–17 June, the Japanese launched a night attack, supported by three or more companies of tanks. The 2d and 6th Marines were ready for them. Both regiments bore the brunt of the assault with 1/6 mostly affected. The attack was stalled by 0700 that next morning on the 17th, primarily from fire by five heavy tanks from Company B, 2d Tank Battalion (Maj Charles W. McCoy). They had arranged for about thirty enemy tanks set ablaze and scattered about the area.

The 2d Division made plans to attack the morning of the 17th, following a ninety-minute artillery and naval gunfire preparation. The 6th Marines were on the left and the 8th Marines on their right. The 2d Marines would constitute their support. However, Gen Smith, at Northern Troops and Landing Force (NTLF), decided to alter the plans for 2d MarDiv's advance on the morning of the 17th. Poor communication resulted in the division regiments moving forward at 0730 as planned. That the 6th Marines, plus attached 2/2 (LtCol Richard C. Nutting, Silver Star), could advance as scheduled just one hour after stopping the Japanese attack, was an example of excellent training. LtCol Hays, 1/8, with Tannyhill, 1/29, had a more difficult time of it. Before them lay the marshy area surrounding Lake Susupe, where men were sinking waist-deep in the muck and the area was replete with snipers. Tannyhill and his men were up against a hill, lying on O-1, containing a series of enemy defensive positions. South of that, directly on the 29th's right flank, lay a coconut grove infested with Japanese. By mid-afternoon they were stymied and no advance had been made, Tannyhill had been wounded, and up came LtCol Rathvon M. Tompkins as his replacement. Tompkins would pick up a Navy Cross for this day's work. He soon spotted four Marine tanks of McCoy's battalion and redirected them. With this base of fire, 1/29 was soon up and at 'em once again. They quickly pushed to the top of the hill and after a quick mop-up, dug in for the night.

Stuart's 2d Marines advanced in a column of battalions, regulating its advance on the 6th Marines to its right. By 1800, 3/2 reached O-2, just a thousand yards south of Garapan's outskirts. It too dug in. All day the 1st, 2d, and 4th Bn's of the 10th Artillery had been supporting the three Marine regiments. VAC 2d Howitzer Bn (LtCol Marvin H. Floom) commenced landing their 155's at 1500, were detached from the 2d MarDiv, and had orders to support the 4th MarDiv.

On the night of 17–18 June, small groups of Japanese soldiers, usually no more than a squad, probed the lines making efforts to locate a spot to penetrate, especially along the 2d MarDiv front. It was raining and observation was poor. At midnight the enemy launched an attack at where the 6th and 8th Marines joined. Though they made a small impression, they were soon driven out and the lines were restored. At 0430, the Japanese tried to go the Marines one better. They were going to attempt an amphibious landing behind the 2d MarDiv's line but they were spotted just north of Garapan and 4/10 opened up on them. Additionally, the U.S. vessels in that area around Mutcho Point also saw the 35 or so enemy barges and opened up, doing the most damage. At least thirteen of the barges, and their passengers, were destroyed, ending any chance of a successful landing.

On the 18th at about 1000 the 165th Infantry of the 27th InfDiv took Aslito Air Field in the far south of the island. On 22 June the airfield would become operational for fighter aircraft. By this time the enemy high command had figured out that their days were numbered and began burning "secret documents." For that day the Northern Troops and Landing Force issued orders for the three divisions to launch an attack. The Marines were to go at 1000 and the 27th at 1200. The latter needed time to move its 105th Infantry to position. The 2d MarDiv was the pivot of the entire line, and since it was a bit farther forward than its cohorts, it moved very little on the 18th. The 4th MarDiv, which was having a difficult time, made up for the lack of activity in the 2d MarDiv with both the 24th and 25th Marines making headway, though the 23d Marines met great opposition.

That night, 18–19 June, was relatively quiet. The NTLF Operational Order for 19 June instructed the three divisions to "complete missions assigned." This order when completed would place the entire southern portion of the island in American hands. Progress beyond Aslito Airfield was good but the 27th was having more difficulty advancing as the enemy reduced their lines. It would be many more days before the entire Nafutan Point was taken. Meanwhile in the northeast, the 4th MarDiv's progress up Magicienne Bay also ground to a halt on the 19th. Meanwhile, the great naval battle of the Philippine Sea was fought and the Japanese navy was essentially destroyed.

On the 20th the two Marine divisions would advance and take the "O-4" line, which included Hill 500 in the 4th's sector. The 2d would have advanced quite a way up the island, with the 2d, 6th, and 8th Marines in line, left to right. At this point in time, the 4th was having greater difficulty but continued making inroads in their sector. (See the 4th Marine Division "biography.") By the end of the day the two divisions were facing northward. Before them, 2,000-plus yards for the 6th and 8th Marines, lay the highest point on the island, Mt. Tapotchau, at 1,554 feet high and lying at the approximate geometric center of the island.

On 22 June, as the island widened eastward, it was planned to call up the 27th to fill the center and advance between the 2d and 4th. It was imagined, at the time, that the 27th, though new and relatively inexperienced, being supported on both wings by divisions already bloodied, would furnish them an easier time. The conception was to have all three divisions abreast, and then to move forward up the island at the same time, leaving no enemies in their rear areas. Unfortunately, the best laid plans often go astray.

On the 23d the 105th Infantry had still not completed the capture of Nafutan Point, while both the 106th and 165th Infantry Regiments had managed to get themselves entangled and made very slow progress to their assigned positions. Holland Smith had issued what he believed were clear and concise orders to Ralph Smith, but somehow communications fell apart.

When the 106th and 165th made it to their positions, they advanced, but began having great difficulty taking on the hills lying before them. To those sites they had some great difficulty with, the men of the 27th quickly assigned nicknames such as "Purple Heart Ridge" and "Death Valley." It isn't deemed appropriate to describe their difficulties nor the controversy between LG Smith and MG Smith. Sufficient to state, the two Marine divisions advanced while the 27th did not. Obviously, both Marine divisions were strung out and on their inner flanks were hurt quite badly by those Japanese that had not been pushed back. After some communication, Smith relieved Smith, and in so doing, created a firestorm, an entire story in and of itself. Ralph Smith was replaced in command of the 27th InfDiv by the designated island commander, MG Sanderford Jarman, USA.

Meanwhile, the 2d MarDiv, with the line-up as before, 2d Marines left and 8th Marines right with the 6th in the middle, continued to advance. Though it was now mostly rubble, the 2d had the fair-sized town of Garapan lying before them. Flametree Hill, to the town's right, provided the 2d Marines with enough difficulty to satisfy them on 24 June. The going

Motormen of the 6th Marines firing at the enemy.

would become more stressful and for the next few days the American advance slowed way down. However, the 4th MarDiv branched out to the east and was headed toward successfully taking the entire Kagman Peninsula.

The 8th Marines and 1/29 completed the capture of Mt. Tapotchau on 25 June, a major event since the height oversaw all of Saipan. On that date Private First Class Harold G. Epperson of Akron, Ohio, a machine gunner with 1/6, fought his post fiercely with his emplacement receiving the full blast of the enemy attack. He is credited with successfully breaking up several attacks. A grenade fell in his hole and he, without hesitation, leaped upon it and absorbed the full blast with his body. He was a posthumous recipient of a Medal of Honor.

In the meantime, the Japanese commanding general sent messages to General Iketa, then located on the island of Yap, that he had only about 1,100 soldiers with no artillery and but three tanks. He also said "… there is no hope for victory," which should have been quite obvious. The 47th Independent Mixed Brigade was commanded by a 1st lieutenant, and the 70 members of the 7th Independent Engineers by a sergeant. American estimates of their troop strength were somewhat higher than this, but the Japanese, regardless of their depleted condition, were doing their best to slow up the Americans.

On the night of 26–27 June, the remnants of the Japanese still holding Nafutan Point broke out and made a dash for Aslito Airfield and Hill 500. Upon arrival they raised hell. Nevertheless, the Japanese found the 25th Marines, a NTLF reserve unit, atop Hill 500, and when the Marines recuperated from their surprise they went to work. By morning the 25th mopped up and counted about 500 enemy dead, some in American uniforms with M-1 rifles. In the north, the 27th InfDiv, under new command, was making good progress.

The NTLF orders issued on 27 June called for a general advance by all three divisions, the 2d still on the left, to Objective line 6. But it would be 30 June before some units, primarily the 4th MarDiv, would approach that line. Fighting south of Garapan and Flame-tree Hill was still difficult for the 2d MarDiv. They did, however, manage to take the site known as the "Four Pimples" lying before the 8th Marines. During this period a Navy flyer mistook a puff of white smoke in the lines of 1/2, and dropped bombs, causing 27 casualties. Both Watson and Smith demanded that Spruance discipline the aviator but Spruance had sense enough to refuse. His theory: discipline this flyer and the rest of them would be chary of providing close-air support in the future.

It was now two weeks into the campaign and all troops were exhausted. Fortunately, the night of 29–30 June was relatively quiet and that gave everyone a little bit of rest. The 2d Marines, as the entire American line's left pivot, had been patrolling and pushing at Garapan; the 6th Marines had pushed north to come alongside; the 8th Marines had a tough row to hoe at Mt. Tapotchau, but managed to come down on the north side, and they too were on line. The 27th InfDiv, under MG Sanderford Jarman, later MG George W. Griner, Jr., was doing well in the middle, and the 4th MarDiv had cleaned up the Kagman Peninsula and was in line up ahead of the others. The entire American force was located at Objective — 6, with the largest part of the island conquered.

From 2 to 4 July the entire line moved forward and swung over toward Tanapag Harbor and Flores Point, and the 2d Marines took Garapan. The 4th MarDiv's 24th and 25th Marines were further north than the other two divisions.

As the days passed, the Japanese on the island began to force the island's civilians to jump off cliffs before the advancing Americans. Nonetheless, the advance continued and Marines did what Marines always do. They earned awards. Private First Class Harold C. Agerholm, of the 4th Battalion, 10th Marines, from Racine, Wisconsin, was awarded a Medal of Honor on 7 July when he helped stem an enemy attack against the regiment and then made numerous personal efforts to retrieve wounded Marines. He evacuated approximately 45 casualties before his race was run when an enemy sniper nailed him. He was awarded a posthumous Medal of Honor.

The enemy ran right into the 10th Artillery's lines, forcing many of the gunners back. They pulled out the firing locks of their guns and fought as infantry as they fell back. The 105th and 165th Infantry were also both hit hard. Their casualties far exceeded those of the 10th Artillerymen but they accounted for nearly 2,300 of the enemy in so doing.

The following day, on 8 July, a 2/6 tank commander, Sgt Grant F. Timmerman, a native of Americus, Kansas, who was way out front, with his body blocked a grenade from going into his tank. He paid the extreme price for his valor and was another posthumous Medal of Honor awardee. The enemy launched several more "*Banzai*" attacks on 8 July but mostly against the 4th MarDiv positions.

The 9th of July would be the final day of this long, grueling campaign. The 4th MarDiv, with the 2d Marines attached, reached Marpi Point, the farthest northern point on the island, killing off most of the surviving Japanese soldiers. Although Saipan Island was declared secured at 1615 on that day, mopping up continued and so did casualties.

However, for all intents, the war on Saipan was over. Its sister island, Tinian, was still held by Japan. But not for long. The entire campaign on Saipan cost the three American divisions nearly 17,000 killed and wounded, of which 6,170 casualties were of the 2d Division.

Order of Battle
Saipan
(15 June to 9 July 1944)

Expeditionary Troops

LG Holland M. Smith	CG
BG Graves B. Erskine	CoS
LtCol Albert F. Metze	G-1
Col St. Julien U. Marshall	G-2
Col John C. McQueen	G-3
Col Raymond E. Knapp	G-4
Col Joseph T. Smith	G-5

Northern Troops and Landing Force

LG Holland M. Smith	CG
BG Graves B. Erskine	CoS
LtCol Albert F. Metze	G-1
LtCol Thomas B. Yancey, USA	G-2
Col Robert E. Hogaboom	G-3
LtCol Joseph C. Anderson, USA	G-4

2d Division (USMC)

MG Thomas E. Watson	CG
BG Merritt A. Edson	ADC
Col David M. Shoup	CoS
LtCol James T. Wilbur	D-1
LtCol Thomas J. Colley	D-2
LtCol Wallace M. Greene, Jr.	D-3
Col Robert J. Straub	D-4

Second Marines

Col Walter J. Stuart	CO
LtCol John H. Griebel	ExO
Capt Leonard O. Hicks	R-1
Capt John L. Schwabe	R-2
Maj Samuel D. Mandeville, Jr.	R-3
Maj Harold "K" Throneson	R-4

1/2

LtCol Wood B. Kyle	CO
Maj Wendell W. Andrews	ExO
Maj Charles P. Lewis, Jr.	B-3

2/2

LtCol Richard C. Nutting	CO
Maj Michael P. Ryan	ExO
lstLt William B. Somerville	B-3

3/2

LtCol Arnold F. Johnston	CO (WIA 21 Jun)
Maj Harold "K" Throneson	CO (To 4 Jul)
LtCol Arnold F. Johnston	CO
Maj Benjamin T. Owens	ExO
Capt Richard Phillippi	B-3

6th Marines

Col James P. Riseley	CO
LtCol Kenneth F. McLeod	ExO
Capt Philip J. Costello	R-1
Capt Donald V. Nahrgang	R-2
Maj Loren E. Haffner	R-3
Maj Cyril C. Sheehan	R-4

1/6

LtCol William K. Jones	CO
Maj James A. Donovan, Jr.	ExO
Capt Charles H. Triplett	B-3

2/6

LtCol Raymond L. Murray	CO (WIA 15 Jun)
Maj LeRoy P. Hunt, Jr.	CO
Maj Howard J. Rice	ExO
Capt Joseph E. Rowland	B-3

3/6

LtCol John W. Easley	CO (WIA 15 Jun)
Maj John E. Rentsch	CO (To 2 Jul)
LtCol John W. Easley	CO
Maj John E. Rentsch	ExO
Capt Edward L. Singletary	B-3

8th Marines

Col Clarence H. Wallace	CO
LtCol Jack P. Juhan	ExO
Capt Lloyd E. Iverson	R-1
lstLt James H. Kavanagh, Jr.	R-2
Maj William H. Souder, Jr.	R-3
Maj Alfred B. Holland	R-4

1/8

LtCol Lawrence C. Hays, Jr.	CO
Maj Robert J. Oddy	ExO
Maj Daniel V. McWethy, Jr.	B-3

2/8

LtCol Henry P. Crowe	CO (WIA 15 Jun)
Maj William C. Chamberlin	CO
Maj William C. Chamberlin	ExO
Capt Arthur J. Rauchle	B-3

3/8

LtCol John C. Miller	CO (WIA 15 Jun)
Maj Stanley E. Larsen	CO
Maj Stanley E. Larsen	ExO
Capt Osborne K. LeBlanc	B-3

1st Bn, 29th Marines

(Attached to 2d Mar Div)

LtCol Guy E. Tannyhill	CO (WIA 17 Jun)
LtCol Rathvon M. Tompkins	CO (WIA 2 Jul)
LtCol Jack P. Juhan	CO (To 4 Jul)
Maj William W. McKinley	CO
Maj William S. Vasconcellos	ExO
Maj William W. McKinley	B-3

10th Marines

Col Raphael Griffin	CO
LtCol Ralph E. Forsyth	ExO
1stLt Russell C. White	R-1
Capt Robert W. Sullivan	R-2
LtCol Howard V. Hiett	R-3
Capt Edward H. Gilbert	R-4

1/10

Col Presley M. Rixey	CO (To 24 Jun)
Maj Wendell H. Best	CO
Maj Wendell H. Best	ExO
Capt Michael J. Bo	B-3

2/10

LtCol George H. E. Shell	CO (WIA 16 Jun)
Maj Kenneth C. Houston	CO
Maj Kenneth C. Houston	ExO
Capt Richard B. Cavnnaugh	B-3

3/10

Maj William L. Crouch	CO (KIA 7 Jul)
Maj James O. Appleyard	CO
Maj Wade H. Hitt	ExO
Capt Alan H. Tully	B-3

4/10

LtCol Kenneth A. Jorgensen	CO
LtCol Harry N. Shea	ExO
Maj James O. Appleyard	B-3

155mm Howitzer Bn, VAC

LtCol Marvin H. Floom	CO
Maj Gene N. Schraeder	ExO
Maj Earl J. Rowse	B-3

18th Marines[1]

LtCol Russell Lloyd	CO (To 25 Jun)
LtCol Ewart S. Laue	CO
LtCol Ewart S. Laue	ExO
Capt Winfield S. Haltom, Jr.	R-1
Capt Murdoch J. McLeod	R-2 & R-3
Capt Walter J. Hulsey	R-4

1/18

LtCol August L. Vogt	CO
Capt Joseph O. Polifka	ExO

2/18

LtCol Chester J. Salazar	CO
Capt Jerome R. Walters	ExO
Capt Jerome R. Walters	B-3

2d Tank Bn

Maj Charles W. McCoy	CO
Capt John C. Richards, Jr.	ExO

24 Amph Trac Bn

Maj Henry O. Lawrence, Jr.	CO (To 2 Jul)[2]
Maj Fenlon A. Durand	CO
Maj Fenlon A. Durand	ExO
Capt William H. Housman, Jr.	B-3

5th Amph Trac Bn

Capt George L. Shead	CO
Capt William C. Stoll	ExO

2d MT Bn

Maj Milton J. Green	CO
Maj Robert H. Sanders	ExO
Capt Harry C. Olson	B-3

2d Service Bn

Capt Robert V. Perkins	CO
1stLt Francis E. McElroy	ExO

2d Medical Bn

LtCmdr Claude R. Bruner	CO

TINIAN

Jig-Day (the reason for the name is unclear) was the 24th of July 1944. The first to land on Beaches White 1 & 2 was the 4th MarDiv. Earlier, from 0557 to 1015, the 2d MarDiv had made a feint toward making a landing at or near Tinian Town, far to the south on the west

---

[1]*Command and staff list of 18th Marines is from the unit's muster roles. A check of other available records and letters from officers gives the following additional information: LtCol Russell Lloyd was also CO 2d Marine Division Shore Party until 25 June 1944 when he was attached to the 6th Marines. Maj G. L. H. Cooper commanded the division shore party from 26 to 30 June 1944 when the beaches were turned over to the Army. LtCol Chester J. Salazar retained administrative command of the 2d Bn, 18th Marines, throughout the period, although his unit, with personnel from other regiments and attached units, functioned as the 2d Division Shore Party. LtCol Ewart S. Laue had administrative command of the 18th Marines until 25 June 1944 and tactical command from 26 June.*
[2]*Transferred to NTLF staff as LVT control officer on 2 July.*

coast. In reality, there were many more casualties to American naval forces, Navy and Marines, in that feint than during the real landing on the northwest coast.

While the BB *Colorado* was engaged in shelling the shoreline, two previously undiscovered 6-inch naval guns managed, within 15 minutes, to score twenty-two direct hits on *Colorado* and six on its destroyer escort, the *Norman Scott*. The crew suffered 62 killed, of which there were 10 Marines, and 223 wounded, of which the Marines constituted 31. The local Japanese commander, Col Kiyochi Ogata, was convinced, as he witnessed the "landing force" turn away, that he had repelled the invasion and so notified his headquarters.

At Beach White 2, 2/25, right flank of the 4th MarDiv, because of botched orders and equipment malfunction, had great difficulty moving ashore. Landing abreast to their left was 3/25 and abreast of them was 2/24. The 23d Marines were kept just offshore as floating reserve. Upon arrival the enemy defense forces put up a stiff fight. On Beach White 1, 2/24 was especially plagued, and at 1515, MG Harry Schmidt, who had replaced Holland Smith in command of NTLF, ordered the 8th Marines ashore to assist. He wanted them ashore at 1600 but because of "transport confusion" the landing was hampered until 2000 when the battalion logged itself as "dug in assigned position." The balance of the 2d MarDiv was still floating offshore. That evening the 24th Marines, backed up by 1/8, was seemingly prepared for whatever the night would bring forth. 1/8 occupied the northernmost part of the defensive line. The enemy launched severe attacks but were decisively defeated. At the end of the day the strip held by the Marines was between 2,000 and 3,000 yards long and 1,500 yards in depth. Not much.

By 25 July, JiG Day plus 1, the balance of the 8th Marines and the 2d Marines were landed. At this time the 6th Marines were also being brought over from Saipan. By nightfall the division had landed on Tinian. The 2d MarDiv took up position to the northeast while the 4th remained in the south. Enemy forces began to retreat southward and into caves and other natural defense locations from which the Marines were once again forced to dig them out. However, this campaign was the first in which the newly arrived napalm was available and that put a different slant on the problem. Now the enemy was driven out or burnt out. Mostly it was the latter. It was a terrible way to die, but then so are most ways.

On 25 July, JiG-Day + 1, the 4th MarDiv moved southward while the 2d MarDiv moved a slight distance along the northern coast and to the east, taking part of Airfield No. 3. On 26 July the 2d MarDiv moved rapidly, taking the balance of the airfield and down to Asigo Point on the east coast.

The most difficulty the 2d MarDiv ran into was on the 27th, when, after an artillery preparation, the division jumped off at 0730. After being harassed by small-arms fire most of the morning, by 1345 the Marines had driven south about 4,000 yards. On the 28th it was the 4th MarDiv's turn to move up while the 2d MarDiv just moved ahead a couple of hundred yards. The following day, JiG + 5, both divisions moved forward against less resistance, although the 2d MarDiv ran into pockets of resistance at Masalog Point. By nightfall more than half of the island was in the hands of the Americans and Tinian Town lay just before the 4th MarDiv. On the east, 3/2 moved against occasional opposition from several machine gun positions and a 70mm howitzer. They quieted that down and drove across open fields chasing a Japanese force and driving them into caves. With the help of a napalm-firing tank they slaughtered 89 Japanese and wiped out 4 machine guns and crews. Now they ran into some difficulty. They came under mortar fire which caused numerous casu-

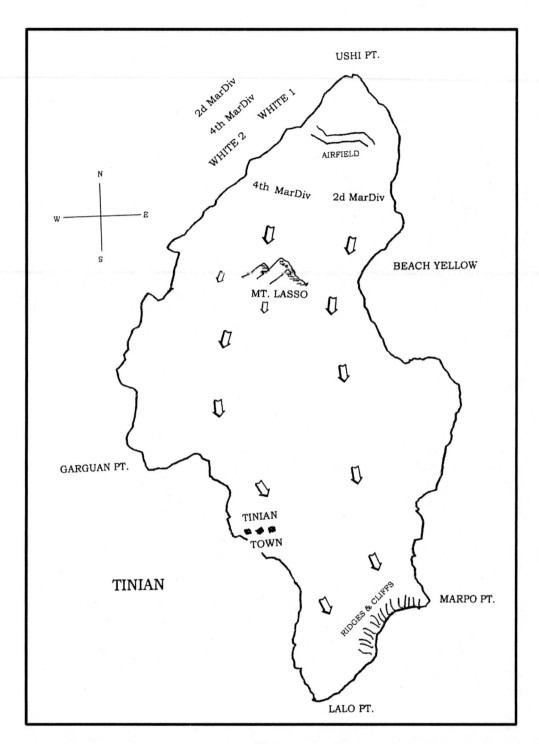

Tinian

alties to the battalion, until tanks and half-tracks came up with supporting fire. But the 2d MarDiv reached its objective by 1830 and now the Marines held 80% of the island.

At 0200 on the morning of 31 July, the Japanese launched a counterattack against both 1/8 and 2/8. All the same, resistance continued to be relatively light until 1 August. In fact, that night a *banzai* attack along the line especially hurt the 8th Marines, which suffered 74

75mm Pack Howitzer firing into a Japanese-held cave in southern Tinian.

casualties. Schmidt was satisfied that the island was secured and so stated at 1855 that night. Hopefully the enemy was listening, but they didn't seem to get the word.

On the morning of 2 August a force of about 200 Japanese attacked 3/6 and after two hours suffered a loss of 119 men. Regardless, LtCol John W. Easley, battalion commander, was a victim, as were other Marines. Shortly after, 100 of the enemy hit 2/6, led by LtCol Edmund B. Games, and withdrew after losing 30 men. One good thing that happened, beginning on 1 August, was the wholesale surrender of civilians. It has been estimated that they numbered between 5,000 and 10,000 before the end. There were freak incidents of civilian casualties. Most were on purpose, such as civilians throwing their children off cliffs, then jumping after them. Groups of civilians were blown up by explosives attached to them by Japanese military forces.

Essentially, though the island was declared secure, the fighting continued for many months to come. The 8th Marines were left on the island to support the new island commander, MG James L. Underhill, and suppress the militant remnants of Japanese. By the end of 1944 it was estimated that the Japanese lost another 500 men while the regiment suffered casualties numbering 38 killed and 125 wounded. It was over, but not quite.

The 4th MarDiv was pulled entirely out of the Marianas, but the 2d remained on Saipan. The 2d and 6th Marines were there when 2/8 and 3/8 joined them on 25 October, while 1/8 remained on Tinian until the end of the year. The total casualties for the 2d MarDiv on Tinian amounted to 107 killed and another 654 wounded. One more Marine of the division, Private First Class Robert Lee Wilson, born in Centralia, Illinois, a member of 2/6, on 4 August threw himself on a grenade while in the process of cleaning up the enemy. Posthumously he was awarded a Medal of Honor.

The island has been acclaimed as providing the U.S. Army Air Force with the airfields capable of providing the necessary location for bombing mainland Japan, just 1200 nautical miles away. The *Enola Gay,* part of the Twentieth Air Force, carried the bomb for bombing Hiroshima, then another plane, the *Bock's,* later flew from Tinian on the second atom-bomb mission to Nagasaki.

Saipan

The division remained on Saipan for the next several months. At the end of the year it was relieved of duty on the island and became part of the III Amphibious Corps under MG Roy S. Geiger. During the Campaign on Iwo Jima the division was made area reserve but was never called upon for that island battle. The IIIAC began preparing for the forthcoming Okinawa campaign.

Okinawa

Second Division embarked in late March as part of Task Group 51.2, which launched a diversion along the southeast coast of Okinawa, at the same time the actual landings were being made elsewhere on 1 April 1945. Shortly before dawn on 1 April 1945 the great and small naval guns, plus numerous aircraft from nearby carriers, blasted the island. The 2d MarDiv was going to make a feint off Minatoga beaches. The reply came swiftly and deadly. Flights of Japanese aircraft began dropping in on transports and warships. The transport *Hinsdale* and LST 884, with members of 3/2, was standing by when struck. Eight Marines were killed, eight missing, and 37 wounded. It was not a good sign for the forthcoming major landings up north on the west coast.

MG Roy S. Geiger, second in command to LG Simon B. Buckner, Jr., USA, urged his CO to land the 2d MarDiv on the southeastern coast, forcing the fiercely defending Japanese forces to disperse. Buckner, however, refused to have another Marine division ashore. Consequently, though the 2d MarDiv was available and an amphibious landing would probably have eased the losses of the American troops, the entire division was never used on Okinawa.

It was, however, directed to land and capture two small islands in the Ryukyu chain, Iheya and Aguni. Under its new CG, MG LeRoy P. Hunt, the 2d MarDiv landed, the 8th Marines supported on 3 June; the regiment, meeting little resistance, captured the island within 24 hours. On 15 June the 8th Marines and supporting units were landed on Okinawa, to relieve the hard-pressed U.S. Army and Marine divisions laboring against fierce resistance. Though they didn't land until nearly the end of the campaign, the regiment suffered 252 casualties, of whom 36 were killed. On 21 June the island was declared secure.

Order of Battle
Okinawa
8th Combat Team, 2d Marine Division
(15 to 22 Jun)

8th Marines Headquarters

Col Clarence R. Wallace	CO
LtCol Martin S. Rahiser	ExO
Maj William C. Chamberlin	S-3 (WIA 18 Jun)
Capt Bob S. Griffin	CO H&S Co
Maj David V. Van Evera	CO Wpns Co
Maj John R. Nelson	CO Div Recon Co
Capt Osman B. Latrobe	CO 2d Eng Bn
Lt Richard L. French	CO 2d Med Bn
1stLt Paul A. Schott	CO 2d MT Bn
Capt James B. Finley	CO 2d Pion Bn
Capt Edward L. Bale, Jr.	CO 2d Tk Bn
Capt James L. George	CO 2d Ampb Trk Co

1/8

LtCol Richard W. Hayward	CO
Maj Robert L. Holderness	ExO
Capt William H. Pickett	S-3 (WIA 22 Jun)
Capt August W. Berning	CO Hdqs Co
Capt Joseph F. Haley, Jr.	CO A Co
Capt John C. Lundrigan	CO B Co
Capt Harry P. Anderson	CO C Co

2/8

LtCol Harry A. Waldorf	CO
Maj William H. Junghans, Jr.	ExO
Capt Martin F. Barrett	S-3 (To 18 Jun)
Capt Robert H. Rogers	CO E Co
Capt Donald L. Walls	CO F Co
1stLt Thurman L. Perkins	CO G Co

3/8

LtCol Paul E. Wallace	CO

Maj Byron V. Thornton	ExO
Maj John I. Warner, Jr.	S-3
Capt Paul Cook	CO Hdqs Co (To 19 Jun)
1stLt Winfield S. Wallace, Jr.	CO Hdqs Co
Capt George S. Skinner	CO I Co
Capt John Adrian, Jr.	CO K Co (WIA 3 Jun)
1stLt David V. Carter	CO K Co
Capt Joseph A. Zielinski	CO L Co (WIA 20 Jun)

10th Marines
2/10

LtCol Richard G. Weede	CO
Maj Kenneth C. Houston	ExO
Capt William M. Spencer, III	S-3
Capt Richard M. H. Harper, Jr.	CO H&S Btry
Capt Robert W. Anderson	CO D Btry
Capt Ralph E. Myer	CO E Btry
Capt Robert H. Hensel	CO F Btry

2d Amph Trac Bn

Maj Fenton A. Durand	CO
Capt Eugene A. Siegel	ExO
Capt William H. Houseman, Jr.	S-3
Capt Wilfred A. Ronck	CO H&S Co
Capt James F. Perry	CO A Co
Capt Philip T. Chaffee	CO B Co
Capt Wallace B. Nygren	CO C Co

JAPAN

In September 1945 the 2d MarDiv landed at Nagasaki, Japan, and became part of the occupation force. Many of the "old-timers," those Marines who had served through much of the war, were sent home, some for other duties, many to be discharged. Those men in Japan helped to demilitarize that nation in the nine months they were there. Afterwards the division, on 15 June 1946, sailed for the United States. Their next home was at Camp Lejeune, North Carolina, where they would be one of the two permanent Marine Divisions.

The division's total casualties for the entire war have been established as 12,395, of which 2,633 were killed or died of wounds, and the balance, 9,137, were wounded in action. They were truly "Second to None."

3d Marine Division

The Third Marine Division was formed in New Zealand in June 1943, although its units had previously organized in the United States before shipping overseas in September 1942. Locations where units formed included Camp Elliott, CA, and New River (Camp Lejeune), NC. Third Division was composed of three infantry regiments, the 3d, the 9th, and the 21st. The artillery regiment was the 12th and the original engineer regiment, until after Guam, was the 19th. Afterwards they were broken down into the Third Engineer Battalion and the Third Pioneer Battalion. Division troops also included a tank battalion, an amphibious tractor battalion, a war dog platoon, a joint assault signal company (Jasco), and motor transport, salvage, and military police. The numeric "Third" preceded all.

At New River, NC, the 3d Marines was the first formed. Composed from cadres of the 5th and 7th Marines and "boots" recently arrived from Parris Island, they sailed on 1 September 1942 under the command of Col Oscar R. "Speed" Cauldwell. Their terminus was American Samoa, where they would relieve the 7th Marines, who were destined for Guadalcanal. The 3d Marines took over the defense of Tutuila and especially the harbor at Pago Pago. Then came the serious training in jungle warfare. Some training they learned after they arrived on Guadalcanal. The island was not the healthiest place and many men were afflicted with disease brought by mosquitoes. However, they were not left on the island forever. On 23 May 1943 they shipped out for New Zealand. There the regiment joined other units that were forming up as the 3d MarDiv.

At Camp Elliott, on 12 February 1942, they formed the Ninth Marines under the command of LtCol William B. Onley. Col Lemuel C. Shepherd, Jr., soon replaced him on 16 March. The regiment was originally composed of cadres left over from the Second and Eighth Marines, and then more boots were added before sailing for New Zealand in January 1943.

The final infantry regiment, the 21st Marines, was formed also at Elliott in July 1942. Nonetheless, they shipped it east to New River, where they gathered in men from the Iceland Detachment, and some old China Marines. On 8 July they officially formed the regiment under LtCol Max D. Smith, who was replaced by Col Daniel E. Campbell on 25 July. On 16 January 1943, Col Evans "Snuffy" O. Ames assumed command of the 21st.

Division artillery, the 12th Marines, was composed in New Zealand, as were the 19th Marines, from various engineer units already there. Col John B. Wilson led the "cannoncockers" and Col Robert Martina Montague, a World War I hero of the 4th Brigade, the "diggers."

The advanced echelon of the division formed up and shipped out on 23 January 1943. Included were: MG Charles D. Barrett, CG; Col Alfred H. Noble, Chief of Staff; LtCol Walter A. Wachtler, D-1; LtCol William F. Coleman, D-2; LtCol Arthur H. Butler, D-3; Col William C. Hall, D-4. Also included were the 9th and 19th Marines, plus assorted administrative personnel. The rear echelon shipped out between 15 and 23 February. Included was the ADC, BG Allen H. Turnage, the 21st and 12th Marines, plus service troops and more administrative personnel.

Their serious training as a division began when they moved into the camps established for them. It was getting onto winter in that hemisphere and their conditioning hikes and exercises were carried out in very inclement weather. Rain was the norm, followed by the usual chill. Generally speaking, the troops were well received by the natives. It was especially wonderful for the 3d Marines, who had been on Samoa for a long time. There were plenty of Caucasian women whose menfolk were in the Middle East.

GUADALCANAL

The division, now trained and considered ready for a combat role, was moved to the nearest appropriate spot for the planned invasion of the island of Bougainville. They left New Zealand in small groups beginning in late June and early July. Their time at the "canal" was taken up with more training, and some clean-up mainly undertaken by the division engineers. The weather was always unpleasant on the island and August was the ultimate in humidity and heat. There were some losses of personnel to Japanese planes which were still paying attention to the island. In October it was learned, by even the lowliest private, that a decision was made by Headquarters 1st Marine Amphibious Corps (IMAC) that D-day at Cape Torokina would be on 1 November. The cape was located at the north end of the Empress of Augusta Bay (known to Marines as Empress Augusta Bay). This is located on the west coast of the island (see map on page 41) and the 3d Marines was selected for the honors. The enemy was estimated to have at least 45,000 and perhaps as many as 70,000 troops on the island. They were somewhat scattered but essentially most were either at the northwestern end or the southeastern end. This should have allowed the Marines a relatively easy landing. Not so.

Following Barrett's death, LG Vandegrift resumed command of IMAC until 9 November. MG Roy S. Geiger would be his replacement. IMAC would have, in addition to the main force, the 3d MarDiv, the 1st Marine Parachute Regiment (LtCol Robert H. Williams), the 2d Marine Raider Regiment (LtCol Alan Shapley), and the 37th InfDiv (MG Robert S. Beightler, USA), in reserve. There had been several changes in the overall command structure of IMAC, before and during the planning, and then in execution of this plan. The first IMAC CG had been MG Clayton B. Vogel, who had some problems adapting to the concept of commanding a Corps and was relieved. LG Alexander A. Vandegrift briefly replaced him, and then was on his way to Washington to become the next Commandant. He in turn was replaced by MG Charles D. Barrett. Barrett was killed at IMAC Headquarters on 8 October, in what has been called an accident, and Vandegrift turned back and again assumed command. Therefore, he was in overall command on 1 November 1943. There were several diversionary landings all about the area. New Zealand troops landed on Mono and Stirling Islands in late October, while on 20 October LtCol Victor H. "Brute" Krulak led his 2d Battalion, 1st Parachute Regiment ashore on Choiseul. The latter was, overall, a near disaster. However, the force managed to get out reasonably well.

BOUGAINVILLE

D-day, 1 November 1943, dawned bright and clear. The 9th Marines would land far-thest from the cape on five beaches and the 3d Marines nearer Cape Torokina on six beaches. The layout for the two regiments was from left, on Red Beaches, Col Edward A. Craig's 9th Marines. From left, 1/9 (LtCol Jaime Sabater), 2/9 (LtCol Robert E. Cushman), and 3/9 (LtCol Walter Asmuth, Jr.). Then on Blue beaches, Col George W. McHenry's 3d Marines. From left, 3/3 (LtCol Ralph M. King), 2/3 (LtCol Hector de Zayas), and on Blue 1, at Cape Torokina, 1/3 (Maj Leonard M. Mason). To 1/3's left was the Buretoni Mission, which was the target of LtCol Alan Shapley's 2d Raiders, landing on Green 2. LtCol Fred D. Bean's 3d Raiders were scheduled to take the island of Puruata, located about a thousand yards off the cape. H-hour was 0715. After a brief but vigorous bombardment the landing party made for shore. At 0726 the first waves hit the beach.

On the right, 1/3, led by LtCol Leonard M. "Spike" Mason, had their work cut out for them. The cape was heavily defended. There had been at least 25 cement pillboxes before the naval gunfire had destroyed most. An estimated 300 Japanese soldiers were dug in, with log and sand bunkers, and they would fight to the death. The rest of the landing force met almost no resistance in comparison and was soon safely ashore. A division headquarters unit suffered the most casualties while still in their boat, hit by three enemy shells: 12 men died and 14 others were wounded. One enemy 75mm gun sited on the cape destroyed 14 boats and caused enormous casualties. Sergeant Robert A. Owens of 1/3, from Greenville, SC, decided to take this gun out. Covered by four comrades and keeping under as much cover as was possible, he approached the bunker. When the firing stopped momentarily, he charged into the gun port, driving out the crew of the gun. Then he destroyed the gun and its capability. Although later that day he paid the ultimate price for his outstanding cour-age, for that one act they awarded him a Medal of Honor.

The Second Raiders supported Mason and his men on their left. To that left, LtCol Hector de Zayas, CO of 2/3, was taken aback when Capt Donald M. Schmuck arrived breath-lessly with his company. It seems that Schmuck's company had, by accident, landed with 1/3 and he and they had to move pronto to be where 2/3 was. De Zayas asked why and Schmuck replied, "Ask the navy." Maps available were next to useless and many command-ers were terribly confused about locations and positions.

In the meantime, Japanese carrier aircraft made every effort to inflict heavy casualties on the landing force. Nonetheless, Marine air plus the hail of antiaircraft fire from the con-verging ships destroyed them instead. Successive flights were beaten off and 26 enemy planes were shot down. On 1/3's beach one of the boats hit contained a legend of the Corps, Gun-ner Milton C. "Slug" Marvin, and his unloading party. When several of his men were killed or wounded, Slug decided to form the rest into a marauding patrol and they made their way into the jungle. In the course of that period, Marvin and company managed to knock out seven pillboxes and killed many Japanese. His reward: a Silver Star.

The 1st Battalion, Third Marines continued having difficulties most of the day. The men that managed to get ashore were forced into combat as soon as they were on dry land. It was one of the first occasions in the Pacific war when the enemy met the invasion force at the beach. The enemy was well dug in and each emplacement had to be taken apart by groups of willing Marines. Early on, Mason was wounded and instead of taking advice to slow his battalion down he exhorted his replacement, Maj John P. Brody, to "get the hell in

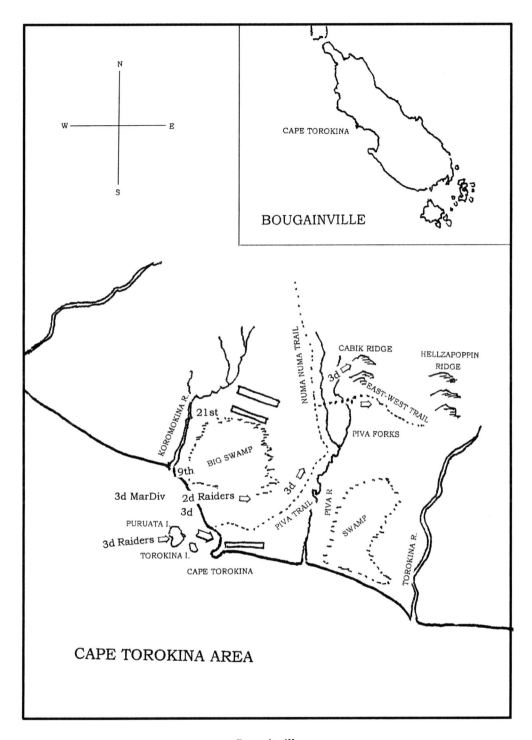

Bougainville

there and fight." It was later reported as "the bloodiest beach of the entire Solomons campaign."

One by one 1/3 knocked out the pillboxes and after three hours at least 270 of the enemy defenders were prone. After an hour of fighting someone foolishly sent a message to the command ship "Old Glory waves on Cape Torokina. Situation well in hand." Old Glory

"Slug" Marvin's unloading party on the beach at Bougainville, just before he was killed.

may very well have waved on Torokina but the "situation" was not well in hand. By the end of the day, however, all the Marines were on their objectives, 600 to 1,000 yards inland. The invasion force quickly learned that they had inadequate maps. There was an impenetrable swamp just beyond the landing site. It made movement nearly impossible, for anyone except Marines. It would be several days before that hazard was overcome. Later, Gen Turnage made a comment: "Never had men in the Marines ever had to fight and maintain themselves over such difficult terrain as was encountered on Bougainville." Though the going would continue to be rough for many days to come they were safely ashore. That was always the most important state of affairs for any invasion force.

On D-Day plus 1, 2 November, the 3d Raider Bn had taken Puruata Island and soon it became the supply "dump" for the invasion force. That fact was soon discovered by the ever-watchful Japanese and shortly it became a major target of their air attacks. Supplies and gasoline blew sky-high on a daily basis. There was not a place available on the part of the main island owned by Marines that was a suitable substitute, so the losses continued for days to come. At the end of the day, the perimeter was about 1,200 yards in depth, at which point was a swamp. The use of amtracs solved some of that difficulty and by the following day, 3 November, the depth had been pushed back another 300 yards. Not very far, but at least Cape Torokina was just about cleaned out.

That day Seabees began building roads through the swampy areas and even prepared to build a fighter strip. Twenty-one days later, Marine fighter planes began landing on it. The hard-hit 1/3 was relieved by a battalion of the 9th Marines on 4 November and went into division reserve. Rain continued without abatement. This was a period when disease was more of an enemy than were the Japanese. Malaria flared up, as did filariasis once again among the Samoan vets. Dysentery was always a problem for men in battle. Combat activity was at a minimum for the 4th, 5th, and the 6th of November.

On D-Day + 5, 6 November, more American ships arrived bringing 1/21, more Seabees,

8. Marines of 1/3 digging graves for their deceased buddies on 2 November.

advance units from the 148th Infantry, USA, and some members of the 3d Defense Battalion. On 7 November the Japanese played the Marines' game. They landed a force estimated at about 500 bodies (accurate word, as it turned out) between the Laruma River and the nearby Koromokina Lagoon, the latter lying about 100 yards west of the river of the same name.

Marine defenses had 3/9 (Asmuth) just across that river as the western perimeter of the division line. Company K, 3/9, located on the western end, was ordered by Asmuth to attack the interlopers. He also directed his mortars and requested help from the 12th Marines to assist in the onslaught. Two platoons of the company, however, were not available, both being on patrol. One platoon ran into a large body of the enemy as they were making their run and though they held their own, were forced to retire away from the fighting. It would be another day and a half before they could rejoin 3/9. Another patrol was also right in the middle of the enemy force on the beach and they had a knock-down fight. Eventually they made their way back to 3/9 by boat.

At 1330 1/3 (Brody), which had been in reserve, was sent forward to relieve 3/9 at the front. Companies B and C were rushed along the beach into a counterattack. No more than thirty yards separated the two enemy forces and a fierce fight raged for hours. The battalion's Sergeant Herbert J. Thomas, of Columbus, Ohio, led his squad through a dense jungle undergrowth against severe machine gun fire. Breaking through the enemy lines the squad fought with grenades and rifles, and destroyed the crews of two guns. Thomas discovered a third gun and began to throw a grenade into that emplacement. However, a Japanese soldier hurled one first and it landed in the midst of Sgt Thomas' men. He, without second thought, hurled himself upon it and absorbed the entire blast, dying in the act. He was selected for a posthumous Medal of Honor.

That night enemy infiltrators broke through to the 3d Medical Battalion's hospital and attempted to halt the life-saving going on within. However, cooks, bakers, and stretcher bearers provided a line and stopped them from interfering with Cmdr Robert R. Callaway and his staff in their operations. Meanwhile, Maj Brody's men of 1/3 kept close to the enemy to their front. Insults were continually exchanged between the forces, such as "Moline you die." Capt Gordon Warner, fluent in Japanese, gave back better, including inciting the Japanese to "Charge."

Turnage realized he would need reinforcements and on 6 November had sent in the 21st Marines, led off by LtCol Ernest W. Fry, Jr.'s, 1/21. Fry, senior man at the scene, was now in direct command. On the eighth, artillery and mortars slammed into the area, 300 yards wide and 600 deep. When Fry's two advance companies went in they found nothing but desolation. The Marines passed over about 250 Japanese lying prostrate as they advanced forward. If there were survivors among them they were soon blasted apart by Marine air from Munda on 9 November.

In the meantime, on 7 November, the Japanese 23d Infantry had arrived before the 2d Raiders at the Buretoni Catholic Mission and provided the latter with some action. Some members of the 9th Marines had previously been sent forward to support the raiders and they too were on hand for the reception. This was at the same time the enemy had made the seaborne Koromokina landing and while the raiders held, the woods before them were full of dead Japanese soldiers.

General Turnage had decided that it was imperative to take and hold the junction of Piva and Numa-Numa Trails lying a few hundred yards east of Piva village. He ordered Col Edward A. Craig of the 9th Marines to do the job. Craig assigned the job to LtCol Alan B. Shapley, CO of the 2d Raider Regiment. The actual attack would be led by LtCol Fred D. Beans and his 3d Raider Battalion, just in from taking Puruata Island. In addition, Beans would have some of the 9th Marines to aid his gang. However, as the saying goes, everything comes to him who waits. The Japanese didn't wait for the Marines. Instead, they launched their own attack. On 8 November they came and it appeared that they would overrun the trail block. Men versus men turned the tide for the Marines. Private First Class Henry Gurke, from Neche, North Dakota, and his comrade, PFC Donald Probst, were holding a position with a BAR when a grenade rolled in upon them. Gurke pushed Probst aside and flung himself on it, taking the full blast but protecting his foxhole mate. For that he was awarded a posthumous Medal of Honor. Probst held on and he was awarded a Silver Star. The post held, the line held and the enemy were driven back. The fighting continued for two days until finally, the enemy could take no more and what was left of them retired. Later count showed 550 enemy dead, with losses of 19 dead and 32 wounded Marines. The 9th Marines sent in more men and aggressively held the positions fought over, thereby ensuring the maintenance of ground paid for. The Battle of Piva Trail was another victory for the 3d MarDiv. Yet the victories were not yet driving the Japanese out of the area, let alone from the island. They were still fighting for every inch of ground.

On the 9th of November the Army's 37th InfDiv (MG Robert S. Beightler, USA) had begun landing their troops and supplies. Marines, lacking nearly everything, managed to openly pilfer (steal) them. It was not a good time for either service.

On 11 November IMAC issued an attack order for the Army (left) and Marine (right) units ashore. Army-Marine artillery would provide support, but under IMAC control, and Marine air would provide close support. The first objective was the junction of the Numa-Numa and East-West Trails. On 13 November, Company E of 2/21 led off the attack, beginning at 0800. But at 1100 it was ambushed by a sizeable enemy force concealed in the coconut palm grove near the trail junction. LtCol Eustace R. Smoak, CO, 2/21, sent his exec, Maj Glenn Fissell, with some 12th Marine artillery observers to find out what was happening. It was bad. Fissell was killed. Smoak moved his battalion closer, through the enemy, and fed his companies into the fight. Smoak ordered Company F forward to cover a withdrawal by E, which was accomplished, but F disappeared and 2/21 was in a very bad state of affairs. Smoak decided that the lateness of the hour and darkness would force him to wait until the following day. With that, 2/21 went into perimeter defense. However, that night, a gunnery sergeant from F came in and told Smoak that F was up front, surrounded by the enemy; it had suffered heavy casualties and had lost its CO. Smoak ordered the sergeant to return to F and lead them around the enemy flank to a position in the rear of the battalion, which the sergeant did.

Next day, 14 November, tanks were brought up and the artillery registered all around Smoak's battalion. He also called in 18 Marine torpedo bombers(?) and his disorganized riflemen were to go forward once again. H-hour was set for 1155 after a twenty-minute artillery preparation, followed by a rolling barrage. The Marines were met by a heavy enemy response. Rifles, machine guns, and mortars began to decimate the advancing Marines. The tanks lost their directions and began firing into and running down the Marines, costing several "friendly" casualties. Capt Sidney J. Altman, "skipper" of E, 2/21, earned himself a Silver Star when he jumped aboard the turret of the lead tank and re-directed the tank commander, who in turn managed to reorient the rest. Smoak's battalion was having a bad time. However, within a few hours the attack was successful; enemy resistance was overcome, the remnants retired and a perimeter defense was established for the night.

On 14 November the 21st Marines came in and relieved the 9th Marines on the front lines. The 129th Infantry, USA, landed and took up a position in the center of the perimeter. However, the newcomers were not ready for front line duty just yet. They inadvertently allowed Japanese patrols to come down the nearby Numa-Numa Trail, which caused trouble in the rear areas, for Army and Marines. Company F of 2/3, just then ingesting some hot stew in their helmets, were rushed to the breach and, to say the least, were very angry with the 129th Infantry. Insults were part of the exchange, which did not hurt the Japanese one little bit but helped to weaken the U.S. forces.

Dry ground was finally discovered and Turnage ordered his troops to move forward rapidly and take it for development of landing fields. The offensive began on 19 November when all troops were pushed beyond the Piva River to establish strong positions. It wasn't easy. The enemy seemed ready and made life very difficult for those trying to advance. Yet 2/3 found high ground and Lt Steve Cibek and his platoon from Company F climbed the 400-foot edifice and occupied it. It gave the Marines a valuable piece of real estate from which they could view much of the surrounding countryside, especially where the offensive was to take place. The advance continued and Cibek and his men managed to hold the height even though continually attacked. The Japanese had been using the same place to spy on the Marines every day, but they should also have remained there at night.

A reconnaissance patrol from 2/3 crossed the Piva River on 21 November but ran into a heavy concentration of fire from enemy bunkers. Fire broke out all along the line and

Officers of the 3d Marine Division planning for airfield construction.

Company B took much of it, suffering numerous casualties. Cibek and his men retained their hold on "Cibek Hill" even though they too were major targets of Japanese assaults. Before the fighting and tensions along the line settled down that day, the 3d Marines sustained severe casualties.

Thanksgiving Day, 24 November, saw more casualties when the Japanese replied to a twenty-minute Marine artillery fire, causing many more dead and wounded amongst the 3d Marines. One company waiting to move forward lost 100 of their 190 men while waiting for H-hour. Nonetheless, at 0900 the 3d Marines moved forward. For 2/3 the first 500 yards was relatively easy; however, after three hundred yards 3/3 ran into serious trouble. Bunkers were slowly being taken by Marines using flamethrowers and by others dropping grenades into their apertures. Meanwhile, enemy mortar shells really gave the Marines in the open a horrible reception. Then the 12th Artillery began shelling the enemy positions again and there were explosions galore. The swamp was waist deep in some places making that route even more difficult as the mortar shells dropped in on the advancing Marines. The explosions tore huge banyan tree limbs free and sent them down upon the Marines. Meanwhile a steady Japanese sniper fire was also coming from the same trees. There was nothing to give thanks for on this day.

Company L, led by Capt John Kovacs, was practically wiped out, including the "skipper" and all the other officers, by sniper fire. Yet, the handful of survivors continued forward. Nevertheless, the back of the Japanese defense was broken, especially when 2/3 plunged far ahead by 1,100 yards and were deep in enemy-held territory. Late in the day the cooks actually managed to get bits and pieces of turkey up to the men on the line, because, after all, it was Thanksgiving Day.

The next day the Japanese launched a major assault against the lines of the 3d Marines; it was, however, broken up and the battle known as Piva Forks was over. The 23d Japanese Infantry was eliminated: over 1,100 enemy dead were counted. The 3d Marines were barely in better shape, with 150 men in 1/3 still on their feet. The regiment had had enough and was relieved by the 9th Marines.

On the right, the 21st Marines were sent in to help the 1st Marine Parachute Regiment, which had gotten into a bit of difficulty. They had stormed a wooded hill and over the next few days had been cut to pieces in so doing. The 21st Marines came up and tried their luck. They too were stopped but after five days up they went and took what is known as "Helzapoppin Ridge," the regiment's first victory.

During December the Marines and Army units kept going forward, creating new landing fields as they took territory. On 24 December the 3d Marines were withdrawn from Bougainville. As they arrived on the beach a violent earthquake startled them and one Marine yelled, "Let's get outta here before anything else happens." The rest of the Marines of the 3d MarDiv were relieved by incoming Army units and all were returned to their beloved encampment on Guadalcanal.

Order of Battle
Bougainville
(15 October 1943 to 28 December 1943)

Headquarters

MG Allen Hal Turnage	CG
BG Oscar R. Cauldwell	ADC
Col Robert Blake	CoS
LtCol Chevey S. White	D-1
LtCol Howard J. Thurton	D-2
LtCol James Snedeker	D-3 (To 11 Nov)
Col Walter A. Wachtler	D-3 (T0 16 Dec)
LtCol Alpha L. Bowser	D-3
Col William C. Hall	D-4

3d Amph Trac Bn

Maj Sylvester L. Stephan	CO (To 5 Dec; 8–9 Dec; from 17 Dec)
Maj Erwin F. Wann	CO (6–7 Dec; 10–16 Dec)
Maj Erwin F. Wann	ExO
2dLt William O. Reid	B-3

3d Medical Bn

LtCmdr Gordon M. Bruce	ExO

3d MT Bn

Maj Stewart W. Purdy	CO
Capt Frank S. Matheny	ExO

3d Service Bn

LtCol Ion M. Bethel	CO

3d Special Weapons Bn

LtCol Durant S. Buchannan	CO
LtCol Walter S. Campbell	ExO
Capt William L. Cerutti	B-3

3d Tank Bn

LtCol Hartnoll J. Withers	CO[1] (To 15 Nov; from 10 Dec)
Maj John I. Williamson, Jr.	ExO (To 30 Nov)
Maj Holly H. Evans	ExO
Maj Holly H. Evans	B-3

Second Raider Regiment (Prov)

LtCol Alan Shapley	CO
Capt Oscar F. Peatross	ExO
1stLt Charles T. Lamb	R-1
Capt James P. Jacobson	R-2
Capt Oscar F. Peatross	R-3
Maj Robert S. Wade	R-4

2d Raider Bn

LtCol Joseph P. McCaffrey	CO (To 1 Nov)
Maj Richard T. Washburn	CO
Maj Richard T. Washburn	ExO (To 1 Nov)
Capt Bernard W. Green	ExO
1stLt Clinton B. Eastman	B-3

3d Raider Bn

LtCol Fred D. Beans	CO

[1]*Muster rolls fail to show a commanding officer by name from 16 November 1943 to 26 December 1943.*

Capt Arthur H. Haake	ExO
Capt Martin Levit	B-3

Third Marines

Col George W. McHenry	CO (To 16 Dec)
Col Walter A. Wachtler	CO (To 27 Dec)
LtCol George O. Van Orden	CO
LtCol George O. Van Orden	ExO (To 27 Dec)
1stLt Clyde T. Brannon	R-1
1stLt John W. Foley, Jr.	R-2
LtCol Sidney S. McMath	R-3
Maj Grant Crane	R-4

1/3

Maj Leonard M. Mason	CO (To 1 Nov)
Maj John P. Brody	CO (To 18 Nov)
Maj Charles J. Bailey, Jr.	CO
Maj John P. Brody	ExO (To 1 Nov)
Maj Charles J. Bailey, Jr.	ExO (To 30 Nov)
Capt Philip C. Roettinger	ExO
Maj Charles J. Bailey, Jr.	B-3 (To 1 Nov)
Capt Donald L. Weiler	B-3 (To 24 Nov)
Maj Robert D. Kenney	B-3

2/3

LtCol Hector de Zayas	CO
Maj William A. Culpepper	ExO
Capt John A. Scott	B-3

3/3

LtCol Ralph M. King	CO
Maj Edwin L. Hamilton	ExO (To 20 Nov)
Maj Wade M. Jackson	ExO
Capt John A. Scott	B-3

Ninth Marines

Col Edward Craig	CO
LtCol James A. Stuart	ExO
Maj Addison B. Overstreet	R-1
Capt Robert A. Campbell	R-2
LtCol Ralph L. Houser	R-3
Maj Frank Shine	R-4

1/9

LtCol Jaime Sabater	CO (To 18 Nov)
LtCol Carey A. Randall	CO
Maj Harold C. Boehm	ExO
Capt Francis H. Bergtholdt	B-3

2/9

LtCol Robert E. Cushman, Jr.	CO
LtCol Wendell H. Duplantis	ExO
Capt Lyle Q. Peterson	B-3

3/9

LtCol Walter Asmuth, Jr.	CO
LtCol Carey A. Randall	ExO (To 18 Nov)
Maj Marlowe C. Williams	ExO
Capt Calvin W. Kunz	B-3

Twenty-first Marines

Col Evans O. Ames	CO
LtCol Arthur H. Butler	ExO
Maj Irving R. Kriendler	R-1

Capt Blair A. Hyde	R-2
Maj James W. Tinsley	R-3
Maj Malcolm K. Beyer	R-4

1/21

LtCol Ernest W. Fry, Jr.	CO
Maj Eugene H. Strayhorn	ExO
Capt Leslie A. Gilson, Jr.	B-3

2/21

LtCol Eustace R. Smoak	CO
Maj Glenn E. Fissel	ExO (To 13 Nov)
Capt Andrew Hedesh	B-3

3/21

LtCol Archie V. Gerard	CO
Maj Henry S. Massie	ExO
Capt Julius H. Flagstad	B-3

Twelfth Marines

Col John B. Wilson	CO
LtCol John S. Letcher	ExO
1stLt Joe A. Inglish	R-1
Maj Claude S. Sanders, Jr.	R-2
LtCol William P. Fairbourn	R-3
LtCol Edmund M. Williams	R-4

1/12

LtCol Raymond F. Crist, Jr.	CO
Maj George B. Thomas	ExO
Maj Edward L. Peoples	B-3

2/12

LtCol Donald M. Weller	CO
LtCol Henry T. Wailer	ExO
Maj Thomas R. Belzer	B-3

3/12

LtCol Jack Tabor	CO
Maj Robert H. Armstrong	ExO
Capt Haddon H. Smiths	B-3 (To 7 Dec)
Maj Thomas C. Jolly, III	B-3

4/12

LtCol Bernard H. Kirk	CO (To 7 Dec)
Maj Andrew H. Rose, Jr.	CO (To 13 Dec)
LtCol Bernard H. Kirk	CO
Maj Andrew H. Rose, Jr.	ExO
Capt George L. Hays	B-3 (To 9 Nov)
Capt Robert S. Rain, Jr.	B-3

Nineteenth Marines

Col Robert M. Montague	CO (To 6 Dec)
LtCol Robert E. Fojt	CO
LtCol Robert E. Fojt	ExO (To 6 Dec)
Maj William V. D. Jewett	ExO
Maj William V. D. Jewett	R-1 (To 6 Dec)
Maj George D. Flood	R-1
Capt Minstree Folkes, Jr.	R-2 & R-3
Maj Virgil M. Davis	R-4

1/19

Maj Ralph W. Bohme	CO
Capt Kenneth M. King	ExO
Capt Joseph W. Beckenstrater	B-3

2/19		Branch No. 3, 4th Base Depot	
LtCol Harold B. West	CO (To 6 Dec)	Col Kenneth A. Inman	CO
Maj Halstead Ellison	CO	Maj Harlan E. Draper	ExO (To 17 Oct)
Maj Halstead Ellison	ExO (To 6 Dec)	LtCol Walter A. Churchill	ExO (From 1
Capt Victor J. Simpson	ExO		Nov)
Capt Charles E. Ingrain	B-3 (To 6 Dec)	Maj Cedric H. Kuhn	ExO (From 1
Capt James R. Ovington	B-3		Dec)

GUADALCANAL

They arrived back at the Canal in January 1944 and remained in this rest area until June. Arrival was sporadic; the other units followed the 3d Marines over a period of nearly one month. Basically, after a few weeks of rest, relaxation, repair, and reorganization, they did what all Marines do: trained for the next campaign. However, the 3d Marines were in bad shape. They had carried most of the load at Bougainville and looked it. Their casualty rate and disease cases had been excessive and they badly needed repair. MG Turnage retained command of the division but the ADC, BG Oscar Cauldwell, was returned to the U.S. and BG Alfred Noble was back once again as ADC. Col Ray A. Robinson became Chief of Staff, replacing Col Robert Blake, who assumed command of the 21st Marines.

The next fight was anticipated to be at Kavieng, on New Ireland, an island in the Bismarck Archipelago about three hundred miles north of Bougainville. Training was brisk and lessons learned at Bougainville were practiced, including tank-infantry attacks, anti-boat firing, self-propelled guns and flamethrowers especially, and assaults on fortified positions. The newly reactivated 4th Marines, now primarily composed of former Raiders, was assigned to the 1st Marine Provisional Brigade, as was the 22d Marines. With aerial reconnaissance and photography, it became apparent that the Bismarcks had been successfully neutralized. Therefore, someplace different than Kavieng had to be selected.

That someplace was Guam, the only American possession in the Marianas group, which had been taken in four hours on 10 December 1941. The token defense force of roughly 150 officers and men of the Marine detachment was surrendered by the island commander, Capt George J. McMillan, USN, to preserve as many island residents as was possible.

The newly organized III Marine Amphibious Corps (MG Roy S. Geiger) consisted of the 3d MarDiv (Turnage) and the 1st Prov Brig (BG Lemuel C. Shepherd). Another division, the 77th InfDiv (MG Andrew D. Bruce, USA) was also assigned to IIIMAC but they were then at Oahu. Plans for the recapture of Guam were received on 11 May 1944. It was directed that the invasion would begin three days after the D-day landings on Saipan, further north in the Marianas. That schedule would, by necessity, have to be changed. The fighting on Saipan had proved to be much more difficult than had been anticipated and the 3d MarDiv had been kept nearby as floating reserve, "just in case." The men had been aboard ship for long periods, some as long as 50 days, and were beginning to find sea service to be less than desirable.

GUAM

On 21 July 1944 the guns of Task Force 53 opened up to support the landing of the IIIMAC. As the Marines loaded into their landing craft, some of their ships played the

Marine's Hymn from loudspeakers. They had already been apprised by MG Geiger that in their selection to retake Guam ... "You have been honored." Bet there were lots of wise-cracks to answer that one.

The Guam beachhead selected was south of Agaña Bay a mile below Agaña town, beginning at Adelup Point further south to opposite Mount Tenjo. All three regiments were to land, the 3d Marines on Beaches Red 1 & 2 on the left, the 21st Marines in the center on a narrow beach, Green, and the 9th Marines on the far right on Beach Blue. Once again it was the ill-fated 3d Marines who had the toughest front. The 3d Bn, 3d Marines was before Chonito Cliff, which rose up from the beach. Next to them on their right was 2/3, located before half of what later became Bundschu Ridge, while 1/3 had the other half. This was where most of the toughest fighting would take place until the Marines managed to get off the beach.

One hero, PFC Luther Skaggs, Jr., from Henderson, KY, while serving as a squad leader of a mortar section of 3/3, proved that he had more than it takes. On that D-day heavy mortar fire caused Skagg's squad leader to become a casualty soon after landing. Skaggs assumed command and led his men forward at least 200 yards off the beach through intense firing. Soon they set up and began dropping shells on a nearby strategic ridge. His command defended their territory that night, and when a grenade lobbed into his hole and shattered his leg, he hurriedly put on a tourniquet and continued firing his M-1 at the enemy. With his rifle and grenades he continued to resist for over eight hours. Skaggs did all this without a complaint or excuse to leave his men during the entire period. For that he was awarded a Medal of Honor.

The 21st Marines (Col Arthur H. Butler, Navy Cross) landed 1/21 (LtCol Marlowe C. Williams, Silver Star) followed by the second (LtCol Eustace R. Smoak) and third (LtCol Wendell H. Duplantis, Silver Star) battalions, all of which pushed ahead. On their right the 9th Marines landed 3/9, then 1/9 and 2/9, all of whom were soon off the beach. Both the 21st and 9th Marines made nifty advances, giving the 3d MarDiv some substantial ground on the first day.

In the south, down below the town of Agat, the 1st Provisional Brigade (BG Lemuel C. Shepherd, Jr.) landed 1/22 (LtCol Walfried H. Fromhold) and 2/22 (LtCol Donn C. Hart) on Beaches Yellow 1 & 2, and from the 4th Marines (LtCol Alan Shapley, Navy Cross), 1/4 (Maj Bernard W. Green) and 2/4 (Maj John S. Messer) on Beaches White, 1 & 2. The 22d (Col Merlin F. Schneider, Navy Cross) moved inward, then turned northward. Inboard went the 4th Marines and then southward. By the end of the day both had taken sufficient territory to ensure the future success of that southern landing.

The next day, up north, Company A of 1/3, led by Capt Geary R. Bundschu, with exceptional bravery, took what became known as "Bundschu Ridge." In so doing, while losing his life he earned a posthumous Navy Cross. With its acquisition, the 3d Marines managed to grab an essential piece of ground and hold it. By the 24th the 3d Marines were onto and holding Fonte Plateau, another tough piece of ground taken by drastic measures. Their left border and front line were now completely on the Fonte River.

Meanwhile, PFC Leonard F. Mason, of 2/3, a BAR man engaged in cleaning out hostile positions, came under fire from two enemy machine guns. Climbing out of his protected position in a gully, Mason, alone and entirely upon his own initiative, moved toward the rear of one gun's position. Wounded repeatedly by enemy rifle fire Mason continued forward until stopped momentarily by a burst of machine gun fire which caused him another

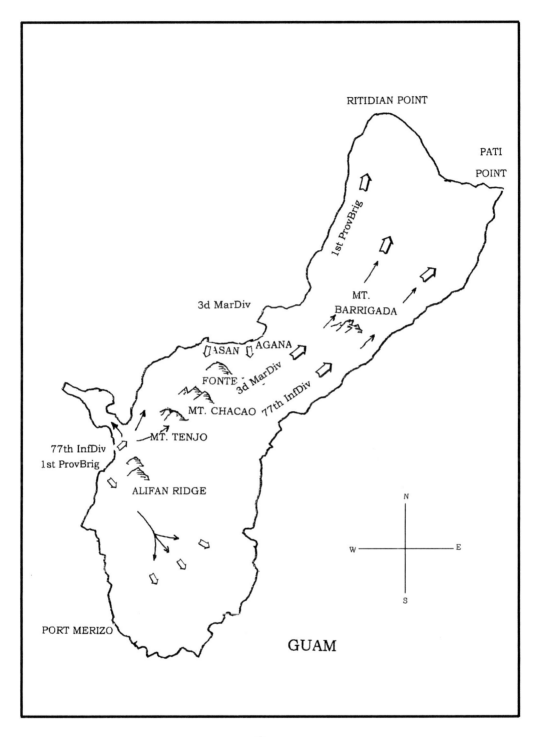

Guam

serious wound. Nevertheless, without personal regard, he continued onward and cleaned out the hostile gun, killing five enemy personnel. Somehow making it back to his company, Mason reported his action, all the while refusing to be evacuated until he had satisfied himself that his mission was duly recorded. He died soon after from that serious wound and was posthumously awarded the Medal of Honor.

18. Upon landing, Marines of 3/9 plant the flag on Guam on 21 July 1944, near Asan Point.

Meanwhile the 9th and 21st Marines were moving at a faster rate. Each was heading in a southeasterly direction and by the 22d, the 21st was almost upon the Radio Towers and the Masso River line. The 9th Marines had also turned right, moving with the sea as their right flank, and had taken ground almost to the Tatgua River line. Continuing to move forward, the 21st had gotten as far south as Mount Chachao while the 9th was assaulting the Piti Navy Yard. In the south, the 305th Infantry landed between the 22d and 4th Marines and quickly moved through them and forward, taking over the major offensive assault into Guam territory. At about 1550 on 25 July a patrol of the 9th Marines reported making contact with the 22d Marines.

Later that evening the Japanese launched a serious counterattack upon the lines of the junction of the 21st Marines and 9th Marines, with others hitting the 3d Marines. At first the attacks were sparse and scattered and it was several hours before the actual intentions of the enemy became known. It actually was a full-blown effort to drive the 3d MarDiv from Guam. Skipper of Company F, 2/9, Captain Louis H. Wilson, Jr., of Brandon, MS, was well aware of the enemy's tenaciousness. He and his command were fighting around Fonte Hill the afternoon of 25 July when he received a direct order to take that portion of the hill which lay before his company. Led by Wilson, F went up the hill over open terrain against horrific enemy rifle and machine gun fire. They advanced three hundred yards and successfully captured their objective. Wilson also assumed command of mixed groups of Marines plus various equipment and prepared a zone for defense for that night. Although he was wounded three times, Wilson continued his work and this enabled the Marines to successfully defend that position for a good five hours under terrific attacks. When it was obvious that his command was safe, he turned over it over to a subordinate and retired for medical attention.

Shortly afterward, when the enemy launched a series of violent attacks upon his men, Wilson voluntarily returned and rejoined his badly handled unit. He repeatedly exposed himself to flying lead and in one instance, ran fifty yards out front to retrieve a wounded Marine. For ten additional hours he and his men, fighting in violent hand-to-hand combat, managed to retain their precarious hold on their real estate. Early the next morning Wilson and his command finally crushed the enemy lying before them.

A strategic slope overlooked his post and for security's sake, it had to be taken. Wilson organized a 17-man patrol and they went and took the slope. In so doing they guaranteed that his unit would retain the high ground, so essential for the success of this operation. For his courage, ability, leadership and conduct, he was awarded a Medal of Honor. General Wilson would also be the twenty-sixth Commandant of the Marine Corps.

About 0100 the Japanese began making small-scale attacks all along the line. They were well armed, equipped with large demolition charges, and used the terrain to great advantage. As they rolled numerous charges down the slopes the Marines had great difficulty escaping them. One position, on the far left of the line, had been relatively quiet until this night. Maj Henry "Hank" Aplington's 1/3, which had been in division reserve, was brought up to maintain in the hills the far left flank position. He later recalled that "with the dark came rain and the Marines huddled under their ponchos ... around midnight there was a probing of the lines of the 21st Marines and slopping over into those of the 9th Marines. My first inkling came at about 0430 when my three companies erupted into fire and called for mortar support.... I talked to my company commanders ... and was told that there were Japanese all around them ... the Japanese had been close. Three of my dead had been killed by bayonet thrusts."

All along the line, the enemy managed to get in deep, almost to the beach, and well into the gun positions of the 12th Marines. Fighting around the guns was fierce, but Marines soon drove away the bulk of the enemy. Offshore navy gun fire was called in to flatten certain areas, especially before the 3d Marines. Many Japanese were crushed as they fell back.

All night the wild attacks continued, but they were unlike the *Banzai* attacks; these were not disorganized suicidal charges. It was later contended that empty enemy canteens smelled of saki, indicating that the Japanese were on a wild drunken rampage. At 0400 all hell broke loose. Enemy troops were opposite the Marines' line and volleys of machine gun and rifle fire plus volumes of hand grenades poured in upon the Marines. The nearly five sleepless nights the Marines had experienced were beginning to tell as morning and daylight came in. The 21st Marines were getting hit as badly as, and in some places worse than, the 3d Marines. Company B of 1/21 was nearly wiped out. By morning there were only about 18 men left for duty and still the Japanese came on them. The mortar platoon of 1/21 was also practically wiped out as the enemy continued their attack where the 21st and 9th Marines joined. Many Japanese had been put down but too many survived and were raising hell behind the lines. Perhaps 600 of their dead were lying before and within the positions of 2/9, commanded by another future commandant, LtCol Robert Cushman, also to be awarded a Navy Cross.

The fighting continued on through the early portion of 26 July. Estimates made at the time claimed as many as 3,200 enemy casualties but they still hadn't been stopped. By this date, Marines and their Army comrades fighting in the Pacific War were well aware that "a live Jap is dangerous" and were intent on killing all of them. Lines were reorganized and Marine casualties sorted out. Between 0900 and 1900 the lines were generally intact. At night there were more infiltrators but the assaults of many enemy seemed to have decreased.

On the morning of 27 July, orders were received for 2/9, which had been attached to the 3d Marines, to go forward and take the military crest of the reverse slope of Fonte Plateau. As the regiment moved forward, "friendly" shells and aerial bombs fell on Company G, disrupting their forward motion. Meanwhile, Company E went forward and retook ground lost the day before. By 1500 all three companies, G, E and F, were on the Plateau and digging in for the night. A *Banzai* attack was launched and Company G stopped it. It was later found that it was composed heavily of officers but that wasn't the end of it. All night the enemy continued their infiltrating and harassment tactics, allowing 2/9 very little rest and no sleep.

The following day, E and F companies advanced and reached their objective after facing modest resistance; but G had a rough time. Just one officer remained and they had replaced their skipper three times in two days. In the afternoon an estimated company-sized enemy attack hit F and G companies but that was soon wiped out. Fonte Plateau was now permanently U.S. Marine. That last attack was soon found to be a last gasp. Many of the deceased were Japanese officers, some quite senior in rank; it was really a suicidal rush, and in that, they were successful. After the 3d and 21st Marines had secured Fonte, the 9th Marines took the Mount Alutom–Mount Chachao massif and saw that the venerable 305th Infantry had taken Mount Tenjo. The Marines had worthy companions in the 77th InfDiv.

In the meantime, the 22d Marines had driven up the coast and was assaulting the Orote Peninsula. That was where the Marines had been housed before 9 December 1941. The southern landing group, 1st Provisional Brigade and 77th InfDiv had been making excellent progress. The Marines were very laudatory of the soldiers, calling them the 77th MarDiv. Probably, if the soldiers ever heard it said, that intended compliment went over like a lead balloon. But our story is the 3d MarDiv, so we digress.

The 3d MarDiv soon found that the majority of remaining enemy forces were retreating up the island. The division pushed toward the enemy and between 31 July and 2 August, 1/3 and 1/9 captured Tiyan Airfield. The honor of liberating the ruins of capital city Agaña fell to 3/3, which they accomplished on 31 July. Meanwhile, the 77th InfDiv came up on the 3d MarDiv's right flank and both divisions then pushed ahead. The 1st Provisional Brigade remained in the south and was responsible for the cleanup of all enemy formations

Marine flamethrower burns an enemy dugout.

in that part of the island. On 3–4 August the 77th captured Mount Barrigada while the 3d was taking Finegayan.

On the 3d of August, in the battle for Finegayan, PFC Frank P. Witek, from Derby, CT, a BAR man with 1/9, stood up and fired at point-blank range into well-hidden Japanese positions, killing at least eight of the enemy. His act allowed the balance of his platoon to take cover. While the platoon was so engaged, Witek remained behind and safeguarded a wounded comrade. After the man was evacuated he then covered the stretcher bearers' withdrawal. After returning to his unit, he again moved forward to support tanks by throwing grenades and firing his BAR as he moved forward to within 10 yards of the enemy. His destruction of another enemy machine gun and eight more Japanese was concluded when he was struck down by Japanese rifle fire. He was posthumously awarded a Medal of Honor for gallantry and giving up his life for his comrades and his country.

Marines and Army continued to press forward. On 8 August, the 22d Marines had reached Ritidian Point, and two days later the Americans had taken almost every inch of Guam. The final day, 10 August, was spent combing the beaches and heavily wooded area on the north shore. The final tally of dead men was estimated at 5,200 Japanese and just over 600 Marines killed in action. Briefly, from the time Turnage returned to the States in September, BG Noble assumed command of the division. He in turn was relieved one month later by MG Graves B. Erskine when Noble was also returned to the U.S. Col John B. Wilson was his ADC and Col Robert E. Hogaboom came with Erskine as the new Chief of Staff and all "G" positions were changed.

From 1 October to the twenty-third, the division was engaged in "cleaning up" the island. Contacts were widely scattered and on 24 October the last major effort began. It lasted until the 3d of November, when it was considered completed, and from now on only small patrols would venture into the brush. This, then, began the "peaceful" occupation of Guam. From now on the 3d MarDiv would prepare for its next engagement, another tough one.

Order of Battle
Guam
(21 July to 10 August 1944)

Headquarters

MG Allen H. Turnage	CG
BG Alfred H. Noble	ADC
Col Ray A. Robinson	CoS
LtCol Chevey S. White	D-1 (KiA 22 Jul)
Maj Irving H. Kriendler	D-1
LtCol Howard J. Turton	D-2 (To 28 Jul)
LtCol Ellsworth N. Murray	D-2
Col James A. Stuart	D-3 (To 28 Jul)
LtCol Howard J. Turton	D-3
LtCol Ellsworth N. Murray	D-4 (To 28 Jul)
Col W. Carvel Hall	D-4

Headquarters Bn

LtCol Newton B. Barkley	CO
Maj William L. Clauset, Jr.	ExO
1stLt George F. De Falco	CO Hdqs Co
1stLt Arthur Salgo	CO Recon Co
Maj Richard Tonis	CO MP Co
Maj William N. Loftin	CO Sig Co
Maj John H. Ellis	CO JAS CO (WIA 21 Jul)

Third Marines

Col W. Carvel Hall	CO (To 28 Jul)
Col James A. Stuart	CO
Col James Snedeker	ExO
Maj John F. MacDonald	R-1
Capt John W. Foley, Sr.	R-2
Maj John A. Scott	R-3 (WIA 6 Aug)
Maj Grant Crane	R-4
Capt Victor J. Bachman	CO H & S Co (WIA 22 Jul)
Capt Francis M. Blodget, Jr.	CO H & S Co
Maj Laurence D. Gammon	CO Wpns Co

1/3

Maj Henry Aplington, II	CO
Maj John A. Ptak	ExO (KIA 1 Aug)
Capt John B. Erickson	B-3
1stLt George R. Nash	CO Hdq Co (To 9 Aug)
2dLt Charles R. Weissberger	CO Hdq Co
Capt Geary B. Bundschu	CO A Co (KIA 21 Jul)
Capt Robert L. Patterson	CO A Co
Capt Joseph V. Millerick	CO B Co
Capt David I. Zeitlin	CO C Co (WIA 25 Jul)

2/3

LtCol Hector de Zayas	CO (KIA 26 Jul)
Maj William A. Culpepper	CO
Maj William A. Culpepper	ExO
Maj Howard J. Smith	ExO
Maj Howard J. Smith	B-3
1stLt Matthew J. Cole, Jr.	CO Hdq Co
Capt William F. Moore, Jr.	CO E Co (WIA 25 Jul)
1stLt French B. Fogle	CO E Co
Capt Paul H. Groth	CO F Co
Capt Stetson S. Holmes	CO G Co (WIA 21 Jul)
1stLt Alex H. Sawyer	CO G Co

3/3

LtCol Ralph L. Houser	CO (WIA 22 Jul)
Maj Royal H. Bastian	CO
Maj Royal R. Bastian	ExO (To 22 Jul)
Capt William B. Bradley	ExO
Capt Paul T. Torian	B-3
Capt William H. Bradley	CO Hdqs Co
Capt Lowell H. Smith	CO I Co
Capt Anthony A. Akstin	CO K Co (WIA 23 Jul)
Capt Paul C. Trammell	CO K Co (WIA 26 Jul)
Capt William G. H. Stephens, Jr.	CO L Co

Ninth Marines

Col Edward A. Craig	CO
LtCol Jaime Sabater	ExO (WIA 21 Jul)
LtCol Ralph M. King	ExO
Capt Charles C. Henderson	R-1 (WIA 21 Jul)
1stLt Charles H. Schofield	R-1
Capt Douglas Whipple	R-2
Capt Evan E. Lips	R-3
LtCol Frank Shine	R-4
Capt James M. Farrington	CO H & S Co
Maj Jess P. Ferrill, Jr.	CO Wpns Co (To 1 Aug)
Capt Robert A. Campbell	CO Wpns Co

1/9

LtCol Carey A. Randall	CO
Maj Harold C. Boehm	ExO
Capt Francis H. Bergholdt	B-3
WO Douglas W. Diggers	CO Hdqs Co

Capt Conrad M. Fowler	CO A Co
Capt Burtis W. Anderson	CO B Co (To 8 Aug)
Capt John B. Glapp	CO B Co
Capt Frank C. Finneran	CO C Co

2/9

LtCol Robert E. Cushman, Jr.	CO
Maj William T. Glass	ExO
Capt Laurance W. Chacroft	B-3
Capt Francis L. Fagan	CO Hdqs Co (To 27 Jul)
Capt Luther S. Kjos	CO Hdqs Co
Capt Lyle Q. Peterson	CO E Co (DOW 25 Jul)
Capt Maynard W. Smith	CO E Co
Capt Louis H. Wilson, Jr.	CO F Co (WIA 25 Jul)
Maj Fraser E. West	CO G Co (WIA 26 Jul)
Capt Francis L. Fagan	CO G Co

3/9

LtCol Walter Asmuth, Jr.	CO (WIA 21 Jul)
Maj Donald B. Hubbard	CO (WIA 1Aug)
Maj Jess P. Ferrill, Jr.	CO
Maj Donald B. Hubbard	ExO (To 22 Jul)
Capt Calvin W. Kunz, Jr.	ExO
Capt Calvin W. Kunz, Jr.	B-3
lstLt George G. Robinson	CO Hdqs Co
Capt Harry B. Parker	CO I Co (KIA 21 Jul)
lstLt Raymond A. Overpeck	CO I Co
Capt William G. Smith	CO K Co (KIA 21 Jul)
lstLt David H. Lewis	CO K Co
Capt Walter K. Crawford	CO L Co

Twenty-first Marines

Col Arthur H. Butler	CO
LtCol Ernest W. Fry, Jr.	ExO
Capt Walter B. White	R-1
Capt Blair A. Hyde	R-2
Maj James H. Tinsley	R-3
Capt Norman S. Chase	R-4
Capt Albert L. Jensen	CO Hdqs Co
Maj Robert H. Houser	CO Wpns Co

1/21

LtCol Marlowe C. Williams	CO
LtCol Ronald R. Van Stockum	ExO
Capt Leslie A. Gilson, Jr.	B-3 (WIA 22 Jul)
Capt Edward H. Voorhees	B-3
Capt Edward H. Voorhees	CO Hdqs Co (To 22 Jul)
Capt William G. Shoemaker	CO A Co (KIA 3 Aug)
Capt Fred F. Harbin	CO A Co
Capt Donald M. Beck	CO B Co (WIA 21 Jul)
Capt Henry M. Helgren, Jr.	CO C Co

2/21

LtCol Eustace R. Smoak	CO
Maj Lowell E. English	ExO
Capt Andrew Hedesh	B-3
Capt James A. Michener	CO Hdqs Co
Capt Sidney J. Altman	CO E Co (WIA 22Jul)
lstLt William R. Williams	CO E Co
Capt Gerald G. Kirby	CO F Co
Capt William H. McDonough	CO G Co (DOW 21 Jul)
lstLt Maurice G. Austin	CO G Co (WIA 5 Aug)
lstLt Howard L. Cousins, Jr.	CO G Co

3/21

LtCol Wendell H. Duplantis	CO
Maj Edward A. Clark	ExO
lstLt James C. Corman	B-3 (To 21 Jul)
Maj Paul M. Jones	B-3
Capt Clayton S. Rockmore	CO Hdqs Co (WIA 26 Jul)
2dLt Coleman C. Jones	CO Hdqs Co (From 4 Aug)
Capt Rodney I. Heinze	CO I Co (WIA 3 Aug)
Capt Clarence W. McCord	CO K Co
Capt Frederick I. Ptucha	CO L Co

Twelfth Marines

Col John B. Wilson	CO
LtCol John S. Letcher	ExO
Capt Edwin M. Gorman	R-1
Maj Oliver E. Robinett	R-2
LtCol William T. Fairbourn	R-3
Maj Lytle G. Williams	R-4 (Rear Echelon)
lstLt Robert Stutz	CO H & S Btry

1/12

LtCol Raymond F. Crist, Jr.	CO (WIA 22 Jul)
Maj George B. Thomas	ExO
Capt Luther A. Bookout, Jr.	B-3
Capt Carl H. Senge	CO H & S Btry
Capt Joshua C. West, III	CO A Btry
Capt James L. Cullen	CO B Btry
Capt Clarence E. Brissenden	CO C Btry

2/12

LtCol Donald M. Weller	CO
Maj Henry E. W. Barnes	ExO
Maj William P. Pala	B-3
Capt Norman V. McElroy	CO H & S Btry
Capt Robert H. Ó Meara	CO D Btry
Capt James Leffers	CO E Btry
Capt David S. Randall	CO F Btry

3/12

LtCol Alpha L. Bowser, Jr.	CO
Maj Claude S. Sanders, Jr.	ExO
Capt Wilbur R. Helmer	B-3
lstLt William G. Reid	CO H & S Btry

Capt Joe B. Wallen	CO G Btry
Capt James H. P. Garnett	CO H Btry
Capt Robert H. Rain, Jr.	CO I Btry (WIA 23 Jul)
1stLt Reuben W. Estopinal	CO I Btry

4/12

LtCol Bernard H. Kirk	CO (WIA 21Jul)
Maj Thomas B. Belzer	ExO
Capt Lewis H. Poggemeyer	B-3
2dLt John T. Nute	CO H & S Btry
Maj Benjamin O. Cantey, Jr.	CO K Btry (WIA 21 Jul)
Capt Charles O. Schrodt	CO K Btry
Capt Robert S. Wilson	CO L Btry (WIA 21Jul)
Capt Lonnle D. McCurry	CO M Btry (WIA 21Jul)

Nineteenth Marines

LtCol Robert H. Fojt	CO
LtCol Edmund M. Williams	ExO
WO John J. Beaumont	R-1 (WIA 22 Jul)
Capt Clarence B. Allen, Jr.	R-2 (WIA 31Jul)
Maj George D. Flood, Jr.	R-3
Capt Julius S. Conrad	R-4
Maj Ward K. Schaub	CO H & S Co

1/19

LtCol Walter S. Campbell	CO
Maj Virgil M. Davis	ExO
Capt Arthur J. Waldrep, Jr.	B-3
Capt Jack B. Wehner	CO Hdqs Co (To 26 Jul)
1stLt Felix D. Kuzwicki	CO Hdqs Co
Capt Charles H. Horn	CO A Co
Capt Robert K. Higgins	CO B Co
Capt Charles M. Hunter, Jr.	CO C Co (To 8 Aug)
1stLt John P. McFadden, Jr.	CO C Co

2/19

Maj Victor J. Simpson	CO
Maj Howard A. Hurst	ExO
Capt Jack R. Edwards	B-3
1stLt Waldemar Meckes	CO Hdqs Co
Capt Claude D. Hamill, Jr.	CO D Co
Capt Charles F. Ingram	CO E Co
Capt Charles Z. Yonce	CO F Co

3d Medical Bn

Cmdr Raymond R. Callaway	CO
LCmdr Delbert H. McNamara	ExO (WIA 26 Jul)
Cmdr Abraham Kaplan	ExO (From 3 Aug)

LCmdr Delhert H. McNamara	S-3
Cmdr Abraham Kaplan	S-3 (From 3 Aug)
LCmdr Delbert H. McNamara	CO H & S Co
Cmdr Abraham Kaplan	CO H & S Co (From 3 Aug)
LCmdr George L. Butler	CO A Co (KIA 21 Jul)
Lt William B. Harkins	CO A Co
LCmdr Julius Simon	CO B Co (WIA 21 Jul)
Lt Edmond A. Utkewicz	CO B Co (From 1 Aug)
LCmdr Daniel B. Landau	CO C Co
LCmdr Clarence C. Piepergerdes	CO D Co
LCmdr Stanley B. Haraburda	CO E Co

3d MT Bn

LtCol Thomas R. Stokes	CO
Maj Ira E. Harrod, Jr.	ExO
1stLt Marshall W. Henry	B-3
Capt Herbert C. Bumgardner	CO H & S Co
Capt Garl A. Wilson	CO A Co
1stLt Donald A. Lloyd	CO B Co
Capt Walter R. Ó Quinn	CO C Co

3d Service Bn

LtCol Durant S. Buchanan	CO
Maj Paul O. Chandler	ExO
Capt Warren E. Smith	B-3
Capt Warren E. Smith	CO Hdq Co
1stLt Joseph M. Broderick	CO Ord Co
Maj William M. Roosevelt	CO S & S Co

3d Tank Bn

LtCol Hartnoll J. Withers	CO
Maj Holly H. Evans	ExO
Capt Victor E. Wade	B-3 (To 22 Jul)
Capt David M. Graham	B-3
Capt David M. Graham	CO H & S Co
Capt William D. Stone	CO A Co (WIA 21 Jul)
Capt Bertram A. Yaffe	CO B Co (WIA 26 Jul)
Capt Julius O. Lemke	CO C Co

25th Naval Const Bn

LCmdr George J. Whelan	CO
LCmdr Brett W. Walker	ExO
Lt John L. Walker, Jr.	CO Hdqs Co
Lt Philip P. Nelson	CO G Co
Lt John V. Frankenthal	CO H Co
Lt Joseph H. Gehring	CO I Co

Iwo Jima

In February 1945 a major landing was made by the V Amphibious Corps (MG Harry Schmidt) on a small island lying a mere 750 miles south of Tokyo. Iwo Jima was selected for a landing in order to provide nearby landing fields for the newly created B-29's, designated to flatten and burn Japan. VAC was created to include three Marine Divisions, the 4th, the brand-new 5th and the 3d MarDiv. However, the latter was to provide, mainly, reserve components with the 4th and 5th MarDivs to land initially.

When the division was aboard ships, the 21st Marines were ordered to move out ahead and provide the 4th and 5th MarDivs with an immediate reserve. The rest of the 3d MarDiv would be a floating reserve. On D-Day morning, 19 February 1945, the initial landing was made by the 4th and 5th while the 3d remained in waiting. It had not been determined if the two divisions would require a third. If not, the 3d MarDiv could return to Guam and more rest and rotation for the old-timers. Col Hartnoll J. Withers and his 21st Marines waited all day. When they learned that evening of the enormous beach casualties suffered on D-Day most members realized they wouldn't be on ships very long.

On 20 February, morning orders were issued for the 21st to prepare to land. In their LCVP's they rode around until late afternoon when, in the rain and rough water, their journey was terminated. Back aboard, on the next afternoon at 1345 they landed in a drizzling rain with orders to dig in. They were now attached to the 4th MarDiv. On the morrow, at 0400 on 22 February, D-Day plus 3, the regiment advanced into the "jaws of hell," later proclaimed as the toughest fight the 3d MarDiv had ever been in. Their orders were to relieve the battered 23d Marines located in the center of the line and at 0815 push northward. In so doing they brought down upon themselves a storm of fire. The men were stunned by the firestorm of artillery and mortar shells as well as the machine gun and rifle fire absorbed.

On the left, LtCol Lowell E. English with 2/21 and LtCol Marlow C. Williams with 1/21 on his right, endeavored to advance, but it was considered impossible; no, rather, it was hopeless. The 21st was nearly surrounded and could see nothing but sand dunes in all directions. Companies suffered losses of their seasoned skippers: F's was killed, G's had his leg blown off, F's was badly wounded and Col Williams was hit. His replacement, Maj Clay M. Murray, was also wounded that same day. His replacement, Maj Robert H. Houser, formerly CO of Weapons Co, and a Navy Cross on Guam, somehow managed to survive.

Meanwhile, the 9th Marines (Col Howard N. Kenyon, Navy Cross) anxiously awaited their opportunity to land, not yet fully realizing quite how bad things were ashore. The 3d Marines were still retained in Expeditionary Troops reserve and Col James A. Stuart and his men were sorely disappointed. They would not land on Iwo Jima; perhaps their previous battering on Bougainville and Guam had been taken into consideration.

Maj George A. Percy, temporarily CO of 2/21, had become involved in a ferocious firefight early on the 23d of February and was unable to advance until 0935. Percy was another Marine who would earn a Navy Cross on Iwo Jima. Houser and 1/21 did advance at 0730. Percy and his men required a second artillery preparation and both battalions had companies that managed to get to the southwest approaches of Airfield No. 2. But heavy enemy fire eventually forced the Marines to fall back and lines were consolidated for the night at the southern edge of the field.

One of the great moments on the 23d was when Cpl Herschel W. Williams, born in Quiet Dell, WV, but now acting as a demolition sergeant with 1/21, went forward to clear obstructions. Those were mainly pillboxes with devastating machine gun fire, causing numerous casualties to Marines. He made it before and behind some of them, and burned the defenders with his flamethrower using their air vents or openings. Time after time, back he went to refresh his flamethrowing weapon's capacity, then forward to destroy more of

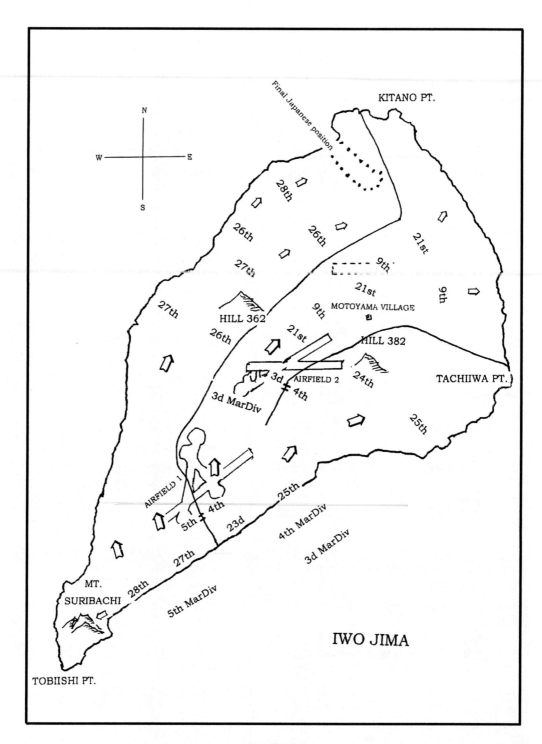

Iwo Jima

the enemy. When the enemy grimly charged him with bayonets he gave them a full blast of flame. He, by dint of extraordinary heroism, cleared out or neutralized the most troublesome of the enemy positions lying before his battalion. Rightfully, he was later awarded a Medal of Honor.

Houser's 1st Battalion was relieved by 3/21 (LtCol Wendell H. Duplantis) on the morning of 24 February and under orders almost immediately, at 0915, advanced. Because of the excellent work of 1/21, the advance was made somewhat easier for 3/21 and they took approximately another 600 yards that day. However, 2/21 was unable to keep pace when they ran into severe mortar and artillery fire. Soon after noon they went forward once again but the severity of 2/21's losses caused their holdup for the balance of that day.

Regardless of the unfortunate situation delaying 2/21, that afternoon 3/21 again went forward even without the support of tanks, which did not arrive on time. It managed to get two companies, I and K, across the center of the airfield. Company K's skipper, Capt Rodney L. Heinze, was wounded, and four minutes later Capt Clayton S. Rockmore of Company I was killed. K's exec, Capt Daniel A. Marshall, assumed command of K and 1stLt Raoul Archambault brought in Company I, and the attack continued. K took most of Hill 199 and the northern edge of the airstrip. "Friendly" artillery fire, however, inadvertently dropped in on them and drove them from their conquest. When the shelling ceased, back up the hill they went. This time the enemy drove them from their conquest. Because their flanking units did not keep abreast, K and I both were taking enfilade fire.

At 1350 Company I went forward once again and, led by Archambault, the Marines went at the Japanese with everything they had. Hand-to-hand combat was ferocious in that severe, hacking and screaming melee that was over in a few short minutes. Fifty enemy soldiers were counted dead. By 1820 the battalion, with severe losses, now held the ground and were ordered to "hold at all costs." Archambault was accordingly awarded a Navy Cross. Col Withers requested relief for his battered regiment and the following day, 25 February, the 9th Marines were called up. Upon relief, the 21st went into reserve.

Division headquarters had landed, and now the 3d MarDiv assumed control of the center of the line. The two other Marine divisions, the 4th on the right and the 5th on the left, compressed, which was just as well since both had already suffered severe losses. That morning of 25 February found the 9th with orders to advance at 0730. On the right was 1/9 (LtCol Carey Randall) and 2/9 (LtCol Robert E. Cushman) to the left. First came artillery preparation, then the regiment began its advance. Cushman's men met the most resistance and were taken in front and left flank by strong enemy fire, making little progress.

Tanks of the 3d Tank Battalion (Maj Holly H. Evans, Silver Star) had been called in to support 1/9 and drew heavy mortar fire and massive artillery shelling, resulting in many casualties to 1/9. Nine tanks were knocked out before they managed to destroy enemy installations, including three heavy guns. Motoyama Airfield No. 2 lay directly in the path of the 9th Marines. It was heavily defended, its flat terrain providing marvelous fields of fire for machine guns, anti-tank guns, and other enemy flat-trajectory weapons. It became obvious to those in charge. This high ground lying before the Marines went across the entire island and gave the enemy undisputed observation of all ground the Marines then occupied. It was necessary, actually obligatory, that the Marines take their front, and soon. Otherwise their losses would become unmanageable. It was decided that all available artillery must be focused upon those positions to provide the cover necessary.

Only three of the 12th Marines' (LtCol Raymond F. Crist) batteries were ashore on 25 February. However, artillery from the 4th and 5th MarDiv's and naval gunfire ably supported the 3d MarDiv. At 1400 the 9th Marines were in a comparative stalemate. A large gap had developed in their center and it was decided that Cushman's badly hurt 2/9 was unable to keep up the pace. LtCol Harold C. Boehm and 3/9 was called up to replace them and immediately push ahead and effect a junction with the 26th Marines (5th MarDiv) on the left.

The 21st Marines making their way toward the Iwo Jima beach on 21 February 1945.

Boehm's battalion got plastered, hit hard on the front and left flank. Casualties rapidly mounted as the companies moved swiftly to take the high ground to their front. By 1700 the assault companies had lost both skippers and a high percentage of officers and non-coms. The battalion was quickly becoming disorganized, lines were wavering and ground taken was being lost. Company K on the right had lost five officers and most NCOs. Captain Joseph T. McFadden, S-3, was ordered to take command of K and reorganize it. Lieutenant Raymond A. Overpeck, senior officer remaining of Company I, was issued similar orders. That was enough for 3/9 and preparations were taken care of for the anticipated counter thrusts that night.

The next morning, 26 February, 1/9 and 2/9, after an artillery preparation, jumped off but the sheet of fire they ran into stopped them from making but modest gains. Boehm's 3/9 was in no shape to continue and was ordered to be pulled back. They went into regimental reserve and occupied a defensive position. Boehm would also earn a Navy Cross for his courage and skills on Iwo Jima. The assault battalions were unable to make any headway, even though several Marine bombers made four close support sorties before their positions. That night a BAR man, Arkansas native Private Wilson D. Watson of 2/9, having been halted with his squad before some heavily defended caves and pillboxes, boldly rushed one of them. Watson fired his weapon into the aperture and threw in a grenade, then ran to the rear of the box waiting for the exiting enemy. He slaughtered as many as possible, enabling his platoon to take its objective. Later, pinned down before a low hill, he and his assistant climbed the rugged incline and then raced about shooting from the hip. Standing fearlessly erect and all the while firing, Watson managed to hold the hill for fifteen minutes. He killed at least 60 Japanese before running dry of ammo, but retained his position until his comrades came up to join him. He survived and was awarded a Medal of Honor.

Kenyon's Ninth Marines had their work cut out for them during the previous few days. While the 12th poured in the artillery, the regiment continued making an effort to break through the well dug-in enemy. Cushman's 2/9 was on the left and Randall's 1/9 on the right. The former reached the north end of the airfield and stopped long enough to catch their collective breath while reorganizing. Boehm's 3/9 pushed through them and advanced a modest distance before they were stopped by massive mortar and artillery fire.

So far, in comparison, the regiment had a relatively easy time of it. From here on the going got really tough. Lying before them was an edifice of at least 100 feet of rough tumbled boulders to climb. Nothing affected the Japanese atop that hill: not artillery, nor gun fire from the ships, not even planes. Once again, it was a job for the infantry. Dig 'em out.

This time 3/9 shone brightly. Up that rugged mass they climbed, and while fiercely engaged in hand-to-hand combat, Col Walter S. Campbell's 3d Engineer Battalion helped the infantry with flamethrowers. The next morning the 21st Marines were back and during the day pushed 500 yards forward through what was left of the pillboxes covering the approaches to incomplete Motoyama Airfield No. 3.

The fighting was slow during the following week and the Marines were able to make but modest gains daily. LtCol Lowell E. English, CO, 2/21, was wounded on 2 March and his Exec, Maj George A. Percy, again assumed command. The greatest artillery preparation was on 6 March, when the guns poured in 45,000 rounds upon the Japanese in a few hundred square yards area. Yet the Marines could barely make another hundred yards' advance that day. It was, and would continue to be, rugged going for all three divisions on Iwo. In many ways it was more like the desperate attempts on the Western Front in World War I than a battle in the more mobile World War II. Advances were reckoned in yards.

The following day, at 0500 on 7 March, the 9th and 21st jumped the Japanese. Surprising the enemy, they gained a valuable several hundred yards of strong positions that had been holding up the regiment. Company B of the 9th suffered numerous casualties, taking one rocky position, but nearly being wiped out in the process. One company officer, 2dLt John H. Leims, a Chicago lad, while launching a surprise attack upon the rock-imbedded fortification of a dominating enemy position, spurred his men forward. With determination he skillfully directed his assault platoons forward against fortified positions and succeeded in capturing the objective in late afternoon. He and his men were cut off from their comrades so he personally advanced across the fire-swept terrain and laid telephone lines to contact his CP. Ordered to withdraw from this exposed position he managed adroitly to effect the withdrawal of his men. Upon arrival he learned that several wounded men had been left behind at another exposed position, whereupon, though worn out physically, he went forward and managed to carry one Marine out, then a second, all the while subjected to intense enemy fire. For his courage, tenacity and leadership during the period, he was awarded a Medal of Honor.

Company F was also isolated from the rest of the 9th Marines for a day and a half, and when relieved by tanks, only 22 Marines remained. The enemy nearly wiped out headquarters of the 9th Marines with land mines and aerial bombs that night. The 9th Marines were paying a heavy price for very poor real estate.

On 6 March, Company G of the 21st was the first Marine unit to spot the far northern end of the island. However, it wasn't until the following day that Percy and 2/21 were on the rocks overlooking the northern coast. The following day Company A sent a 28-man platoon down the cliff to the seashore, cutting the enemy positions in half. They deserved being first. The platoon sent a can of sea water back to Gen Erskine with a message: "Forward for approval, not for consumption." As an example of the losses, Company A, 1/21, had on that final day only three Marines left of the original landing force. The rest of the men came from two replacement drafts.

But the campaign was not as yet over. The entire island was loaded with live Japanese still within caves and it was now time to mop them up. With all the firing the island was nearly as dangerous to life and limb as before being "secured." As soon as the 3rd MarDiv's area was cleared they then helped the 4th and 5th MarDiv's with their areas. The final fighting occurred around Kitano point and it wasn't until 16 March that the entire island was considered secured.

This was the final call for the 3d MarDiv. They would be on Guam when the war ended in August 1945.

Order of Battle
Iwo Jima
(19 February to 17 March 1945)

Headquarters

MG Graves B. Erskine	CG
Col John B. Wilson	ADC
Col Robert E. Hogaboom	CoS
Maj Irving R. Kriendler	D-1
LtCol Howard J. Turton	D-2
Col Arthur H. Butler	D-3
LtCol James D. Hittle	D-4
LtCol Jack F. Warner	CO Hdqs Bn (To 14 Mar)
LtCol Carey A. Randall	CO Hdqs Bn

Ninth Marines

Col Howard N. Kenyon	CO
LtCol Paul W. Russell	ExO
Maj Calvin W. Kunz	R-3

1/9

LtCol Carey A. Randall	CO (To 6 Mar)
Maj William T. Glass	CO (To 14 Mar)
LtCol Jack F. Warner	CO
Capt Frank K. Finneran	ExO
Capt James R. Harper	B-3 (To 27 Feb)
Capt Robert R. Fairburn	B-3

2/9

LtCol Robert E. Cushman, Jr.	CO
Maj William T. Glass	ExO (To 6 Mar; from 15 Mar)
Capt Laurance W. Cracroft	B-3

3/9

LtCol Harold C. Boehm	CO
Maj Donald B. Hubbard	ExO
Capt Joseph T. McFadden	B-3

Twenty-first Marines

Col Hartnoll J. Withers	CO
LtCol Eustace R. Smoak	ExO
Capt Andrew Hedesh	B-3

1/21

LtCol Marlowe C. Williams	CO (WIA 22 Feb)
Maj Clay M. Murray	CO (WIA 22 Feb)
Maj Robert H. Houser	CO
Maj Clay M. Murray	ExO (To 22 Feb)
Maj George D. Flood, Jr.	ExO
Maj George D. Flood, Jr.	B-3

2/21

LtCol Lowell E. English	CO (WIA 2 Mar)
Maj George A. Percy	CO
Maj George A. Percy	ExO (To 2 Mar)
Maj Michael V. DiVita	ExO
Capt Thomas E. Norpell	B-3

3/21

LtCol Wendell H. Duplantis	CO
Maj Paul M. Jones	ExO
1stLt James C. Corman	B-3

Twelfth Marines

LtCol Raymond F. Crist, Jr.	CO
LtCol Bernard H. Kirk	ExO
LtCol Thomas R. Belzer	B-3

1/12

Maj George B. Thomas	CO
Maj William P. Pala	ExO
Maj Clarence E. Brissenden	B-3

2/12

LtCol William T. Fairbourn	CO

Maj Oliver E. Robinett	ExO
Capt Joseph F. Fogg	B-3

3/12

LtCol Alpha L. Bowser, Jr.	CO
Maj Claude S. Sanders, Jr.	ExO
Maj Wilbur R. Helmer	B-3

4/12

Maj Joe B. Wallen	CO (To 20 Mar)
LtCol Thomas R. Belzer	CO
Maj David S. Randall	ExO (To 20 Mar)
Capt Lewis F. Poggemeyer	B-3

3d Tank Bn

Maj Holly H. Evans	CO
Capt Gerald F. Foster	ExO
Capt Bertram A. Yaffe	B-3

3d Eng Bn

LtCol Walter S. Campbell	CO
Maj Eldon J. C. Rogers	ExO
Capt Arthur J. Wardrep, Jr.	B-3

3d Pioneer Bn

LtCol Edmund M. Williams	CO
Maj Howard A. Hurst	ExO
Capt Jack R. Edwards	B-3

Service Troops, 3d Division[2]

Col James O. Brauer	CO (To 6 Mar)
Col Lewis A. Hohn	CO
Maj Reginald G. Sauls, III	ExO

3d Service Bn

LtCol Paul G. Chandler	CO
Maj William E. Cullen	ExO
Capt Warren E. Smith	B-3

3d MT Bn

LtCol Ernest W. Fry, Jr.	CO
Maj Ira E. Harrod, Jr.	ExO
Maj Ira E. Harrod, Jr.	B-3

3d Medical Bn

Cmdr Anthony E. Reymont	CO
Cmdr Owen Deuby	ExO

GUAM

The 3d MarDiv division replaced its losses in manpower and reorganized, and went back to what all Marines expect: re-training. The few surviving old-timers, those with twenty-seven months or three campaigns, were sent home. Some replacements arrived but the division lost many to the wear and tear at Okinawa, which got first claim. Meanwhile, the 3d Marines were utilized to patrol Guam and in so doing found and killed a few Japanese stragglers. It wasn't until the peace was signed that another five hundred came forward, but even then many more remained in the boonies.

The Division had been scheduled for the landings on the island of Kyushu in Japan. But with modest replacements to fill the many holes, Headquarters decided not to continue the 3d Marine Division in peacetime. When Gen Erskine left Guam for the States in October 1945, his ADC was his replacement. BG William E. Riley was the last CG of the division and he "closed the books" on the 3d MarDiv on 28 December 1945.

---

[2]This command was superimposed upon and coordinated the activities of the Service, MT, and Medical Bns.

4th Marine Division

In July 1942, the 23d Marines was activated under the command of LtCol William B. Onley. The regiment was in fact the earliest unit to eventually become a part of the Fourth Marine Division (4th MarDiv). It was first assigned to the 3d MarDiv, its original parent unit. In September 1942, Col Louis R. Jones replaced Onley in command. In January 1943 the 23d Marines had the unpleasant experience of amphibious training in the cold Chesapeake Bay, hardly an improvement over infantry training at New River, NC. The regiment was detached from the 3d MarDiv on 15 February 1943 and five days later became part of the infant 4th MarDiv.

The other regiments, like the 23d, all had origins in the Marine Reserve program: 24th Marines (Col Franklin A. Hart), 25th Marines (Col Samuel Cumming), 14th Marines (Col Louis G. DeHaven), plus assorted service troops, filled out the division on 16 August 1943. Many reservists mingled with veteran Marines to create the wartime units which were to perform so admirably.

The following month training at Camp Pendleton began in earnest. That November, the 14th Marines moved to Camp Dunlap, in Niland, CA, for extensive artillery firing of their 75mm pack howitzers and few 105mm howitzers. Soon afterward, the division, now composed of nearly 18,000 Marines, began practice landings on Aliso Beach near San Diego. Then they went aboard transports for storming beaches at San Clemente Island with Task Force 53 giving fire support. Their training was basically much the same as all their predecessors.

Then came the cold weather experiences at Las Pulgas Canyon, where the troops were exposed to subarctic temperatures while living in tents. Finally came the time to board combat-loaded ships for a long journey. On the evening of 6–7 January, ships with the 14th Marines and their guns, and amphibious tractor units aboard, sailed out of San Diego harbor in their LSDs and LSTs. Six days later, on the morning of the 13th, the balance of the 4th MarDiv sailed away into the unknown. The senior brass knew they were on their way to assault a Japanese stronghold but not exactly where. Operation Flintlock was underway. This would be the first Marine division to load up in the U.S. and sail directly to land upon enemy-held territory, on islands among those mandated to Japan post–World War I. In other words, when successful, they would be the first to capture an enemy province.

Before World War I, the Marshall Islands had been held by Germany. The "islands" were really small rocks jutting out of the ocean. They were usually classified as atolls with just the westernmost being of interest to the U.S. high command. The distances between them were considerable. It was about 250 miles between Majuro on the east to Kwajalein located nearly in the center of the group. There were eight primary atolls with but two of interest. The two were, from east to west, Kwajalein and farthest west, Eniwetok. All ground operations were to be under the control of V Amphibious Corps (MG Holland McT. Smith).

Kwajalein was to be the first attacked. The entire atoll consisted of about 85 islands and extended 65 miles in length and was 18 miles across at its widest. The island named Kwajalein lies at the far eastern southern tip. That landing was to be effected by the venerable 7th InfDiv, a veteran of the Attu campaign and well versed in amphibious landings as taught by the Marine Corps.

Forty miles almost directly north lies the dual islands of Roi–Namur. That was the 4th MarDiv's target. The division was part of the Northern Landing Force (MG Harry Schmidt). This is the one we will concentrate upon. Roi on the left was 1200 by 1250 yards at its widest, Namur on the right was 800 by 900 yards. Roi had an airfield, one of the finest in that part of the Pacific. Namur was primarily covered with pillboxes and other man-made defensive structures. A decision had been made to land the 23d Marines on Roi and the 24th Marines on Namur. Both islands were well defended and the first operation of the 4th MarDiv would be quite costly in manpower.

ROI-NAMUR

Two days before D-day, the *Tennessee, Maryland,* and *Colorado,* along with 5 cruisers and 19 destroyers, shelled both islands, nonstop for twenty-four hours. They were aided by aircraft flying from the Fast Carrier Task Force, which planes continued to paste Roi and Namur as the landing boats were launched. It was also planned to take two smaller nearby islands to land most of the pack howitzers for ground operational support. The seizure of Ennuebing fell to the division's Scout Company. Mellu, somewhat larger and further away, was the target of 1/25 (LtCol Clarence J. O'Donnell). Both were secured by noontime on D-day, 1 February 1944. Three other islands, lying on the opposite eastern string of the atoll, were taken when 2/25 (LtCol Lewis C. Hudson, Jr.) and 3/25 (LtCol Justis M. Chambers) landed on Ennugarret, Ennumennet, and Ennubrr. Phase two of the operation, the landing on Roi and Namur, from the lagoon side, was now ready for initiation.

H-hour was 1000, but the actual landing time was delayed until 1100. Naval gunfire and aerial attack once again preceded the landing. The first landings began at 1200 and the 23d Marines found that most of the occupants of Roi had fled to Namur for protection. It seemed, at that time, to be too good to be true. Marines already landed proceeded without major mishap. One Marine of the 23d, from Tacoma, WA, PFC Richard B. Anderson, began to toss a live grenade but it slipped down into the shell hole and his buddies looked aghast. Without hesitation, Anderson flung his body on the grenade and absorbed the blast, saving the lives of his comrades. His selfless act brought forth a posthumous Medal of Honor.

The original Phase-line 1 was reached in barely more than a quarter of an hour. When Col Jones had the good news relayed back to MG Schmidt, he ordered the regiment to halt and reorganize. During the intervening time, two tanks and two supporting companies had moved forward and had to be recalled.

Franklin Hart's 24th Marines going onto Namur did not have life quite as rosy. The strongest defenses were already established on that island and the heavy vegetation provided splendid cover. LtCol Francis H. Brink's 2/24 had landed on Green Beach 2, the right, and managed to move forward at least 200 yards. LtCol Austin B. Brunelli's 3/24 was to their left and had a terrible time. The fire from undamaged pillboxes hit many Marines and effectively slowed down the battalion. It wasn't until 1400 that the main body reached Phase-line 1. At that point they awaited the arrival of tanks to soften the defenses.

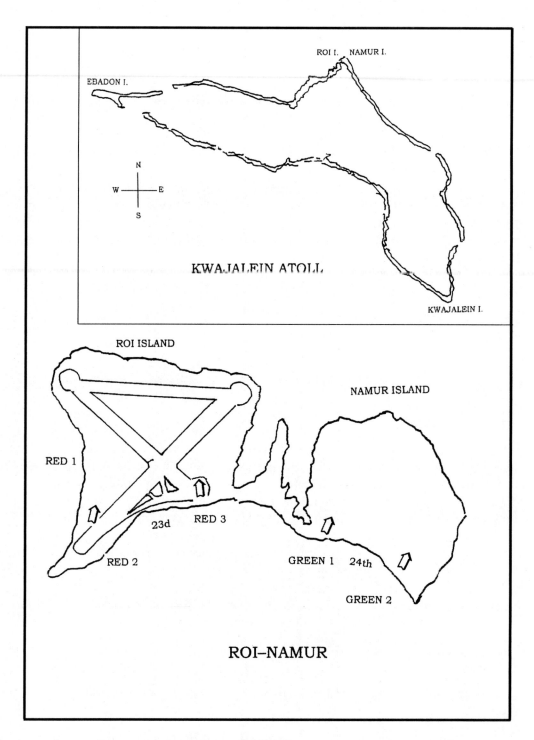

Roi-Namur

On the right 2/24 ran into what has been remembered vividly by many veterans of that campaign, both Navy and Marines. The battalion arrived at a large blockhouse which, unknown to them, housed torpedoes and aerial bombs. Something caused the explosion of this ordnance, which set off an enormous cloud and killed some and concussed other Marines as they fell to the ground. Metal fragments and concrete caught many before they were under cover. One officer described the scene as "an ink blackness spread over the island so that the hand could not be seen in front of the face." Debris continued to fall, steel and concrete, and many Marines without protection fell. Those in nearby boats also suffered from flying debris. During the following half hour two more explosions went off and expanded the list of casualties. That battalion suffered more than half its total island casualties at this one time.

With tanks in support, 3/24 began to push ahead at 1630. 1stLt John V. Power, a reserve officer from Worcester, MA, was badly wounded in the stomach while engaged in knocking out pillboxes. To everyone's amazement, Power held his wound with one hand and charged forward, emptying his carbine into the narrow slot on one door. His effort doomed the occupants because his platoon continued his work and finished off the pillbox, while others pulled him to a shell hole, where he died a few moments later. He was awarded a posthumous Medal of Honor.

A tank commanded by Capt James L. Denig was the victim of five Japanese, one of whom tossed a grenade through an aperture; the explosion set off a gasoline fire. BAR man Cpl Howard E. Smith bravely ran onto the tank, pulled Denig out, then hauled Cpl Bill Taylor and finally Cpl Ben Smith, dragging all to relative safety. Howard Smith unsuccessfully tried to reach an already dead fourth man. He was awarded a Navy Cross for his courage.

Sgt Frank A. Tucker, using "Kentucky windage," pulled a Sgt York on a trench full of Japanese soldiers, about 75 in all. Getting into a position looking directly down the trench he killed 38 of the enemy. His helmet, canteen and binoculars each took a bullet but with no scratches to himself. His reward was a Navy Cross. This island battle was a series of individual fights, with many heroes.

Brink's 2/24 began moving again at 1700 but found the going difficult in taking the well-defended extensive rubble. After moving about 300 yards the battalion called it a night. Whereas 3/24 was within a couple of hundred yards of the northern shore, they had to angle their right flank back to join with 2/24.

The 23d Marines on Roi were moving rapidly ahead but found many Japanese popping up behind them. Though their position was hopeless, no one had told them and they continued to cause heavy Marine casualties with those tactics. However, flamethrowers and demolitions men managed to make it more obvious they were finished. As a result the enemy began blowing themselves up with their own grenades. At 1800, just six hours after landing, the island of Roi was declared secured.

A few Japanese nestled against that northern shore hadn't yet received the word. They planned and executed a *Banzai* attack against 3/24. Companies I and L received the brunt and the Marines' line was compelled to fall back a short distance to a more secure position. Pharmacist's Mate Second Class James V. Kirby of Pontiac, MI, along with numerous wounded Marines he had gathered together, were caught between the lines. That night he and his charges sat out the fighting going all around them and as the Marines came forward again, additional wounded men were dragged into his hole for care. One of those men was a private from Anoka, MN, Richard K. Sorenson, who had sat on a Japanese grenade to protect his fellow Marines. Kirby managed to make his way to Sorenson and was able to stop the bleeding to save Sorenson's life by tying up a severed artery. The former was awarded a Bronze Star and Sorenson was a recipient of a Medal of Honor.

LtCol Aquilla J. Dyess, from Augusta, GA, and his command, 1/24, had landed, still

24th Marines Weapons Company 37mm Anti-Tank gun firing on enemy pillboxes on Namur.

in support, at 1325 on 1 February. On the morning of 2 February they, and the remnants of 2/24, were given the task of cleaning up the enemy remnants on Namur. Placing himself between the enemy and his battalion to point out objectives and avenues of approach, Dyess led a charge against the defending force. Concentrated enemy machine gun fire eventually brought him down as he was standing upon a parapet of an anti-tank gun site. He was posthumously awarded a Medal of Honor.

The Marines continued going forward and so effectively did they sweep northward they were able to declare Namur secured by 1215 of 2 February 1944. In two days a brand-new, untried Marine division had overwhelmed an enemy-occupied, over many years, and well-fortified island. Like many Marines in World War II, they were mainly officially listed as reserves. Yet they would always be in the forefront of Marine assaults in the Pacific War.

The 20th Marines (Engineers), commanded by Col Lucius W. Burnham, arrived and began the massive job of restoring the islands, especially the airfield. LtCol Francis B. Loomis, Jr., and his 15th Defense Battalion, landed and were to take up the task of remaining and clearing up the die-hard Japanese who hadn't already died.

Meanwhile, in the south, the praiseworthy 7th InfDiv had landed on Kawajalein Island, and by 1330 on 4 February that island was also secured. That division then continued to take various smaller islands within the atoll until finalization on 7 February. Next was Eniwetok Atoll, but the 4th MarDiv was not involved in that operation. Within a week the division was off the island and aboard transports.

23d Marines on Roi Island, 2 February 1944, near the shattered hulk of a three-story concrete block-house.

Order of Battle
Kwajalein–Marshall Islands
Roi–Namur
(1 to 2 February 1944)

Headquarters

MG Harry Schmidt	CG
BG James L. Underhill	ADC
Col William W. Rogers	CoS
Col Merton J. Batchelder	D-1
Maj Gooderham L. McCormick	D-2
Col Walter W. Wensinger	D-3
Col William F. Brown	D-4

Twenty-third Marines

Col Louis R. Jones	CO
LtCol John R. Lanigan	ExO
Capt Frank E. Phillips, Jr.	R-1
Capt Richard W. Mirick	R-2
Maj Edward W. Wells	R-3
Capt Henry S. Campbell	R-4

1/23

LtCol Hewin O. Hammond	CO
Maj Hollis U. Mustain	ExO
Capt James R. Miller	B-3

2/23

LtCol Edward J. Dillon	CO
Maj Lawrence V. Patterson	ExO
Capt James W. Sperry	B-3

3/23

LtCol John J. Cosgrove, Jr.	CO
LtCol Ralph Haag	ExO
Maj Robert J. J. Picardi	B-3

Regimental Weapons Company

Capt George W. E. Daughtry	CO
Capt Raymond C. Kraus	ExO

Twenty-fourth Marines

Col Franklin A. Hart	CO
LtCol Homer L. Litzenberg, Jr.	ExO
Capt Kenneth N. Hilton	R-1
Capt Arthur B. Hanson	R-2

LtCol Charles D. Roberts	R-3
Maj Clyde T. Smith	R-4

1/24

LtCol Aquilla J. Dysss	CO (KIA 2 Feb)
Maj Maynard C. Schultz	CO
Maj Maynard C. Schultz	ExO (To 2 Feb)
Capt Gene G. Mundy	B-3

2/24

LtCol Francis H. Brink	CO
LtCol Richard Rothwell	ExO
Maj Claude M. Cappelmann	B-3

3/24

LtCol Austin B. Brunelli	CO
Maj John V. V. Veeder	ExO
Capt Webb D. Sawyer	B-3

Regimental Weapons Company

Maj Richard McCarthy, Jr.	CO
Capt Edward J. Schofield	ExO

Twenty-fifth Marines

Col Samuel C. Cumming	CO
LtCol Walter I. Jordan	ExO
WO Daniel H. Nelson	R-1
Capt Charles D. Gray	R-2
LtCol William F. Thyson, Jr.	R-3
Capt Edward Sherman	R-4

1/25

LtCol Clarence J. Ó Donnell	CO
Maj Michael Davidowitch, Jr.	ExO
Capt Fenton J. Mee	B-3

2/25

LtCol Lewis C. Hudson, Jr.	CO
Maj William P. Kaempfer	ExO
Capt Victor J. Barringer	B-3

3/25

LtCol Justice M. Chambers	CO
Maj James Taul	ExO
Maj John H. Jones	B-3

Regimental Weapons Company

Capt James T. Kisgen	CO
Capt Thomas H. Rogers	ExO (To 1 Feb)
Capt Delbert A. Graham	ExO

Fourteenth Marines

Col Louis O. DeHaven	CO
LtCol Randall M. Victory	ExO
lstLt Cecil D. Snyder	R-1
Capt Harrison L. Rogers	R-2
Maj Frederick J. Karch	R-3
Maj Richard J. Winsborough	R-4

1/14

LtCol Harry J. Zimmer	CO

Maj Clifford B. Drake	ExO
Maj Thomas M. Fry	B-3

2/14

LtCol George B. Wilson, Jr.	CO
Maj William McReynolds	ExO
Capt Ralph W. Boyer, Jr.	B-3

3/14

LtCol Robert E. MacFarlane	CO
Maj Harvey A. Feehan	ExO
Maj Donald M. Love, Jr.	B-3

4/14

Maj Carl A. Youngdale	CO
Maj John B. Edgar, Jr.	ExO
Maj Roland J. Spritzen	B-3

Twentieth Marines

Col Lucian W. Burnham	CO
LtCol Nelson K. Brown	ExO
Capt Martin M. Calcaterra	R-1
Capt Carl A. Sachs	R-2
Maj Melvin D. Henderson	R-3
Capt Samuel O. Thompson	R-4

1/20

Maj Richard O. Ruby	CO
Capt George F. Williamson	ExO
Capt Martin H. Glover	B-3

2/20

LtCol Otto Lessing	CO
Maj John H. Partridge	ExO
Capt George I. Smith	B-3

3/20 (Seabees)

LtCmdr William O. Byrne	CO
LtCmdr Thomas H. Flinn	ExO

1st Armored Amph Bn

Maj Louis Metzger	CO
Capt Richard G. Warga	ExO
1stLt Thomas M. Crosby	B-3

4th Amph Trac Bn

LtCol Clovis C. Coffman	CO

10th Amph Trac Bn

Maj Victor J. Croizat	CO
Maj Warren H. Edwards	ExO

4th Tank Bn

Maj Richard K. Schmidt	CO
Capt Francis L. Orgain	ExO
Capt Leo B. Case	B-3

15th Defense Bn

LtCol Francis B. Loomis, Jr.	CO
LtCol Peter J. Negri	ExO
Capt Guy L. Wharton	B-3

MAUI

The division's next stop was the Hawaiian island of Maui; at least, the remnants of the division. Their total loss was 737 officers and men of whom 190 were killed or died of wounds. Most of those were from the 24th Marines. Otherwise the organization was in relatively good shape and easily absorbed the replacements. After a brief period of rest and relaxation, they were back to the Marine Corps' specialty: training. After a few short months the division began seriously preparing for additional work in their chosen field. It would be a major undertaking this time. On 29 May the division boarded their transports for an invasion of Saipan, a large island in the Marianas chain.

Saipan lay less than 1500 miles south of Japan proper and taking it would place B-29s within bombing range. All the islands of the Marianas chain, except Guam, had been in Japanese possession for many years and taking them would prove costly. There was an estimated 30,000 Japanese soldiers on Saipan, of which a third were Special Naval Landing Force (Marines). As all Marines were well aware, they would tenaciously fight to the death, taking many Americans with them. Additionally, the perils to health were many. In the sea were sharks and barracudas. On the reefs were razor-sharp coral, sea snakes, and giant clams which could grab a man in their "jaws." Ashore, presuming the Marines would bypass all the other hazards, would be snakes, giant lizards, dysentery, dengue fever, typhus, leprosy, filariasis, and typhoid. In other words, who wanted it anyway? The US Army Air Force, that's who.

The Northern Landing Force (NLF) of the V Amphibious Corps (VAC), commanded ashore by MG Holland McT. Smith, consisted of three divisions, the 2d MarDiv, the 4th MarDiv and the 27th InfDiv, all of which were experienced and considered sufficiently so to warrant a successful invasion. However, the 3d MarDiv, slated to invade Guam, another island in the Marianas, rode transports offshore for a number of days. This was surety for the men ashore, just in case the invasion got into trouble.

SAIPAN

D-day was scheduled for 15 June 1944 and H-hour originally at 0800, later changed to 0840. The 4th MarDiv (MG Harry Schmidt) would land on the southwest coast, from the town of Charon Kanoa down to Agingan Point, supported by the 27th InfDiv (MG Ralph C. Smith, USA). MG Thomas E. Watson's 2d Division, with BG Merritt A. Edson as ADC, would land just north of the 4th and below Garapan, the capital. Order of Battle for the 4th MarDiv was: 2/23 (LtCol Edward J. Dillon) and 3/23 (LtCol John J. Cosgrove) landing on Beaches Blue, 1 and 2; on Beaches Yellow, 1 and 2, were 1/25 (LtCol Hollis U. Mustain) and 2/25 (LtCol Lewis C. Hudson, Jr.). Meanwhile, Franklin Hart's 24th Marines would stage a diversionary demonstration north of Garapan, then revert to division reserve.

The 4th MarDiv was ably supported by the U.S. Army's 534th and 773d Amphibian Tractor Battalions, which placed 4,000 Marines ashore within twenty minutes. Another good unit, the U.S. Army's 708th Armored Amphibian Tractor Battalion, with 75mm guns aboard, pounded the enemy fortified ridge line running about a mile inland. When the Marines landed they came under intense artillery and mortar fire from weapons well placed. It had been planned that the armored vehicles would continue to carry their human cargo to the ridge line, but due to organizational and communication error, they stopped at the beach.

The plan to drive inland and take Mount Fina Susa only partially succeeded. Vehicles pushed ahead but trod swampy ground, and the attendant enemy gunfire made their travail much worse than had been expected. The Susupe Swamp hurt the 23d Marines badly, slowing down all their movements, leaving them stuck on the artillery-targeted beach. A mortar platoon of 3/23 did move forward and set up near Fina Susa, and with good observation plus concentrated fire, gave the Japanese artillery and mortars on the mountain almost as good as they were given. Late that afternoon the Marines were ordered to retire but the mortar men stayed behind to cover their withdrawal. When it was their turn to fall back their tubes were too hot to handle; no vehicles were nearby to assist, so they had to leave their guns behind.

LtCol Ralph Haas and 1/23 had landed behind 3/23 and that night occupied the town of Charan Kanoa, which was a constant target of Japanese artillery fire all through the night. The Marine casualties mounted as the town was being destroyed. So too was the pier which the Marines had anticipated utilizing for unloading incoming supplies. The enemy use of artillery was frightfully effective and it soon became apparent that, contrary to previous experience, the Japanese were trying to defeat the Americans on the beach. That night, at 2000, the enemy launched a serious counterattack. It was where the two Marine divisions joined, and they generally drove quite deep into the 2d MarDiv's lines. That was stopped, however, and the enemy thrown back.

On 16 June, the day began nearly as one-sided as the previous day. The Japanese had the advantages of thirty years of ownership (since 1914), the best terrain (the ridge line), scores of well-prepared caves and dugouts, and many heavy weapons already pre-targeted. The 14th Marine artillery, to the tune of 15 batteries of 75mm pack howitzers, were ashore, but the enemy's accuracy knocked out four batteries, creating havoc amongst the others. Accurate enemy mortar fire in the south had slowed 1/25 to just 700 yards' advancement. The bombardment on Charan Kanoa and the beaches continued all day and casualties mounted. During that day, PltSgt Robert H. McCard, tank commander of Company A, 4th Tank Battalion, found himself nearly out of business when enemy 77mm's put his tank down. Putting all the tank's weapons upon the Japanese, they continued the unequal fight until McCard finally ordered his crew to use the escape hatch. Meanwhile, this Syracuse, NY, native exposed himself by hurling grenades at the enemy to cover the escape of his men. Seriously wounded and out of grenades, McCard then dismantled a machine gun and delivered a vigorous fire into their positions, destroying sixteen of the enemy. He was finally overcome by his wounds and gallantly gave his life for his country. Posthumously he was awarded a Medal of Honor. At the end of the day one company of the 25th Marines was down to just 13 men, while overall the total down was about 2,000 Marines.

That night the 27th InfDiv was landed and the 165th Infantry moved into line to support the drive on Aslito Airfield. That day word came through that the enemy fleet was heading for Saipan and as a consequence, the U.S. warships congregated and headed out to intercept them. Supply ships also left their immediate location and made for safety. Just when the ammo and food were most necessary, they were gone. Another interesting phenomenon was the huge numbers of Japanese and Chamorro civilians coming into the American lines to surrender. Many required food and medical supplies, which their artillery, and fleet, had nearly eliminated for the American fighting men ashore.

Difficulties accumulated and the Marines and their Army comrades had to virtually hack their way into the island. The enemy still had all the advantages of observation. Mount Tapochau, lying in the center of the island, was by far the worst (or best, depending upon your point of view) location for that purpose. By the 18th of June the hard-driving 25th Marines had managed to get to a point where they could see Magicienne Bay on the east coast. The 165th Infantry had already managed to take the Aslito Airfield, thereby covering the Marines' southern flank. Counter-battery fire, air support, and the digging out of so many enemy artillery positions by the ground grunt had well-nigh eliminated that vicious weapon. The Japanese had no air or sea support, and most if not all of his inadequate tanks had already been disposed of. In other words, the enemy was still playing the game, but on nerve only. The Americans had cut the island and taken most of the south, and were now in a position to turn northward and take the balance of it.

Meanwhile, the war on the island was still knockdown and drag-out for all Marines and soldiers. The 23d Marines were having an especially bad time of it. For three days the regiment attacked an exceptionally well dug-in enemy force in a village near Charan Kanoa. The enemy was nearly invisible, and the Marines, being unable to establish an adequate defensive system each night, were forced to pull back to the lines from which they began that day's assault. The next day they started in all over again. This was truly a battle of extermination; only the complete destruction of the Japanese fortified positions and annihilation of them would suffice. And that is what happened. LtCol John J. Cosgrove was wounded on the 19th while directing 3/23 in their attack and he too was awarded a Navy Cross. His replacement was his exec, Maj Paul S. Treitel.

That same day saw the 25th Marines attacking Hill 500, which lay nearly in the middle of the island between Charan Kanoa on the west and Magicienne Bay on the east (see map on page 89). With it in the Marines' possession, the greater height of Tapochau would be somewhat negated. LtCol Justice Chambers' 2/25 made the attack with a company commanded by Capt James Headley leading. They ran into a nest of six machine guns that tore into the company and wounded Headley twice, though not seriously. Of his 100 Marines, 51 became casualties, and it was all they could do to withdraw to safety, eventually getting back down the hill. Throughout the day the Marines of the 25th also suffered intensely from artillery fire.

The next morning, 20 June, Chambers, nicknamed "Jumping Joe," personally directed another assault by Headley and his men. Up the hill they went, as was later said, in a "Hell-bent-for-leather" charge. The enemy machine guns were knocked out by grenades, the flamethrowers burned those Japanese in caves, and those trying to escape were caught on bayonets. This was an old-fashioned example of hand-to-hand combat. After an hour and a half, Headley and company weren't forced downward; instead, they took Hill 500. In the meantime, Chambers, with a concussion from an exploded land mine, was taken unconscious to a field hospital. But he'd be back and would really do his stuff on Iwo Jima.

Capt Headley, from Cincinnati, OH, would be awarded a Navy Cross for his consistent courage and leadership while at Saipan; and he would also pick up an Oak Leaf Cluster in lieu of a second Navy Cross on Iwo Jima. That was the kind of men who were leading Marines in the Pacific War.

During the next week, the pace of the advance picked up. On 22 June the Americans advanced 2,500 yards, and the 4th MarDiv was at the base of Kagman Peninsula. The 27th

InfDiv had been brought up and was now in the center position between the 2d MarDiv on the west and the 4th on the east. Unfortunately the 27th initially failed to keep up with the Marines' advance. The 4th MarDiv was forced to fill in that blank space with three support battalions and could not continue their forward motion. This was followed by some serious altercation between the Marine and U.S. Army Pacific command when MG Ralph Smith, the 27th's CG, was relieved. That relief is still, even today, causing a rift between the two services. It was Smith versus Smith, and no one was completely happy with the hullabaloo.

Eventually, once again all three divisions began forward motion. The next major obstacle was Mount Tapochau, and a real obstacle it was. Although the 6th Marines of the 2d MarDiv actually took the mountain, a reconnaissance patrol from the 25th Marines made that possible. SgtMaj Gilbert L. Morton led it and reached the top on 22 June. That was almost the easy part. When they reached the summit all of a sudden they found they were surrounded by the enemy. After digging in and creating a modest defensive position they beat off continual attacks. Morton, of New Orleans, LA, planned to withdraw under cover of darkness; however, there were too many wounded, so he and his men decided to stick it out. All night the Japanese came for them but each time were beaten back. Morton managed to personally strangle two of them himself. In the morning another patrol saved them, but only five Marines were still alive. Gilbert L. Morton was one of the living and was awarded a Navy Cross for his courage and leadership.

Both Tapochau and the major city of Garapan had fallen to the 2d MarDiv and the Japanese were on the run. Marine and Navy fighters and bombers were now using Aslito Airfield and providing close air support for the three divisions. Still the enemy, defeated but unwilling to acknowledge that fact, took his wounded and dead with him as he fell back. Marines wondered where all the dead Japanese were, and found out at the campaign's end. They had brought them back to the end of the island and dumped them off the high cliffs into the rocks and sea below. Perhaps they decided it was better than burying them.

By 2 July, the half-way mark had been achieved. The three divisions were now nearly on line equally. The 4th MarDiv spent two days taking two hills, Hill 721 and 767, calling the latter "Fourth of July Hill." Three-fourths of the island was in American hands but the casualties continued; the troops were exhausted and combat efficiency was rated down to 75%. Now the enemy was bottled up on Marpi Point and tenuously holding a modest strip of ground south along the west coast to Tanapag Harbor. That was not in the 4th MarDiv's sector. However, they and the 27th InfDiv pivoted on their left flank and headed down from the hills westward to more level ground. All three divisions advanced toward the western coast with the 4th's three regiments abreast on the northern flank.

Before General Saito committed hara-kiri he exhorted his troops to "utilize this opportunity to exalt true Japanese manhood." They did, and the resulting *Banzai* attack against the 27th InfDiv drove them in at least 3,000 yards. They then pierced the 2d MarDiv's lines far into the 10th Artillery's lines, where the latter finally stopped them and the enemy died to the last man. Losses to the Americans were about 1,500 and to the enemy 3,000. The lucky 4th wasn't touched during this attack.

Following this last effort, the 23d Marines smashed into what few Japanese remained along the coast, and the 24th and 25th drove northward to Marpi Point. What followed was one of the most dramatic events in the entire Pacific War. As the Americans looked on

Beach Yellow and 1/25 preparing to make their way inland on 15 June 1944.

in horror, thousands of Japanese civilians slaughtered their children with knives or guns, then threw them off the cliffs to the rocks and sea below. That was followed by the civilians committing suicide the same way, followed by many of the troops. The few civilians that tried to surrender to the Americans were shot down by the Japanese troops.

On 9 July the island was officially declared secured, marking the end of twenty-five grueling days of combat. The division's casualties numbered nearly 6,000, or 28% of its total strength. The enemy losses totaled a known 23,811 dead with 1,810 captured. Radio Tokyo proclaimed a national week of mourning for the loss of Saipan. Next on the Americans' agenda: Tinian, Saipan's sister island, lying just three and one half miles south.

Order of Battle
Saipan
(15 June to 9 July 1944)

Headquarters		Twenty-third Marines	
MG Harry Schmidt	CG	Col Louis B. Jones	CO
BG Samuel C. Cumming	ADC	LtCol John H. Lanigan	ExO
Col William W. Rogers	CoS	Capt Charlie J. Talbert	R-1
Col Walter I. Jordan	D-1	Capt Richard W. Mirick	R-2
LtCol Gooderham L.		Maj Edward W. Wells	R-3
McCormick	D-2	Capt Henry S. Campbell	R-4
Col Walter W. Wensinger	D-3	*1/23*	
Col William F. Brown	D-4	LtCol Ralph Haas	CO

Maj James S. Scales	ExO
Capt James H. Miller	B-3

2/23

LtCol Edward J. Dillon	CO
Maj Albert H. Follmar	ExO
Maj Robert H. Davidson	B-3

3/23

LtCol John J. Cosgrove	CO (WIA 19 Jun)
Maj Paul S. Treitel	CO
Maj Paul S. Treitel	ExO
Maj Robert J. J. Picardi	B-3

Twenty-fourth Marines

Col Franklin A. Hart	CO
LtCol Austin H. Brunelli	ExO
Capt Kenneth N. Hilton	R-1
Capt Arthur B. Hanson	R-2
LtCol Charles D. Roberts	R-3
Maj Clyde T. Smith	R-4

1/24

LtCol Maynard C. Schultz	CO (DOW 16 Jun)
Maj Robert N. Fricke	CO (To 18 Jun)
LtCol Austin H. Brunelli	CO (To 4 Jul)
LtCol Otto Lessing	CO
Maj Robert N. Fricke	ExO
1stLt Gene O. Mundy	B-3

2/24

LtCol Richard Rothwell	CO
Capt Claude M. Cappelmann	ExO
Capt Charles C. Berkeley	B-3

3/24

LtCol Alexander A. Vandegrift, Jr.	CO (WIA 27 Jun)
LtCol Otto Lessing	CO (To 3 Jul)
Capt Webb D. Sawyer	ExO
Capt Webb D. Sawyer	B-3

Twenty-fifth Marines

Col Merton J. Batchelder	CO
LtCol Clarence J. Ó Donnell	ExO
Capt Francis A. Norton	R-1
Capt Charles D. Gray	R-2
LtCol William F. Thyson, Jr.	R-3
Maj Arthur E. Buck, Jr.	R-4

1/25

LtCol Hollis U. Mustain	CO
Maj Henry D. Strunk	ExO
Capt Fenton J. Mee	B-3

2/25

LtCol Levis C. Hudson, Jr.	CO
Maj William P. Kaempfer	ExO
Capt Victor J. Barringer	B-3

3/25

LtCol Justice M. Chambers	CO (WIA 22 Jun. * 24 Jun)
Maj James Taul	CO (To 23 Jun)

Maj James Taul	ExO
Capt James O. Headley	B-3

Fourteenth Marines

Col Louis G. DeHaven	CO
LtCol Randall M. Victory	ExO
1stLt Cecil D. Snyder	R-1
Capt Harrison L. Rogers	R-2
Maj Frederick J. Karch	R-3
Maj Richard J. Winsborough	R-4

1/14

LtCol Harry J. Zimmer	CO
Maj Clifford B. Drake	ExO
Maj Thomas McE. Fry	B-3

2/14

LtCol George B. Wilson, Jr.	CO
Maj William McReynolds	ExO
Capt Jack H. Riddle	B-3

3/14

LtCol Robert E. MacFarlane	CO
Maj Harvey A. Feehan	ExO
Capt Fenton H. Elliott	B-3

4/14

LtCol Carl A. Youngdale	CO
Maj John B. Edgar, Jr.	ExO
Maj Roland J. Spritzen	B-3

Twentieth Marines

LtCol Nelson K. Brown	CO
Capt William M. Anderson	ExO
Capt Martin M. Calcaterra	R-1
Capt Carl A. Sachs	R-2
Maj Melvin D. Henderson	R-3
Capt Samuel O. Thompson	R-4

1/20

Maj Richard G. Ruby	CO
Maj George F. Williamson	ExO
Capt Martin H. Glover	B-3

2/20

Maj John H. Partridge	CO
Capt Howard M. Dowling	ExO
Capt George A. Smith	B-3

4th 105mm Howitzer Bn, VAC

LtCol Douglas E. Reeve	CO
Maj Marvin H. Burdett	ExO
Capt Joe H. Daniel	B-3

4th Tank Bn

Maj Richard K. Schmidt	CO
Maj Francis L. Orgain	ExO
Capt Leo B. Chase	B-3

10th Amph Trac Bn

Maj Victor J. Croizat	CO
Maj Harry T. Marshall, Jr.	ExO

4th MT Bn

LtCol Ralph L. Schiesswohl	CO

Maj Vaughan H. Huse	ExO
1stLt Walter W. Alford	B-3

4th Service Bn

Col Richard H. Schubert	CO
2dLt James T. Willis	B-3

4th Medical Bn

LtCmdr George W. Mast	CO
LtCmdr George M. Davis, Jr.	ExO

TINIAN

From a slew of captured documents, the Americans were able to quickly piece together the layout of Tinian; the order of battle, fortifications, layout of dumps, and the plan for defense. Essentially, this would be a shore-to-shore operation, utilizing small landing craft, with LSTs the principal mode of transportation. Reconnaissance patrols were sent over in rubber boats to look around. It would also be a U.S. Marine operation, with the 27th Inf-Div assuming occupation duty on Saipan.

Beginning on 11 June, Task Force 58 began a systematic destruction of anything above ground useful to the defenders. A rubber boat landing by the VAC Recon Battalion on the night of 10–11 July discovered that two proposed landing beaches, White one and two, were lightly defended and the rough coral could be easily surmounted by troops. The highest point was Mt. Lasso, a mere 540 feet at its peak. Elsewhere, Tinian was relatively flat with cane fields. It was decided that Regimental Combat Team (RCT) 24 would go ashore, in a column of battalions, on Beach White One. RCT 25 would land to their south by a few hundred yards. RCT 23 would be briefly in division reserve and not land until later; the same was true for the 14th Marines. The latter had 4 battalions of 75mm howitzers loaded in DUKWs also for a Jig-day landing. The 2d MarDiv was to create a diversion off Tinian Town. (See 2d MarDiv for details.)

Jig-day, 24 July 1944, and H-hour at 0740, was entirely a 4th MarDiv show. The 24th Marines struck at Ushi Point and immediately took the airfield. The 25th Marines moved onto White Beach Two and fanned out. The 23d Marines landed at noon, and in the meantime, supplies were moved inland to create dumps. Tanks, half-tracks and other vehicles were unloaded. Everything was going extremely well on the first day. All batteries of the 14th Marines were ashore, as were the attached (2d MarDiv) 10th Marines' batteries. Casualties were extremely light with 15 killed and 150 wounded by nightfall with a gain of 4,000 yards wide and 2,000 yards deep.

The anticipated counterattack came that night, beginning at 0200 on the 25th, but the Marines were well dug-in. It was a true, well-organized and executed *Banzai* that hit the perimeter at several points simultaneously. It was preceded by the usual artillery and mortar fire falling upon the Marine lines. Six tanks, followed by infantry, hit the center, which was held by the 23d Marines. Of the six tanks, all but one were destroyed, and that one somehow escaped.

Nonetheless, the infantry continued coming and soon they and the Marines of 2/23 were in close hand-to-hand combat. Some of the Japanese penetrated the lines, some as deep as into the artillery positions. Howitzer crews lowered the muzzles and fired point-blank, slaughtering most and then liquidating the remnants with small arms fire. One machine gun crew piled up 250 bodies before their position. In front of one company, 350 enemy dead were counted.

On the left, before the 24th Marines, a platoon lead by Sgt John F. Fritts, Jr., killed 150

4th MarDiv troops landing on Tinian's north shore.

of the enemy. By morning, overall at least 1250 Japanese were dead, and that wasn't counting those bodies retrieved by their comrades, an estimated 700 or 800 more. It was calculated at about one-fifth of the enemy's total strength on that island.

On 25 July the 2d MarDiv landed to the left of the 4th and was assigned the east side
of the island (see map on page 98). Four RCTs moved south, led by tanks providing a base
of fire and partial cover for the infantry. By 28 July the airfield near Garguan Point was
taken, and two days later Tinian Town fell to the Americans. In six days the Marines had
taken three-fourths of the island. The ground was conducive to advancing but not for
defense. With all possible haste the Japanese began to seriously dig in and contest each inch
of ground. Straightaway the Marines would have to dig them out, with the consequent
casualties that always brought. In the meantime, on 31 July, Col Ogata mustered about a
company-sized strike force and, preceded by a mortar barrage, attacked the 24th Marines.
They were, however, quickly repulsed with Ogata as one of their casualties.

Down at the southern tip, between Lalo and Marpi Points, on difficult ground, the
enemy awaited the Marines. Two battleships, a heavy and two light cruisers, plus loads of
destroyers and bombing planes shelled the area heavily. The ground grunts went in with
flamethrowers and a liberal use of demolitions, with BARs covering them. On 30 July, one
group of five, including Pvt Joseph W. Ozbourn from Herrin, IL, was having a difficult time
of it. Their job was to clear out the remaining enemy from pillboxes hindering their final
moves on the island. Ozbourn, with four others, moved forward to throw a grenade into
one opening when a blast from the entrance severely wounded three Marines. Ozbourn
had the armed grenade in his hand. Unable to throw the grenade into the opening of the
pillbox, he grasped it tight to his own body, absorbing the full blast and saving his four
comrades. He was awarded a posthumous Medal of Honor for this courageous act.

On 1 August 1944 Tinian Island was declared secured. Still, some Japanese, civilians and soldiers, went over the cliffs as on Saipan. Notwithstanding, the Marines managed to get a prominent citizen to broadcast an appeal to the civilians and at least 13,262 were saved from extinction.

At least six thousand known enemy soldiers died on Tinian, not counting those buried by their comrades. The 4th MarDiv losses were 290 killed and 1,515 wounded with 24 missing. The division, because of its performance on Saipan and Tinian, was the third Marine division to be awarded the coveted Presidential Unit Citation. By 14 August the last of the division troops boarded transports for the ride back to Maui. Rest, relaxation, and exercise were ahead, with training being the main thing. It would allow the members of the division some time before getting back into harness.

Order of Battle
Tinian
(24 July to 1 August 1944)

Headquarters		Twenty-fourth Marines	
MG Clifton B. Cates	CG	Col Franklin A. Hart	CO
BG Samuel C. Cumming	ADC	LtCol Austin R. Brunelli	ExO
Col William W. Rogers	CoS	Capt Kenneth N. Hilton	R-1
Col Walter I. Jordan	D-1	Capt Arthur B. Hanson	R-2
LtCol Gooderham L.		LtCol Charles D. Roberts	R-3
McCormick	D-2	Maj Clyde T. Smith	R-4
Col Walter W. Wensinger	D-3		
Col William F. Brown	D-4	**1/24**	
		LtCol Otto Lessing	CO
Support Group[1]		Maj Robert N. Fricke	ExO
Col Orin H. Wheeler	CO	Capt Gene G. Mundy	B-3
Twenty-third Marines		**2/24**	
Col Louis H. Jones	CO	Maj Frank E. Garretson	CO (until 27 Jul)
LtCol John B. Lanigan	ExO	LtCol Richard Rothwell	CO
Capt Charlie S. Talbert	R-1	Maj George D. Webster	ExO
Capt Richard W. Mirick	R-2	Capt Charles C. Berkeley, Jr.	B-3
Capt William E. Buron	R-3		
Capt Henry S. Campbell	R-4	**3/24**	
		LtCol Alexander A.	
1/23		Vandegrift, Jr.	CO
LtCol Ralph Haas	CO	Capt Doyle A. Stout	ExO
Maj James S. Scales	ExO	Capt Webb O. Sawyer	B-3
Capt William L. Dick	B-3		
		Twenty-fifth Marines	
2/23		Col Merton J. Batchelder	CO
LtCol Edward S. Dillon	CO	LtCol Clarence S. Ó Donnell	ExO
Maj Robert H. Davidson	ExO	Capt George K. Dunn	R-1
Capt James W. Sperry	B-3	Capt Charles D. Gray	R-2
		LtCol William F. Thyson, Jr.	R-3
3/23		Maj Arthur E. Buck, Jr.	R-4
Maj Paul S. Treitel	CO	**1/25**	
Capt Philip S. Maloney	ExO	LtCol Hollis U. Mustain	CO
Capt Donald S. Callaham	B-3		

[1]*The division's Task Organization for Tiinian listed the following units under the Support Group: Hdq Bn (less dets); 4th MT Bn (less dets); 4th Tk Bn (less Cos A, B, and C, and dets CoD); 4th Med Bn (less dets); 4th Serv Bn; VMO-4; 1st JASCO (less dets); 2d Tk Bn; and the Prov LVT Gp, V Phib Corps (less dets), which included the 5th, 715th and 534th AmphTrac Bns (all less dets).*

Company headquarters personnel of the 24th Marines communicating with superiors on Tinian.

Maj Henry D. Strunk	ExO
Capt Fenton S. Mee	B-3

2/25

LtCol Lewis C. Hudson, Jr.	CO
Maj William P. Kaempfer	ExO
Capt Victor S. Barringer	B-3

3/25

LtCol Justice M. Chambers	CO
Maj James Taul	ExO

Fourteenth Marines

Col Louis G. DeHaven	CO
LtCol Randall M. Victory	ExO
Capt Cecil D. Snyder	R-1
Capt Harrison L. Rogers	R-2
Maj Frederick J. Karch	R-3
Maj Richard J. Winsborough	R-4

1/14

LtCol Harry J. Zimmer	CO (KIA 25 Jul)
Maj Clifford B. Drake	CO
Maj Clifford B. Drake	ExO
Maj Thomas McE. Fry	B-3

2/14

LtCol George B. Wilson, Jr.	CO

Maj William McReynolds	ExO
Capt Jack H. Riddle	B-3

3/14

LtCol Robert E. MacFarlane	CO
Maj Harvey A. Feehan	ExO
Capt Benton H. Elliott	B-3

4/14

LtCol Carl A. Youngdale	CO
Maj John B. Edgar, Jr.	ExO
lstLt Russell F. Schoenbeck	B-3

4th 105mm Howitzer Bn, VAC

LtCol Douglas E. Reeve	CO
Maj Marvin R. Burdett	ExO
Capt Joe H. Daniel	B-3

Twentieth Marines

LtCol Nelson K. Brown	CO
Maj Richard O. Ruby	ExO
Capt Martin M. Calcaterra	R-1
Capt Carl A. Sachs	R-2
Maj Melvin O. Henderson	R-3
Capt Samuel G. Thompson	R-4

1/20

Maj Richard O. Ruby	CO

| Maj George F. Williamson | ExO |
| Capt Martin H. Glover | B-3 |

2/20

Maj John H. Partridge	CO
Capt Howard M. Dowling	ExO
Capt George A. Smith	B-3

4th Tank Bn

| Maj Richard K. Schmidt | CO |
| Maj Francis L. Orgain | ExO & B-3 |

10th Amph Trac Bn

| Maj Victor S. Croizat | CO |
| Maj Harry T. Marshall, Jr. | ExO |

4th MT Bn

LtCol Ralph L. Schiesswohl	CO
Maj Vaughan H. Huse	ExO
1stLt Walter W. Alford	B-3

4th Service Bn

| Col Richard H. Schubert[2] | CO |
| 2dLt James T. Willis | B-3 |

4th Medical Bn

| Cmdr Stewart W. Shimonek | CO |
| LtCmdr George W. Mast | ExO |

MAUI

While the division was back "home" there were some changes to the most senior positions. BG Franklin A. Hart had become the ADC; Col Walter D. Wensinger assumed command of the 23d Marines; Col Walter I. Jordan CO of the 24th Marines; and Col John R. Lanigan of the 25th Marines. Col Merton J. Batchelder became the Chief of Staff of the division; Lt Col Melvin L. Krulewitch assumed command of the Support Group.

While at Maui plans were developed to utilize the 4th MarDiv once again, this time as part of a three-division Marine assault upon a small island with two functioning airfields and one under construction. The need was expressed by the U.S. Army Air Force command at the Joint Chiefs of Staff in Washington. Their new B-29 aircraft were very expensive and being shot to pieces over Japan, thereby requiring a closer place to land upon return from bombing raids, to save crews (about 1500 to 1600 in number as later calculated) and aircraft. There were something like 22,000 to 23,000 Japanese soldiers on this small island, most of them already dug in. At least 22,000 Marines (roughly a full division) paid a heavy price for the island, not all killed in action, of course. As later events proved, this was going to be one hell of a fight.

IWO JIMA

D-day for two divisions, the 4th and newly created 5th MarDiv, was on 19 February 1945. Plans developed were for the two divisions to land abreast on 3500 yards of beach: the 4th, on Beaches Yellow 1 and 2, were for 1/23 (LtCol Ralph Haas) and 2/23 (Maj Robert H. Davidson), while 1/25 (LtCol Hollis U. Mustain) and 3/25 (LtCol Justice M. Chambers) would land on Blue 2. Division Reserve would be the 24th Marines (Col Walter I. Jordan). The 5th MarDiv would land on the southernmost beaches, from Mount Suribachi north on Beaches Green and Red. Not landing that day, but kept in Corps Reserve, would be the 3d MarDiv less the 3d Marines.

Initially the leadership, Navy and Marine, thought the landing would be smooth and the fight equally so. The sea was relatively calm, visibility excellent, waves of B-29's were overhead to drop blockbusters and napalm, and a record number of heavy warships were

---

[2]*Schubert remained with rear echelon at Maui, Hawaiian Islands, during Marianas campaign.*

at hand to blast the island out of the ocean. As the division history proclaimed: "From all directions, from every type of weapon, molten steel rained on the island." Only trouble was the enemy had umbrellas and raincoats: holes in the earth.

Before H-hour, 0900, the boats were nearing a landing and, though no one knew why, the landing seemed unopposed. No fire was coming from Iwo Jima. When the tractors began landing on their beaches, however, all hell broke loose. Japanese artillery pieces were well registered and the shells landed on the tractors as they arrived. A few of them went down in the water, as did a few planes strafing the ground near the beaches. The Marines landed exactly at 0900 and found they were ankle deep in volcanic ash, which greatly impeded forward movement. Not enough to dig into, just a complete lack of cover and concealment. Nonetheless, for some reason most of the assault landing force, in the first hour, made it ashore with little trouble. Even the valuable support services, medical aid and a contingent of Seabees, also made it in the first hour or so.

At 1000, the honeymoon terminated, as did many Americans, exposed to everything the enemy had planned for them. Big guns depressed, as did little guns, machine guns, and mortars; and lack of cover became disastrous for the Marines. It appeared, to those taking it, as though the Navy's big guns and the enemy's big guns were dueling with the Marines in between. Later the Marines counted over 50 pillboxes in 500 yards of beach, plus two huge blockhouses, numerous tank traps and scores of rifle pits. Fortunately the USN shelling had destroyed many and that was probably the only reason the Marines could get ashore.

By noon the Marine assault companies were driving hard despite the volcanic ash and made it to Motoyama Airfield No. 1. In so doing, they had lost many men, including numerous officers and non-coms. Many platoons were now commanded by sergeants; and numerous corpsmen were killed off or wounded, leaving the hundreds of wounded Marines without any chance for repairs. One field music (Marine terminology for a musician), Sgt Darrell S. Cole, who was tired of being behind the lines, begged for a post with a line company. He showed what a Field Music could do when enraged. Cole made three trips forward with grenades to a pillbox, dropped them into a slot and put it out of action. On his way back a sniper cut him down. His parents received the Navy Cross he was awarded.

There were no rear areas on Iwo. Seabees were taking as heavy casualties as their Marine comrades. By 1600 3/25 reported fifty percent casualties. All tanks were ashore by 1300, as were two battalions of artillery; they were able to fire later that afternoon. By 1700 more than a thousand wounded 4th MarDiv men had been transported to ships. When the order came to "dig in" the lines were inland by 500 yards, not very far for a successful landing, and leaving the Marines little defense capability.

No matter where the Marines were to go, no matter how far they might advance, the enemy always had the best sites and positions. They always had the highest ground, always the best observation. The Japanese were good, very good, but fortunately the Marines were always better. Nevertheless, the latter had to take heavy losses in order to be better. But, then, so did the Japanese to try to keep up.

During the night there was no counterattack, as expected, but the enemy continued firing, mainly his well-positioned artillery. One battalion CP, that of 1/23, was wiped out almost entirely, including its CO, LtCol Ralph Haas, from heavy artillery fire. On 20 February, the 23d Marines (Col Walter W. Wensinger) captured the entire Airfield No. 1. The 25th Marines were able to move ahead but took enormous casualties in so doing. So much so, that the reserve 24th Marines (Col Walter I. Jordan) were landed in order to try to cease the flow of Marine blood and stabilize the very difficult situation. This was an entirely different kind of fight that the enemy was fighting. No great *Banzai* charges with numerous casualties to the Japanese. He was fighting from down deep and causing the Marines to come and dig him out. The price was very high. By the end of the second day Marine casualties reached over 2,000.

During the period 19 to 22 February, no matter what obstacles were encountered, LtCol Justice M. "Jumping Joe" Chambers, CO of 3/25, was the main instrument keeping his battalion moving. Soon after landing he found his men stymied and stopped. He, by personal leadership from the front, managed to get them moving against fierce machine gun and rifle fire from the cliffs ahead. In eight hours of savage fighting he led his men upward and eventually took that ridge, forcing the enemy to give way. This freed up the regiment and it began moving forward once again. He continued his hands-on leadership and his fighting spirit never diminished even in the face of overwhelming losses to personnel, including most of his senior officers. On 22 February, while directing the fire of a rocket platoon, he was seriously wounded and evacuated under heavy enemy fire. He was rewarded with the Medal of Honor for his distinguished leadership and courage.

Bad seas also created excessive problems. Boats with supplies overturned, as did several with one battalion of howitzers, losing seven of twelve guns. Japanese artillery still had the beach well-covered. By day three, 21 February, the beach was so littered with wreckage that few boat lanes were opened to moving traffic. Combat efficiency for the 4th MarDiv was calculated at 68%. Regardless, Capt Joseph J. McCarthy, the "skipper" of Company G, 2/24, decided to open up the way before Motoyama Airfield No. 2. Acting on his own to break the determined enemy resistance before the airfield, he pulled together a demolitions crew, flamethrower personnel, and a picked rifle squad. Then he led the way across seventy-five yards of fire-swept ground, charging a heavily fortified pillbox on the ridge to his front. McCarthy hurled grenades into the emplacement while directing the operations of his small group in destroying the hostile position. Two enemy soldiers tried to escape but Joe boldly stood upright in full view of the enemy and shot both down. The next position was demolished by the demo team; when Joe entered he found a live enemy aiming toward one of his men. He jumped the man, disarmed him and then shot him with his weapon. He then rallied his men and with him in the lead, they launched a furious attack upon the other positions remaining on the ridge. An inspiring and indomitable fighter, McCarthy was mainly responsible for capturing the ridge. He was appropriately awarded a Medal of Honor for these actions, "above and beyond the call of duty."

The 25th Marines had another hero of substance come forward on 21 February. He was Sgt Ross F. Gray, and he was born in Marvel Valley, AL. A member of Company A, 1/25, Gray shrewdly gauged the opposition's tactics and positions on high ground lying northeast of Airfield No. 1. Having just received a bunch of grenades, Gray hastily withdrew his men and then moved out alone to reconnoiter the ground ahead. He discovered a network of mines laid before a strong fortified position. Alone and carrying just a satchel charge, Gray crept up to it and hurled the charge; the explosion sealed the entrance. He repeated his actions and sealed a second opening, even though all the while under intense machine gun fire. Gray managed to destroy six enemy emplacements, a quantity of ammo and ordnance gear, plus taking out at least 25 enemy soldiers. He personally had destroyed a minefield and a strong enemy position, allowing his fellow Marines a somewhat less dan-

On 19 February 1945, Marines of the 25th finding the way forward through volcanic ash.

gerous forward path. For this he was awarded a Medal of Honor, but did not live to receive it; he was killed in action on 27 February 1945.

That same day, in late afternoon, the 21st Marines, 3d MarDiv came ashore to relieve the badly battered 23d Marines in the center. On 22 February, the 21st Marines (Col Hartnoll J. Withers, Silver Star), in line alongside the 24th Marines and attached to the 4th MarDiv, moved forward with the 26th Marines (Col John R. Lanigan, Navy Cross) of the 5th MarDiv on their left. The two fresh battalions in the center made all the difference in the world. (See 3d MarDiv for 21st Marines details.)

On 23 February the 24th Marines fought a bloody battle for Charlie–Dog Ridge and on 24 February captured it after some of the toughest fighting on the island, so far. They and the 21st Marines drove in to, and on the 25th captured, Motoyama Airfield No. 2. The 25th Marines were still moving, slowly, on the east coast toward Tachiiwa Point. The 24th Marines had one of the island's chief strong points in their path to overcome: Hill 382, the second highest point on the island after Mt. Suribachi, loaded with natural and man-made crevices 15 to 50 feet deep. It was the backbone and nerve center for the northern portion of the island's defense. There were three other difficult points within the sector of the 4th MarDiv; they were branded "Turkey Knob," "Amphitheater," and Minami Village. Because each was interdependent with the others, the entire position would have to be assaulted at the same time.

On 26 February, to the 23d Marines went the task of Hill 382; to the 25th Marines went Turkey Knob and the Amphitheater. Both locations were later considered to be the most difficult and most costly operation for the 4th MarDiv. It was described as the backbone of Japanese defense and their nerve center of the entire island. The defensive positions included four tanks buried up to their turrets, at least twenty pillboxes, several 75mm anti-aircraft guns with muzzles depressed to fire horizontally, and many machine guns, light and heavy. Maj James S. Scales and 3/23 went up the hill, and after a knock-down day-long fight, two companies took the high ground. One of their men, PFC Douglas T. Jacobson of Rochester, NY, wiped out a 20mm AA Gun and crew with his newly acquired bazooka. Not satisfied with that, he pushed himself to the summit of Hill 382 and when his platoon was halted he used his weapon with accuracy. He first destroyed two machine gun positions, then attacked a large blockhouse. He neutralized that by killing off the occupants. Then he went after another pillbox, killing more Japanese before destroying the site with an explosion. From then on he became a one-man battalion. Next he wiped out six more positions, killing off all ten occupants, then volunteered his help to another nearby company. First he knocked out another pillbox, then destroyed an enemy tank, then went and destroyed another blockhouse. All-in-all, he is credited with knocking out at least 16 positions and killing approximately 75 of the enemy. He survived and, rightly so, was awarded a Medal of Honor.

But the numbers of Marines were so depleted that they were forced to retire and the enemy then went up the hill and reclaimed it. Then, once more the 23d Marines went up and again were forced to retire, and once again the Japanese regained the hill. The Marines' casualties taking the height didn't allow them to hold it, and every night the positions were reversed.

A battalion of the 24th Marines tried the Amphitheater with similar results. The 25th Marines caught the same treatment at Turkey Knob, from all sides. Day after day, each regiment received the same handling and for four days it continued. On 1 March, Col Walter W. Wensinger's (Navy Cross, 19 February to 16 March 1945) badly handled 23d Marines were relieved by LtCol Richard Rothwell (Silver Star) and 2/24. This battalion succeeded in scaling Hill 382, but no fewer than six company commanders became casualties during the four days of battle. Capt Walter Ridlon and Company F, plus the remnants of Company E, were credited with the hill's capture. Ridlon earned a Navy Cross for the period 19 February to 16 March 1945. Sergeant James Beddingfield and a squad of Marines came up from behind and surprised the eight remaining enemy still on the hill. "They never had a chance," said Beddingfield, "they couldn't get their gun wheeled around before we had them." Consequently, Turkey Knob and the Amphitheater became untenable for the Japanese. In thirteen days of fighting the division had suffered 6,591 casualties, and though some replacements had arrived, the combat efficiency was rated at only 50%.

Another Marine who earned the Navy Cross was LtCol Austin R. Brunelli, CO of 1/24, for extraordinary heroism in action against the enemy, as commander of a Marine infantry battalion from 8 to 16 March 1945. Brunelli, whose regular duties were as regimental executive officer, had been painfully wounded and evacuated 20 February, but through his own efforts, returned on 21 February. On 9 March he was ordered to assume command of 1/24, an infantry battalion which had suffered heavy casualties and was disorganized. Upon assuming command from Maj Paul S. Treitel, he made a personal reconnaissance of his entire front lines, and reorganized his badly depleted units into two rifle companies. By his heroic conduct he restored the fighting spirit of his men and was able to resume the attack in coordination with units on his flanks. Under his fearless and inspiring leadership the battalion made substantial gains against the fanatical resistance of the enemy. This advance

Marines of 3/23 trying to move forward without taking too many losses on 27 February 1945.

of his battalion eliminated a salient, and thereafter the general advance continued daily until the resistance of the enemy was completely overcome. Throughout the action LtCol Brunelli repeatedly exposed himself, with utter disregard for his own personal safety, to strong enemy fire in order to direct and encourage the men of his battalion. His conduct throughout was in keeping with the highest traditions of the United States Naval Service.

But it still wasn't over. General Kuribayashi, the island CG, was still alive and the defense went on. The Marines continued to "dig 'em out," blasting caves, knocking out bunkers, locating and destroying mortar positions, and the same for OPs. Nights were cold, since it was late winter in the north Pacific, and everyone desired, no needed, hot coffee. The front changed and the 25th Marines were the pivot. They continued holding the enemy's southern flank while the rest of the division tried to clean up the northern edges. But it was still the same old story. After a half hour preparatory artillery barrage, the 23d went forward and barely eked out a 100-yard gain. The 24th Marines attacked in conjunction but fared no better. One platoon of the 23d was ambushed and only one man survived uninjured.

On the night of 8–9 March the Japanese tried the only organized counterattack of the entire campaign. After an artillery, mortar and machine gun barrage, at 2200 they began trying to infiltrate the Marines' lines. That continued all night, all along the lines. Some got through to the OPs. Some with land mines strapped to their chests charged into a group of Marines. Others blew themselves up with grenades as they witnessed their comrades' failures. The next morning 784 enemy bodies were counted all along the front, but the lines had held. Now the division's casualties numbered 8,100 and combat efficiency was down to 45%. On 10 March the Marines' final push began. Later that day patrols reached the shore and on 11 March the division had managed to reached the ocean. In the meantime, some Japanese had been bypassed, which group the 25th Marines crushed by the following day. By 16 March all three divisions had cleaned up their sectors and the island was declared secured.

The division's total casualties numbered 9,090, of which 1,731 had been killed. Of the 22,000 Japanese killed on the island, 8,982 were counted in the 4th MarDiv's sector. Perhaps another 1,000, uncounted for obvious reasons, had been sealed up in cave closings. The division's POW's numbered just 44. On 4 March, while the fighting was going on, the first crippled B-29 had landed on Airfield No. 1.

Order of Battle
Iwo Jima
19 February to 16 March 1945

Headquarters

MG Clifton B. Cates	CG
BG Franklin A. Hart	ADC
Col Merton J. Batchelder	CoS
Col Orin H. Wheeler	D-1
LtCol Gooderham L. McCormick	D-2
Col Edwin A. Pollock	D-3
Col Matthew C. Horner	D-4
Col Bertrand T. Fay	CO Hdqs Bn
LtCol Melvin L. Krulewitch	CO Support Group[3]

Twenty-third Marines

Col Walter W. Wensinger	CO
LtCol Edward J. Dillon	ExO
Maj Henry S. Campbell	B-3

1/23

LtCol Ralph Haas	CO (KIA 20 Feb)
LtCol Louis B. Blissard	CO
LtCol Louis B. Blissard	ExO (To 20 Feb)
Capt Fred C. Eberhardt	B-3 (KIA 20 Feb)
Maj James W. Sperry	B-3

2/23

Maj Robert H. Davidson	CO (WIA 7 March, * from 11 Mar)
LtCol Edward J. Dillon	CO (From 7 to 11 Mar)
Maj John J. Padley	ExO (WIA 7 Mar)

Capt Carl O. J. Grussendorf	ExO
Capt Edward J. Schofield	B-3 (WIA 7 Mar)

3/23

Maj James S. Scales	CO
Maj Philip J. Maloney	ExO
Maj William H. Cushing	B-3

Twenty-fourth Marines

Col Walter I. Jordan	CO
LtCol Austin R. Brunelli	ExO (To 8 Mar)
Maj Webb D. Sawyer	R-3

1/24

Maj Paul S. Treitel	CO (To 8 Mar)
LtCol Austin R. Brunelli	CO
Maj Horace C. Parks	ExO
Maj Irving Schechter	B-3 (To 8 Mar)
Maj George D. Webster	B-3

2/24

LtCol Richard Rothwell	CO
Maj Frank E. Garretson	ExO
Capt John F. Ross, Jr.	B-3 (WIA 20 Feb)
Maj Charles C. Berkeley, Jr.	B-3 3/24
LtCol Alexander A. Vandegrift, Jr.	CO (WIA 23 Feb)
Maj Doyle A. Stout	CO
Maj Doyle A. Stout	ExO (To 23 Feb)
Maj Albert Arsenault	ExO
Maj Albert Arsenault	B-3 (To 23 Feb)
Maj William C. Esterline	B-3

[3]*The 4th MarDiv Support Group task organization for Iwo Jima was as follows: Hdqs Bn (less dets); 4th MT Bn (less Cos A, B, and C); 4th Tank Bn (less Cos A, B, and C plus Main Plt, Ord Co, 4th Serv Bn) 4th Serv Bn (less dets); 4th Med Bn (less Cos A, B, and C); 4th Engr Bn (less Cos A, B, and C); 2d Arm Amph Bn (less Cos A, B, C, D, and det of Bn Hdqs); Div Ren Cc; 1st JASCO (less dets); 1st Prov Rocket Det (less 1st and 2d Secs); Det 726th SAW Co); JICPOA Int Team; Det Sig Bn, VAC; Corps Ln Grp. After the landing the following groups were also attached: 5th Amph Trac Bn; 10th Amph Trac Bn; 24th and 30th Repl Drafts.*

Twenty-fifth Marines

Col John R. Lanigan	CO
LtCol Clarence J. Ó Donnell	ExO
Maj John H. Jones	B-3

1/25

LtCol Hollis U. Mustain	CO (KIA 21 Feb)
Maj Fenton J. Mee	CO
Maj Henry D. Strunk	ExO (WIA 19 Feb)
Maj Fenton J. Mee	ExO (To 21 Feb)
Maj Edward L. Asbill	ExO
Maj Fenton J. Mee	B-3 (To 21 Feb)
Capt William J. Weinstein	B-3

2/25

LtCol Lewis C. Hudson, Jr.	CO (WIA 20 Feb)
LtCol James Taul	CO
Maj William P. Kaempfer	ExO (WIA 20 Feb)
Maj Donald K. Ellis	B-3 (WIA 20 Feb)
Capt Edward H. Birkenmeier, Jr.	B-3

3/25

LtCol Justice M. Chambers	CO (WIA 22 Feb)
Capt James C. Headley	CO
LtCol James Taul	ExO (To 20 Feb)
Capt James Antink	ExO
Maj Lawrence M. Rulison	B-3 WIA 19 Feb)
Capt Elwyn W. Woods	B-3 (After 12 Mar)

Fourteenth Marines

Col Louis O. De Haven	CO
LtCol Randall M. Victory	ExO
Maj Frederick J. Karch	R-3

1/14

Maj John B. Edgar, Jr.	CO
Maj Charles V. Watson	Exo
Capt Raymond Jenkins	B-3

2/14

Maj Clifford B. Drake	CO
Maj Donald E. Noll	ExO
Maj Ralph W. Boyer	B-3

3/14

LtCol Robert E. MacFarlane	CO (WIA 19 Feb)
Maj Harvey A. Feehan	CO (To 23 Feb)
LtCol Carl A. Youngdale	CO (To 10 Mar)
Maj Harvey A. Feehan	CO
Maj Harvey A. Feehan	ExO (To 19 Feb; from 28 Feb to 10 Mar)
1stLt Bernard J. Diggs	B-3

4/14

LtCol Carl A. Youngdale	CO (To 23 Feb)
Maj Roland J. Spritzen	CO (To 10 Mar)
LtCol Carl A. Youngdale	CO
Maj Roland J. Spritzen	ExO
Capt Russell F. Schoenbeck	B-3

4th Tank Bn

LtCol Richard K. Schmidt	CO
Maj Francis L. Orgain	ExO
Maj Leo B. Case	B-3

4th Eng Bn

LtCol Nelson K. Brown	CO
Maj Melvin D. Henderson	ExO
Maj Melvin D. Henderson	B-3

4th Pioneer Bn

LtCol Richard G. Ruby	CO
Maj John H. Partridge	ExO
Capt George A. Smith	B-3

4th Service Bn

LtCol John F. Fondahl	CO
Maj Henry P. Welton	ExO
1stLt James T. Willis	B-3

4th MT Bn

LtCol Ralph L. Schiesswohl	CO
Maj Michael J. Danneker	ExO

4th Medical Bn

Cmdr Reuben L. Sharp	CO
LCmdr Eugene G. McCarthy	ExO

5th Amph Trac Bn

Maj George L. Shead	CO
Capt William C. Stoll, Jr.	ExO
Capt William S. Clark	B-3

10th Amph Trac Bn

Maj Victor J. Croizat	CO
Maj Harry T. Marshall, Jr.	ExO
Capt George A. Vradenburg, Jr.	B-3

MAUI

The 4th MarDiv returned "home" to Camp Maui and a great welcome from the proud citizenry, who declared the division its own. After some rest and relaxation, not too much, the division began preparing for Operation Olympic, the planned invasion of Japan. The surrender of Japan saw the division still on Maui, and in the following month, September 1945, members began preparing for a return to the United States mainland. With its record of twenty-one months overseas, four invasions with sixty-three days of combat, and five months aboard ship, plus 17,722 total casualties, it had served the nation well.

5th Marine Division

On 21 January 1944 the 5th MarDiv was activated at Camp Pendleton, CA, with its first CG, BG Thomas E. Bourke, an artilleryman. He wasn't the only veteran Marine in the division. At least forty percent of its enlisted personnel and some officers were combat veterans, including paratroops and raiders. Many were survivors of wounds or diseases like malaria. But only one regimental commander, the 28th Marines' Col Harry B. (Harry the Horse) Liversedge, had combat experience.

Bourke was reassigned as ADC when on 4 February MG Keller E. Rockey, a veteran of the 4th Brigade in France, replaced him as CG. Col William A. Worton, another 4th Brigade survivor, became Chief of Staff. Worton came up with a list of officers he recommended for bringing the 5th MarDiv quickly into shape. They included such luminaries as Col Ray A. Robinson, another World War I veteran, for operations and training; Col Benjamin W. Gally, chief of personnel assignments, and his assistant, LtCol Thomas A. Wornham, plus Col John Beckett, who became D-1. Rockey was also lucky because the CMC released a number of bright younger officers at HQMC for duty with the division.

The 26th Marines was activated on 21 January 1944 at Camp Pendleton. Its main cadre for the regiment was the disbanded 1st Marine Parachute Regiment. The 26th Marines (Col Chester B. Graham) departed for the Pacific on 22 July 1944 and was assigned as reserve for the 1st Provisional Brigade then engaged on Guam. Not being required for service, the regiment was returned to Hawaii, where it disembarked on 31 July 1944. At Camp Tarawa the 26th was joined by the balance of the 5th MarDiv which was undergoing training with the Amphibious Training Command in the Pacific.

The 27th Marines (Col Thomas A. Wornham) was activated on 21 January 1944, also at Pendleton. The 28th Marines (LtCol Chandler W. Johnson) was activated on 8 February 1944, at Pendleton, as were the other division troops. LtCol Charles E. Shepard replaced Johnson on 11 February, and on that same day, Col Harry B. Liversedge replaced him, eventually taking the regiment to Iwo Jima.

On 21 January 1944 the 13th Marines (Artillery) was activated with Col James D. Waller in command. The 13th was the only formation of the division that had a history before its association with the 5th MarDiv. It was formed in 1918 at Quantico as an infantry regiment and its first CO was Col Smedley D. Butler, who took the regiment to France in October 1918. It was among the many regiments disbanded in 1919. Its World War II activation began with 2/13, formed on 16 October 1943 as a separate artillery regiment. But, along with the other battalions, it was reactivated on 10 January 1944 at Pendleton.

On 8 February General Rockey handed his regimental and battalion commanders their activation orders and to begin training at once. The first was the 28th and service troops, on the 8th of February. The 28th, which absorbed most of the veteran Marines of the Guadalcanal campaign, the 1st Parachute Regiment, moved to Tent Camp No. 1 in Las Pulgas Canyon. LtCol (later Col) Chester B. Graham assumed command of the 26th Marines, while Col Thomas A. Wornham took over the 27th Marines. Col James D. Waller was handed command of the 13th Marines, the division's artillery unit, while on 25 May the 16th Marines was split into the 5th Engineer Bn and the 5th Pioneer Bn. LtCol William Collins was made CO of the 5th Tank Bn.

The division's training at Pendleton ceased in the summer, and the 26th Marines, first to boat up, was sent out on 22 July from San Diego. Initially the regiment was assigned to reserve status during the Marianas campaign but, when everything seemed in order, it was then released for reassignment to Hawaii. The other regiments "saddled up" and headed directly for Camp Tarawa on the island of Hawaii. There, by 1 October, the division, back together, was in fairly good shape and preparing for something, they weren't quite sure what. Everyone had seen a map of an island that was shaped like a gourd; actually something like the continent of South America. By Christmas, the signs were obvious to everyone. They were going someplace very soon, but most if not all members of the division had no idea where.

By mid-January 1945 the division was on its way someplace. That someplace was also the target for the already bloodstained 3rd and 4th MarDivs. The men of the 5th, aboard the various ships, were preparing for D-day, the 19th of February. Some Marine humor was prevalent. One man is quoted as yelling, "Do you think I'm a coward? That I'm scared to go down that cargo net? Do you think I'm that kind of guy? You're goddamn right I am."

The island is 8 square miles in area, and 5½ miles long. That would be an out-of-the-ordinary unpleasant 8 square miles for the men of the three divisions. The 28th Marines were slated to land at the southern end, right below 556-foot Mount Suribachi; and then they were to move up and take it. The 27th Marines would land to their right and go directly across the island's southernmost narrow waist to the west coast and then drive northward. The 26th Marines would be held in reserve, but not for long.

Iwo Jima

Every Marine had been prepared for the worst. This island, though under constant bombardment by the U.S. Navy's big guns and air bombing for months, which should have depopulated the island completely, was still heavily defended and well fortified. Gun crews of the *North Carolina,* the *Washington,* the *New York,* and the *Texas*, plus two ancients, the *Arkansas* and a Pearl Harbor relic, the *Nevada,* added their voices to the din. They worked hard in trying to blow the island off the ocean, but they didn't succeed. On D-day, 19 February 1945, the Marines of the 4th and 5th MarDivs began their movement from ship to shore. The 26th Marines had been selected to remain aboard ship as Division reserve.

At H-hour, actually one minute before 0900, the first wave of the 27th Marines landed on Beach Red. At exactly H-hour men of 1/28 (LtCol Jackson B. Butterfield) raced onto Beach Green and began moving at a rapid pace for the west coast. It was just minutes before the Japanese recovered from the awful pasting the island had received and began firing upon the landing beaches. This was when the Marines learned that this was going to be the worst island they had yet landed upon. Every inch of the beach was sited and the enemy artillery didn't waste any shells; each scored numerous Marine casualties. The 5th and 4th MarDivs were moving as rapidly as they could, in the shifting volcanic sand, but to little avail. Being unable to move rapidly, they were taking terrible punishment (see map on page 124).

One of those that died on the beach that day was "Manila John" Basilone, the MoH man from Guadalcanal. He had been offered a soft berth back in the States but was tired of the quiet pace and asked to be given a machine gun platoon in combat instead. He got his wish.

Capt Dwayne "Bobo" Mears, a former 3d Raider man now skipper of Company B, 1/28, a huge man of great physical strength, caught a bullet in his back. It was a non-fatal wound, and when patched up, he was next hit in his jaw while he was in the process of attacking a pillbox singlehanded. Loss of blood caused him to be unable to talk or move. He was half buried in the sand by one of his men, but died later aboard ship, a recipient of a Navy Cross. To Mears' right, Capt Phil E. Roach, skipper of Company C, was wounded and earned a Silver Star.

Another man from 1/28, Company A's Cpl Tony Stein, of Dayton, OH, had personally improvised a machine gun stripped from a damaged Navy plane in Hawaii. He called it his "stinger" gun and with it he loosed a torrent of bullets to cover his company going into position. When his company was pinned down he leaped up, exposing himself to the enemy, and loosed another blast from the "stinger." Then, as his company moved forward he personally attacked several pillboxes, killing at least twenty Japanese soldiers. Needing ammo, he stripped off his shoes and jacket and ran back for more ammo, making eight trips in all. Later he directed the fire of a half-track, helping them destroy a pillbox. Then, when his company was forced to withdraw, he covered their retreat even though his "stinger" was shot out of his hands twice. Tony Stein died fighting and his mother was the recipient of a Medal of Honor awarded to him.

At 1035 1stLt Frank J. Wright, PFC Remo A. Bechelli, and PFC Lee H. Zuck, reached the opposite shore, effectively cutting Suribachi off from the rest of the island. Note the cross-section of American names in that small group. They, and their comrades from Company B, 1/28, had great difficulty keeping it. In fact, Wright lost four of his officers and many of his men, along the way. Wright later received a Navy Cross. The battalion was badly extended across the island with one flank in the air. It was in no position to help 2/28 (LtCol Chandler W. Johnson) with their job of taking the mountain. At 1245, 3/28 (LtCol Charles E. Shepard), released from its division reserve status, landed. Too soon they were also taking heavy losses.

LtCol William R. "Rip" Collins and his 5th Tank Battalion landed and began to advance while cleaning up by-passed positions behind 1/28. But almost as soon as they landed, five tanks crossed land mines and were knocked out just beyond the beach. Half-tracks with 75mm guns and Weasels with 37mm anti-tank guns were hit hard coming ashore and afterwards. One PFC, Hillery E. Windham, an ammo carrier, assumed command when a gun commander was wounded. Directing the piece into position across 200 yards inland, Windham then began firing into Suribachi, giving the men of 2/28 great support. He was awarded a Silver Star for leadership and courage.

At 1430, Division ADC, BG Leo D. Hermle, a hero of the 4th Brigade in France, was the first general officer ashore on Iwo. He brought ashore his ADC group as well as a headquarters reconnaissance party, and set up an advance Division command post. Still courageous, Hermle went forward to his front line units around Motoyama Airfield No. 1 just to see what was happening. Meanwhile, many wounded Marines were making their way back to the beaches, but there was no cover to protect them from enemy fire. The chaplains and doctors were doing their best, but being wounded wasn't any protection. Men died from the constant exposure to enemy fire and many were given the last rites on the beach as they waited for boats to take them off. Hermle decided that his men had already taken enough for that day and at 1700 issued orders for the divisions to "button up" for the night.

In the meantime, late that afternoon the 26th Marines were also called in. Upon arrival they faced worse attrition from enemy fire than either of the other two regiments. The Japanese had succeeded in intensifying the conflagration on the beach. Some elements of the 13th Marines (Col James D. Waller) managed to get ashore with their 75mm pack howitzers, plus a few 105mm howitzers, and moved into position. According to the records, Sgt Joe L. Pipes, commanding a 105mm howitzer, was the first artillery piece to land on Iwo and within minutes of arrival began firing upon Suribachi. As the other guns started firing they were soon on the receiving end of counter-battery fire and several of the guns were lost.

TAKING SURIBACHI

Suribachi was one gigantic observation post which served the Japanese well, until the 28th Marines began climbing upward and eliminating observation posts as they wiped out the well-dug-in defenders. It is the opinion of those in the know that the enemy never considered that the mountain could be taken. Its capacity for bringing down death and destruction was constant. The Japanese could see all over the island and a mere phone call to the artillery would plunge a shell crashing into the mass of targeted Marines. It could only be taken from the land side and that was where all the remaining heavy stuff was located. Unfortunately for the Japanese, the 28th Marines weren't privy to their philosophy. So, they went up the hill, fighting all the way.

One member of Company E, 1/28, PFC Donald J. Ruhl, from Columbus, MT, went after a blockhouse and killed all eight occupants, with his bayonet and by rifle fire. The next morning, under heavy mortar and machine gun fire, he moved out to rescue a wounded Marine. Dragging the casualty about forty yards under severe fire, he then got up, and running, he carried the wounded man 300 yards to an aid station on the beach. Returning to his platoon he at once volunteered to go forward and investigate an abandoned enemy gun position. He remained there all night to prevent the enemy from repossessing the weapon they left behind. The next morning he and his platoon guide worked their way to the top of a bunker to fire at the enemy on the far side. When a grenade was thrown between them Ruhl pulled it to himself, protecting his comrade. He was posthumously awarded a Medal of Honor.

On 20 February, LtCol Johnson and 2/28 were on the left. LtCol Shepard and 3/28 were in the center while Butterfield's well-worn 1/28 was on the far right. Before the Marines jumped off, once more the ships offshore and planes overhead bombarded the mountain. When the 28th headed forward they ran into a hailstorm of return fire. That slowed them down a bit. But, once again, up they went, burning out defenders, blasting with grenades and satchel charges those in caves or blockhouses, and engaging in hand-to-hand combat. Other Marines followed the leading companies and took out the by-passed hard spots. It was slow but was the only way to do it, and the 28th did it. The 28th Marines' exec, LtCol Robert H. Williams, a former paratrooper, obeyed Liversedge's command to establish the CP practically in the front lines. Williams then wisecracked that "it's a hell of a good way to make your battalions move faster."

Men of the 5th MarDiv dug in on the beach.

By night the bypassed enemy came out looking for Marines to kill. They utilized their bodies packed with grenades or demolition charges to explode amidst any group of Marines they could happen upon. Since it was generally a one-way trip, few of the Japanese ever made it back to their lines. They did manage to hurt a number of Marines that way. One platoon, led by 1stLt Harold H. Stirling, met one such group at dawn and slaughtered at least fifty Japanese, with the loss of two Marines killed and several wounded. There were many individual encounters. Private Leo Jez, a Marine from Chicago, caught an enemy officer's samurai sword in mid-air and tore it from his grasp. Jez then cut the man's head off. He almost lost a thumb and suffered a cut on his back, but made it back to an aid station with the sword. Plus, he received a Silver Star. One Marine was in the process of bayoneting a Japanese soldier in his rear as the latter ran. A BAR man caught the man before he was bayoneted to death. Marine witnesses laughed aloud at the incongruity or humor of the situation. Another situation which the Marines also found funny was when a Japanese soldier ran into a Marine mortar section yelling, "Cease firing." "Who the hell are you?" asked a Marine, and the enemy took off with bullets whizzing after him. When engineers placed a charge in a cave, a soldier walked out carrying the charge in his arms. They shot him and returned the charge to its rightful place.

Suribachi still hadn't been taken four days after the landing. The work of the 28th Marines, digging out the enemy, sealing up his caves and pillboxes, and killing them, was slow and painful. On 23 February the climb began in earnest. A four-man patrol from Company F, led by Sgt Sherman Watson, almost made it to the top. His comrades on the climb were PFC's Ted White, George Mercer and Louis Carlo. Another patrol of forty men was led by 1stLt Harold G. Schrier, from Company E. Up they went with a small flag which he had been instructed to place on top of the volcano. Schrier had gained fame as a Raider in a one-man recon in the Solomons. For this patrol he would receive a Navy Cross. Behind him was PltSgt Ernest I. Thomas and the rest of the patrol. They made their way to the very top without incident. Upon reaching it, they found a battery of heavy machine guns, with ammo stacked, but no enemy around anywhere.

As the flag was being implanted a Japanese soldier raced out of hiding and made an effort to hurl a grenade. He was soon destroyed and most of the patrol went down into the crater to attend to other enemy soldiers down there. This was the first flag planted on top of Suribachi, and a cheer went up from the Marines down below. That raising was photographed by SSgt Lou Lowry, who went with the patrol and had exposed himself to danger numerous times past. However, as most of us know, a few hours later another and much larger flag was purposely sent up with a crew of men to install it. That was the subject of a most famous photograph which has generally thrilled Americans ever since. Nearly everyone has forgotten the first picture, except the men that planted the first flag.

At this point, with the taking of Suribachi, many of the members of the 28th Marines assumed, or wished, their job was finished. It wasn't. Three days after the foregoing events, the regiment was back in the war.

THE REST OF THE ISLAND

On 20 February a very young Marine much like Johnny Kelly from the 6th Marines back in 1918 France, and trouble for everyone, especially the Japanese, went big-time. He was Pvt Jaclyn H. Lucas, from Bellhaven, NC, and he was a member of 1/26. He was technically a deserter who had joined the unit when he stowed away aboard ship. Four days before the landing he turned seventeen. On D-day plus one, Lucas and three other men were moving up a ravine when they were ambushed by a Japanese patrol. Grenades were thrown and Lucas grabbed one, pulling it under him. He saved the lives of his comrades, survived somehow, and was awarded a Medal of Honor, the youngest Marine ever to be so honored.

Even with 1/26 (LtCol Daniel C. Pollock) attached, the fighting going north was tough for the 27th Marines. They advanced in a two-battalion formation, 3/27 led by LtCol Donn J. Robertson on the right and 1/26 on the left. Robertson would earn a Navy Cross for these first few days on the island. His battalion ran into stout resistance, finding upwards of 135 pillboxes in their sector. Both battalions, however, with tanks from the 5th Tank Bn, moved ahead and together overran the Motoyama Airfield No. 1. One of the first groups to cross the airfield was Capt John K. Hogan's company, known far and wide as "Hogan's Goats." A platoon of tanks from Company A (1stLt John J. Stemkoski, Silver Star) probed deep, at least 1,000 yards up the beach. There they quickly silenced numerous machine guns and an ammunition dump, inflicting much harm on the Japanese.

One thing that the troops had been finding were mounds of sand with phony fire ports. These appeared in photos as real pillboxes and had received much attention from artillery and naval gunfire. The Marines also found numerous dummy tanks, most constructed of wood, all of which had also drawn extensive shellfire. But the men also ran into genuine

Unloading supplies on the beach for the 5th Marine Division.

massive artillery, machine gun, and small arms concentrations, including depressed AA guns firing air-burst shells. It was sufficient to slow down any advance.

Another man with 1/26, the skipper of Company C, Capt Robert H. Dunlap of Galesburg, IL, fought his company hard. Nothing seemed to slow them down. A key terrain feature facing the western beaches was a steep, cave-pocked cliff out of which poured a stream of accurate fire. At the face of this cliff, from which the enemy was pouring down death and destruction, Dunlap led Company C upward. After moving them up as far as they could physically go, Dunlap decided to leave his force and personally moved ahead another 200 yards. There he observed what the enemy was doing, and also located their gun positions. With that data he returned to his own lines and relayed the information gained to supporting artillery. They in turn passed the coordinates to naval gunfire. Placing himself in an exposed vantage point where he could observe the results, and working without respite for two days and two nights, he skillfully directed the bombardment. His courageous effort was a primary reason that Dunlap became a recipient of the Medal of Honor.

The 27th Marines had swamped the Japanese in the so-called battle of the "Boat Basin," where the enemy's primary water supply was located, and they had also pushed past Airfield No. 1. But eventually they ran into one of the most important defensive positions on the island, Hill 362. Basically, the enemy's defensive lines ran across the island from there to Hill 382, where the 4th MarDiv would be so badly bloodied. By this time, the enemy was well aware of what punishment they could expect from the heavy artillery and naval gunfire each day. VAC headquarters had a pattern which remained the same: each morning at 0800 Marine artillery and naval gunfire laid down a barrage into the enemy lines which lasted until 0830. By the clock, the enemy then came out of their deepest blockhouses and dugouts to re-occupy their defensive positions and waited for the unfortified Marines to once again assault them. It never failed, and it never changed.

By D-day + 7 (26 February), and after suffering heavy casualties, the 26th Marines had managed a day's rest before going back into action. The 3d MarDiv had been having a difficult time in their sector. They had not yet taken the bluff to their left, the one which made the advance of the 26th Marines nearly impossible. On 27 February, GySgt William G. Walsh, a native of Roxbury, MA, led an assault platoon from Company G, 3/27th, against the enemy stronghold. Up they went and though driven back, up again he went. The fire from the enemy made any advance seemingly impossible, but Walsh went and his men followed. Their losses were horrendous but they followed their sergeant. They finally made it to the top and into a hole they went, the few survivors. Just then a grenade was tossed in and Walsh absorbed the terrific blast, saving his few remaining men. His posthumous award was a Medal of Honor. The 27th Marines, badly hurt but not yet out of the game, were relieved by the 28th Marines after their resounding victory at Suribachi. They would find the going up Hill 326 much more difficult than even the former.

Tactics as outlined by VAC didn't change. It was still a general advance straight against the well-dug-in enemy. Consequently, casualties among the Marines of all three divisions continued to mount. Hill 362, with all its caves and pillboxes, in twisted terrain, was just as bad as Suribachi, which the 28th learned to their regret. Each seemed to have many entrances and probably each could have held a battalion. As efforts were made to seal an opening, the Japanese continued to come out of others and fire at those attempting to close one. Digging them out was a never-ending job, and costly in manpower. While trying to cross open ground in front of a cave, Company F of 2/28, Capt Arthur H. Naylor, Jr. CO (Silver Star on 21 February), lost ninety-four men in an hour. Naylor set up his CP only 25 yards from the opening and established a 24-hour guard at the mouth. However, that didn't trouble the Japanese. They hurled grenades directly into Naylor's CP.

The worst times were when the Marines advanced and as they pushed ahead the enemy came out of their digs, fired upon them and threw grenades from behind. Launched from trucks, hundreds of rockets were rained on the reverse of each slope, which happened to be just as well-fortified as the forward slope. Finally, on 1 March 1945 (D-day plus 10), the 5th MarDiv took Hill 362. Paying the bill included the loss of LtCol Tom M. Trotti, 3/26, killed in action by a mortar burst on 22 February; and LtCol Chandler W. Johnson, 2/28, killed in action on 2 March as he was returning to his CP from a forward observation post. Johnson was awarded a Navy Cross for his exploits during the period from 19 February until his death.

On 3 March two Marines, one from Lorain, OH, and the other from Quincey, MA, absorbed grenades to save the lives of their fellows. The former was machine gunner Charles J. Berry of 1/26, who had been engaged in a hand grenade duel during a night attack. The second was PFC William R. Caddy, a rifleman with Company I, 3/26. Both were posthumous recipients of the Medal of Honor. Many Marines died taking grenades, giving up their lives for their fellow Marines during the war. That same day another Marine, Sgt William G. Harrell, of 1/28, a native of Rio Grande City, TX, got even for loads of Marines. He was standing watch when, near dawn, the enemy tried to infiltrate the defense around the CP. He quickly put paid to two of them and, seemingly unmindful of the danger he was in, Harrell waged a knock-down-and-drag-out lone battle until a grenade blast tore off his left hand and fractured his thigh. Another Japanese wounded him with a saber but Harrell finished him with his pistol. Though bleeding fiercely he saw to it that a wounded comrade fell back while he maintained covering fire. Two more enemy soldiers rushed upon him, one holding a grenade to his head. Killing that man, he grabbed the grenade and blew up his second enemy while losing his right hand in the ensuing blast. He had, however, managed to kill a dozen of the enemy while fearlessly holding on to his position defending the Command Post. Harrell was fitted with two claws and a Medal of Honor.

By the 6th of March, the ground action and terrain were such that the division's intelligence officer decided that the artillery of the 13th Marines was no longer effective, it being a "grunt's war." The Japanese had finally given up the center of the island and were now in residence at the northwest corner. This was even worse territory to fight over and the enemy made the Marines pay heavily for every inch of ground they gained. The condition of the division no longer allowed it to be a fighting unit. It was there and would stay because the situation required it, but it was no longer an effective fighting division.

Casualties were close to 100% in some units. So many officers and non-coms had become casualties that privates were leading in their stead. One company had had six different skippers since D-day. One first sergeant related later that he had landed with seventeen sergeants and none were left. A few hours later he too was evacuated, with a wounded leg. Cooks, bakers, candlestick makers, were now part of the infantry teams, as were company clerks, and because each was a Marine, he was also a rifleman.

A 2/27 Marine lieutenant, Platoon Leader Jack Lummus, from Ennie, TX, fought continuously for two days and nights. He was leading his platoon forward when they were suddenly halted by a terrific concentration of hostile fire. Lummus moved forward and was momentarily halted when a grenade exploded nearby. Back on his feet he went forward and took out one emplacement but was taken under fire by a second. Another grenade felled him, but even though he had several severe wounds he was once again back on his feet. In a one-man assault he took on the emplacement and killed off all the occupants.

Lummus managed to get back to his command and encouraged them to advance. While directing a nearby tank firing at another emplacement, Lummus then rushed a third heavily fortified position, again killing all the defending troops. Then he went back to leading his men against all the enemy within their sector, systematically eliminating all opposition. This time he stepped on a land mine and was himself fatally wounded. He was the posthumous recipient of a Medal of Honor.

Another Marine member of the 27th, PFC James D. LaBelle of Weapons Company, born in Columbia Heights, MN, was one more Marine that decided to hazard his life for several others. He and two other Marines were in a foxhole on 9 March when a grenade fell in upon them. LaBelle, without hesitation, dragged the grenade under him and saved the life of his comrades. For that he too was awarded a posthumous Medal of Honor.

This northwest pocket was nicknamed "Death Valley" by the Marines. The ratio of living and dead climbed rapidly, especially the dead to wounded. Because the Marines grabbed every bit of cover they could find, many caught the big one in the head. Consequently, Corpsmen had less to do since more Marines died than lived. The enemy was still dug in and waiting for the advancing Marine to come into his sights. At such close quarters, the heavy stuff, on both sides, was useless. No close air support, no heavy naval guns or even ground artillery was used. Even mortars were of little help.

Tanks moved up and fired directly into the cave mouths. Gasoline was dumped into the caves in an effort to burn the Japanese out. Rockets were fired directly into caves. Explosives were also tried. The best weapon was the flamethrowing tank, which burned the defenders and was the only successful weapon utilized. Still the enemy fought back, falling back and piling up Marine bodies as his were also being piled up.

The 27th Marines were in a bad way but Col Wornham managed to scrape together enough remaining men to form a provisional battalion. One of his men, PlSgt Joseph R. Julian, from Sturbridge, MA, was another one-man Marine expeditionary force. On 9 March Julian and his men faced a determined enemy effort to slow down and defeat his battalion's advance. The terrific mortar and machine gun barrage forced Julian to place his men in defensive positions, but he continued forward in a one-man assault. Against the nearest pillbox he hurled both phosphorus and regular grenades, killing two and driving the other five enemy out of the emplacement. Grabbing a discarded rifle, he quickly took those five out.

Obtaining more explosives, with another Marine, he went forward and took out two more emplacements. Then, unassisted, he took a bazooka and, firing four rounds, ended the last remaining pillbox. He was, however, mortally wounded by a burst of enemy fire. His courageous and daring tactics eliminated many of the enemy and made Julian another posthumous recipient of a Medal of Honor.

The fighting continued. The gorge before them was littered with enemy caves and dead bodies of Marines and their foe. The audacity and especially bravery of men on both sides was exemplary or discouraging, depending upon one's point of view. Out of the two hundred plus men of one Marine company, only one hundred remained after attempts to take the gorge. As one captain said, "It was easier to go into the gorge than climb out." The enemy targets were the wounded Marines. Whenever anyone tried to save one, he and the potential savior were usually hit numerous times.

The fighting went on. On 14 March two more Marines earned the highest honor their nation could bestow. One, Pvt George Phillips of Rich Hill, MO, a member of 2/28, courageously pulled an enemy grenade to himself to save the lives of his comrades. Another, Pvt Franklin E. Sigler, born in Little Falls, NJ, now of 2/26, voluntarily took command of his rifle squad when his leader became a casualty. He fearlessly led them against an enemy machine gun emplacement that had managed to hold up his company for several days. Arriving first, he managed to throw numerous grenades, personally annihilating the entire crew. From the heights above, many more Japanese guns opened up on him and his men. He courageously scaled the heights, surprising the enemy with his one-man assault. Though severely wounded, he crawled back to his squad and continued to direct their operations. His wounds notwithstanding, Sigler went out to drag in wounded Marines, carrying in three. It wasn't until he was ordered to the rear for medical attention that he gave that up. His was a hard-earned award of a Medal of Honor.

It wasn't until 26 March that the final battle for Iwo Jima was fought. On that morning a last charge by the Japanese ended their possession of the island. It also led to the final Medal of Honor awarded during the campaign for the 5th MarDiv. Most of the Japanese were members of the medical corps; one was a doctor (dedicated to saving lives), others were medicos. Many carried M-1's or grenades taken from dead Marines. The 5th Pioneer

Wounded Marine of 2/26 being helped to the rear by a buddy.

Battalion, led by Maj Robert Riddell, had a big hand in stopping this last desperate sortie. Their casualties numbered nine dead and forty wounded.

One outstanding individual from that group, 1stLt Harry L. Martin, from Bucyrus, OH, instantly organized a firing line and succeeded in repulsing an attack upon his small group. Realizing the depth of penetration of their lines, and the numbers of Marines surrounded, Martin defied the intense fire to work his way through the enemy. Sustaining two severe wounds, he continued, dropping numerous Japanese as he made his way forward. Arriving at where his men were surrounded, he directed them back to their lines. Meanwhile a few of the enemy had taken possession of a machine gun, which Martin, with just his pistol, charged and killed all the occupants. Realizing that his men were the main target and that they could no longer resist a major assault he called to his men to follow him. They charged into the strong enemy formation with Martin leading and he fearlessly killed as many as he could before he was felled by a grenade. His posthumous award was the Medal of Honor.

Essentially, the fighting on Iwo had ceased, though over the next few months scores of individuals and a few groups of Japanese would attack Americans and be killed in so doing. In the meantime, the Air Force had already landed and established a repair base for returning damaged B-29s, of which at least forty had been saved. The cost to the 5th Mar-Div was severe. Nearly 2,500 5th MarDiv or attached Marines were buried on the island and another 6,218 had been wounded, with most removed offshore.

Order of Battle
Iwo Jima
(19 February to 26 March 1945)

Headquarters

MG Keller F. Rockey	CG
BG Leo D. Hermle	ADC
Col Ray A. Robinson	CoS
Col John W. Beckett	D-1
LtCol George A. Roll	D-2
Col James F. Shaw, Jr.	D-3
Col Earl S. Piper	D-4
LtCol Frederick H. Dowsett	D-5
Maj John Ayrault, Jr.	CO Hdqs Bn

Twenty-sixth Marines

Col Chester B. Graham	CO
Col Lester S. Hamel	ExO
LtCol William K. Davenport, Jr.	R-3

1/26

LtCol Daniel C. Pollock	CO (WIA 19 Mar)
Maj Albert V. K. Gary	CO
Maj Albert V. K. Gary	ExO (To 19 Mar)
Capt Aram S. Rejebian	B-3

2/26

LtCol Joseph P. Sayers	CO (WIA 23 Feb)
Maj Amedeo Rea	CO
Maj Amedeo Rea	ExO (To 23 Feb)
Capt Thomas M. Fields	ExO
1stLt Royer G. Warren	B-3 (WIA 26 Feb)
2dLt William M. Adams, Jr.	B-3

3/26

LtCol Tom M. Trotti	CO (KIA 22 Feb)
Capt Richard M. Cook	CO (On 22 Feb)
Maj Richard Fagan	CO (From 23 Feb)
Maj George F. Waters, Jr.	ExO (WIA 20 Feb)
Maj Chester E. Bennett	ExO (From 6 Mar)
Maj William R. Day	B-3 (KIA 22 Feb)
Capt Conrad A. Pearson	B-3

Twenty-seventh Marines

Col Thomas A. Wornham	CO
Col Louis C. Plain	ExO (WIA 19 Feb)
LtCol James P. Berkeley	ExO
LtCol Justin G. Duryea	R-3 (To 5 Mar)
Capt Franklin L. Smith	R-3

1/27

LtCol John A. Butler	CO (KIA 5 Mar)
LtCol Justin C. Duryea	CO (WIA 9 Mar)
Maj William H. Tumbelston	CO (WIA 14 Mar)
Maj William H. Tumbelston	ExO (To 9 Mar)
Maj William H. Kennedy, Jr.	ExO (To 14 Mar)
Maj Ronald F. Adams	ExO
Capt Thomas R. Shepard	B-3 (WIA 14 Mar)

2/27

Maj John W. Antonelli	CO (WIA 9 Mar)
Maj Gerald F. Russell	CO
Maj Gerald F. Russell	CO (To 9 Mar)
Maj C. J. Chandler, Jr.	B-3

3/27

LtCol Donn J. Robertson	CO
Maj Frederick J. Mix, Jr.	ExO
Maj William H. Kennedy, Jr.	B-3 (To 9 Mar)
Maj Frederick J. Mix, Jr.	B-3

Twenty-eighth Marines

Col Harry B. Liversedge	CO
LtCol Robert H. Williams	ExO
Maj Oscar F. Peatross	R-3 (To 14 Mar)
LtCol Charles F. Shepard, Jr.	R-3 (To 25 Mar)

1/28

LtCol Jackson B. Butterfield	CO
Maj William A. Wood	ExO
1stLt William R. Henderson	B-3

2/28

LtCol Chandler W. Johnson	CO (KIA 2 Mar)
Maj Thomas B. Pearce, Jr.	CO
Maj Thomas B. Pearce, Jr.	ExO (To 2 Mar)
Maj James H. Finch	ExO
Capt Martin W. Reinemann	B-3

3/28

LtCol Charles E. Shepard, Jr.	CO (To 14 Mar)
Maj Tolson A. Smoak	CO (To 25 Mar)
LtCol Charles E. Shepard, Jr.	CO
Maj Tolson A. Smoak	ExO (To 14 Mar)
Maj Oscar P. Peatross	ExO (To 25 Mar)
Maj Tolson A. Smoak	ExO
Capt Robert N. Spangler	B-3

Thirteenth Marines			*5th Engineer Bn*	
Col James D. Waller	CO		LtCol Clifford H. Shuey	CO
LtCol Kenyth A. Damke	ExO		Maj Herbert I. McCoy	ExO
LtCol Jack Tabor	B-3		Capt Richard S. MacLaury	B-3

1/13			*5th Pioneer Bn*	
LtCol John S. Oldfield	CO		Maj Robert S. Riddell	CO
Maj Edward O. Cerf	ExO		Maj Rupert C Henley	ExO
Maj James R. Crockett	B-3		Capt Harold A. Hayes, Jr.	B-3

2/13			*5th Service Bn*	
Maj Carl W. Hjerpe	CO		Maj Francis P. Daly	CO (KIA 22 Feb)
Maj Olin W. Jones, Jr.	ExO		Maj Gardelle Lewis	CO (From 26 Feb)
Maj George E. Moore	B-3		1stLt William A. Brokaw	Adjutant

3/13			*5th Motor Transport Bn*	
LtCol Henry T. Waller	CO		Maj Arthur F. Torgler, Jr.	CO
Maj William M. Miller	ExO		Capt Herbert E. Pierce	ExO
Maj Edwin N. Kittrell, Jr.	B-3		Capt William Montagna	B-3

4/13			*5th Medical Bn*	
Maj James F. Coady	CO		LCmdr William W. Ayres	CO
Maj William W. Mitchell	ExO		LCmdr John E. Gorman	ExO
Capt Jackson C. Turnacliff	B-3			

Service Troops[1]			*3d Amphibian Tractor Bn*	
Col Benjamin W. Gaily	CO		LtCol Sylvester L. Stephan	CO
LtCol Robert L. Cooper	ExO		Maj Erwin F. Wann, Jr.	ExO
			Maj George M. Foote	B-3

5th Tank Bn			*11th Amphibian Tractor Bn*	
LtCol William R. Collins	CO		LtCol Albert J. Roose	CO
Maj Gardelle Lewis	ExO (To 26 Feb)		Maj Robert W. Dyer	ExO
Maj John L. Frothingham	ExO		Capt Leopold Fiske	B-3
1stLt George C. Moore	B-3			

HAWAII

On 12 April the ships carrying division headquarters and the 28th Marines arrived at Hilo, and immediately began unloading. The Navy band played the Marines ashore, civilians honked their horns and the Red Cross distributed candy and cigarettes. They were "home." The Commandant, General Vandegrift, visited Camp Tarawa and thanked the division for its collective heroics. Even girls showed up, as part of various entertainment shows and in local USO clubs. The men of the 5th MarDiv began to feel like they were at home.

Regardless, they were still Marines and the war was still ongoing. In early May the division was rewarded with their next assignment, a landing on the Chusan Archipelago on the China coast. But by the end of the month, that was cancelled and they were reapportioned to a landing on the coast of Japan. The division was to be attached to the Sixth Army, USA, then based in the Philippines. In the meantime they went directly to what Marines always go to: training. However, the members of the division did receive awards for heroics on Iwo. Ninety-four members were awarded the Navy Cross, 39 of them posthumously; three hundred thirty-seven the Silver Star; 79 posthumously. Fourteen were awarded the Medal of Honor, 10 posthumously.

---

[1]*The Service Troops command controlled and coordinated the activities of the following units of the 5th Division: Hdqs Co, Hdqs Bn; Recon Co; Sig Co; MP Co; 5th Serv Bn; 5th MT Bn; 5th Tk Bn; 5th Engr Bn; 5th Pion Bn; and 5th Med Bn.*

The war was over before the division was forced into making a second assault landing. Twelve days after the signing of the peace treaty, the 5th MarDiv loaded up, and on 22 September they arrived off the coast of Kyushu. After a reconnaissance mission the ships headed into Sasebo's harbor and the passengers got a first look at what had happened to Japan: destruction galore everywhere. Ships were listing, if afloat; three of them were aircraft carriers, all in bad shape.

The first unit to climb down the nets was Col Chester B. Graham's 26th Marines. The ADC, BG Ray Robinson, had gone ashore with his staff to make housing arrangements. The 27th Marines debarked in the Navy Yard, while 1/13 went ashore to provide any artillery fire, if necessary. It was a city of 200,000 and it was nearly dead. No one attempted to interfere with the landing; it went well.

The occupation by the 5th MarDiv lasted until early December. In the interim many high-point men were already on their way to the States. Relieved of their occupation duties, the transporting of the division began. From the 20th of December, every day of the month, and during January 1946, ships arrived at San Diego and unloaded their human cargo. By then 500 officers and 11,000 men had been discharged from active duty. That same month the 13th and 27th Marines had been disbanded, the division CG, now BG Robinson, had been detached, and Col Liversedge was his replacement. The rear elements of the division arrived in mid-January, and after disbanding the active units, on 5 February 1946, the 5th Marine Division passed into history. And what a history it had produced in its short life.

6th Marine Division

Officially activated in September 1944 on Guadalcanal, the 6th MarDiv was, at least to the Japanese intelligence, "a fresh unit. Among the badly mauled enemy it is a tiger's cub and their morale is high." As a division, that was a correct estimate; it was the last Marine division organized. However, most of the infantry units were composed from veterans of the Pacific war. It was the only division almost completely organized around battle-tested units.

The 4th Marines, a resurrected regimental number from the unit surrendered at Corregidor, was created almost exclusively from disbanded Raider units. They were the 1st Raiders, which had served at Tulagi and Guadalcanal; the 2d, which served at Makin and on Guadalcanal; the 3d, at New Georgia and Bougainville; and finally the 4th, also on New Georgia. Gathered into what became the 4th Marine Raider Regiment, LtCol Alan Shapley, the four units ultimately became the 4th Marines. And the 22d Marines had already been engaged at Eniwetok in the Marshalls. One battalion of the 29th Marines was under fire at Mt. Tapotchau on Saipan. The 15th Artillery, as well as all subordinate units bearing the numeral "6," was composed of veterans, like the Raiders, who had served elsewhere. It was almost entirely composed of veteran Marines.

"The Old 4th" goes back to its original organization at Camp Thomas, CA, in March 1911, Col Charles A. Doyen in command. Its history really began with the intervention at Vera Cruz in 1914, and the intervention in Santo Domingo in June 1916. During the latter period, Col Joseph "Uncle Joe" Pendleton successfully commanded until December 1916. The 4th remained on duty on that island until Col Alexander S. Williams eventually brought the regiment back to San Diego in August 1924. Its next duty overseas was in China with the 3d Brigade under BG Smedley Darlington Butler in February 1927. That was the beginning of a 14-year-long involvement in Shanghai. In late November 1941 the 4th was pulled out of Shanghai and shipped to Cavite in the Philippines. Afterwards, when the war commenced, they were sent to Bataan and later to Corregidor, where the Army commander surrendered all U.S. and Filipino forces in May 1942. With a minimal chance to fight, by circumstances, the regiment was given little chance to make its mark. However, in February 1944, on Guadalcanal, the number was assigned to a new gathering of Marines, led by Col Shapley. In March the regiment landed on Emirau, with an important air base awaiting them. By mid-April they returned to the "canal."

The 22d Marines also had a history. It was the first independent regiment founded after the war began, at Linda Vista, a tent camp near San Diego, CA, in early 1942. Colonel John T. Walker was its first CO. Approximately one third of the regiment was formed from remnants of the 6th Marines recently returned from Iceland. In June 1942 the 22d was shipped to Samoa for garrison duty. While there, they were scattered around the islands, and it wasn't until 1 November 1943 that the regiment was pulled together at Maui in Hawaii under orders to prepare for action. Assigned to the 4th MarDiv, its first action was at Eniwetok Atoll in the Marshalls, where it was assigned the task of taking Parry Island and assisting in taking Engebi, both in the atoll.

MARSHALL ISLANDS

On the night of 19–20 February, Corporal Anthony P. Damato, born in Shenandoah, PA, landed on Engebi with 2/22. Damato pounced upon a grenade that landed in a hole he occupied with two other Marines. He earned a posthumous Medal of Honor.

Parry, lying just north of Eniwetok Island, was important for the 4,000-foot runway the Japanese had built on it. After a devastating bombardment, and the surprise landing which drove the Japanese underground, the 22nd landed. Two battalions, 1/22 and 2/22, landed abreast on the northern shores of the island on 18 February 1944. They were closely supported by 3/22, which arrived at noon. The ground was covered with heavy undergrowth which made viewing the enemy nearly impossible. The fighting was especially bitter in so congested a location and it took nearly two days to complete the conquest of Parry. The regiment's losses were severe for the limited period: 184 killed and 540 wounded. The enemy's losses were nearly 2,000 dead. The 22d completed its task by taking numerous small islands within the atoll, many of which had small detachments of Japanese, all of whom had to be destroyed.

In April the regiment arrived at Guadalcanal, where they joined the 4th Marines. They were formed into the 1st Provisional Brigade, commanded by BG Lemuel Shepherd, Jr. The Brigade served notably at Guam under the overall direction of MG Roy S. Geiger, CG, IIIMAC. Their task was to support the main landing by the 3dMarDiv on the northern shores by taking the southern part of the island. The Brigade landed on Yellow and White Beaches, just south of Agat, while the 77th InfDiv (MG Andrew D. Bruce) was held in reserve. However, one RCT, the 305th, was assigned to directly support the 1st Provisional Brigade.

GUAM

The 22d Marines (Col Merlin F. Schneider, awarded a Navy Cross for Guam) were on the left and the 4th Marines (LtCol Alan Shapley, awarded a Navy Cross for Guam) on the right, with the latter's right at Bangi Point. Plans were for the amtracs to bring the troops in as far as 1,000 yards beyond the beach. However, the enemy artillery and mining on the beaches precluded success in that endeavor. Many of the vehicles were destroyed with their crews and passengers, while moving toward the beaches. Too many, in fact. When later in the day it became necessary to move in supplies, the seagoing carriers weren't available. By the end of the day, the Brigade had pushed in 2,000 yards and established a front 4,500 yards long.

Japanese defenses had been well prepared, especially at and about Agat in the north. The 22d Marines were badly battered by mortar and artillery fire around Agat as they made efforts to expand the beachhead northward. Fighting was desperate but the Marines managed to drive most of the enemy out of the gutted town of Agat and were at the northern edge of the town by nightfall. In the southeast, Shapley's 4th Marines, with a strong tank force in support, worked their way toward Mt. Alifan. That night several times the enemy attacked the 4th Marines, but without major success. One platoon of Maj Bernard "Barney" W. Green's (Silver Star, Guam) 1/4 suffered heavily and was forced to withdraw from Hill 40. At 0230 the next morning a more serious Japanese attack was launched by tanks and trucks mounted with guns at the point near where the 4th and 22d Marines' flanks joined. A few were knocked out by bazooka men, which gave several Sherman tanks time to get to the scene. They caught the enemy tanks coming down Harmon Road in a column and destroyed all before they could maneuver. Another major attack began at 0400 against LtCol Hamilton M. Hoyler's (Silver Star Guam) 3/4. Some Japanese managed to get through the Marines, who were now low on ammo, and infiltrate the pack howitzers' positions.

In mid-afternoon of 22 February, BG Shepherd requested the 305th RCT, 77th InfDiv, to come ashore. The first elements, 2/305, arrived late afternoon, and more later that day and early evening. Upon arrival they went into support. On the north flank, the 22d Marines were entertained by the enemy that night. One infiltrating Japanese company managed to get close to the regimental CP before being discovered at dawn. Cooks and bakers and clerks grabbed their weapons and before the fight ended, three Japanese officers and 66 of the enemy soldiers lay dead within the Marine lines. At 0900, with the lines fairly stabilized, the 4th Marines resumed their advance up the heights of Alifan. Then they were all over it, blasting the enemy in their caves. By evening the mountain had been conquered with most of the enemy dead.

The 22d had reached the base of Orote, from Apaca Point east along the Old Agat Road. Before them lay two large rice paddies, and a rather narrow roadway to advance upon. Behind this bunched-up formation was the Hdqs of the 4th Marines, though that regiment's task was to cover the 22d's right flank when it advanced on the peninsula. The 77th InfDiv had landed and took over the majority of the already occupied territory which enabled the 1st Provisional Brigade to take the peninsula.

On 24 July the 22d Marines advanced toward the peninsula, with 1/22 (LtCol Walfried H. Fromhold, Silver Star, Engebi) in the lead. They were closely followed by 3/22 (LtCol Clair W. Shisler, Silver Star, Engebi) which spread to the right when the land opened up. LtCol Donn C. Hart, Silver Star, Engebi) and his men of 2/22 were in support. The ground was too narrow and heavily mined for tanks; therefore the grunts had to lead the way. *Banzai* attacks were commonplace. The Marines welcomed them. That allowed them to slaughter the enemy quickly. The regiment continued its advance that day up the peninsula while the 4th Marines covered their right flank.

Positions changed on 25 July when the 4th Marines occupied a narrow left flank while the 22d took the right as they continued to advance. That night, a few minutes before midnight, 3/22 absorbed the largest night attack. They were, however, supported by artillery and tanks. The shelling began dropping fragmentation shells on the closely assembled Japanese, and as one participant, 1stLt Paul J. Dunfey, a native of Lowell, MA, said: "Arms and legs flew like snowflakes … Japs ran amuck. They screamed in terror till they died." Shelling lasted until about 0300; afterward the Marines counted upwards of four hundred dead Japanese. Fruitless though their losses may have been, they still didn't consider giving up.

The enemy, however, gave up those tactics and instead began sniping the Marines as they advanced, causing grievous casualties. For the next few days the two Marine regiments continued their advance, taking the old Marine barracks on 28 July, followed by the village of Sumay. On 29 July they had taken all of the peninsula except for a small section on the narrow north coast. By 30 July the Marines had killed off all the enemy, except for the few wounded captives taken. The solid 77th, led by the very solid MG Andrew Bruce, had taken their place in line and forced their way north through the eastern part of the island, joining the venerable 3d MarDiv as it came down. The island of Guam, lost in the first few days of the war, had been retaken by the Americans. Elements of the 4th Marines began leaving Guam on 22 August, and by early September the entire 1st Provisional Brigade was on its way back "home" to Guadalcanal.

GUADALCANAL

What else does any Marine unit engage in when not in battle? Why, training, of course. This was formulated and managed by LtCol Victor "Brute" Krulak, now Division G-3. That, after a brief catching of breath, is what happened to the gathering of old units and new units on the "canal." In the meantime, now Major General Lemuel C. Shepherd, Jr., became the CG of the newly created 6th MarDiv and BG William T. Clement, his ADC, with Col John C. McQueen as CoS. Incoming units, besides the usual numeric "6" support groups, was the 29th Marines under Col Victor F. Bleasdale, a heroic veteran of the 6th Machine Gun Battalion, 4th Marine Brigade in France.

The 29th Marines had been activated at Camp Lejeune as a separate reinforced regiment on 1 May 1944 and assigned to the 6th MarDiv on 10 September 1944. Its 1st Battalion had been organized on Guadalcanal on the same date from cadres from the 2d MarDiv and had been attached to the 4th MarDiv until assigned to the 6th MarDiv. While with the 4th MarDiv on Saipan the regiment had been attached to the 8th Marines, 2d MarDiv. They had suffered severe casualties in the attack upon Mt. Tapochau, losing their regimental commander, LtCol Guy E. Tannyhill, in the process.

Training was especially hard on the 29th Marines. Its commanding officer, Bleasdale, was classified by a historian as having "what might be called a Calvinistic conception of education — that man being essentially evil did not want to learn by nature, but had to have the desire and knowledge beaten into him." Unfortunately, he wasn't the most popular officer in the Division.

The artillery regiment of the division, the 15th Marines, which had previously been attached to the 4th and 22d Marines, was commanded by Col Robert B. Luckey. Other units included the 6th Tank Bn (LtCol Robert L. Denig, Jr.), 6th Engineer Bn (Maj Paul F. Sackett), 6th Motor Transport Bn (LtCol Ernest H. Gould), 6th Pioneer Bn (LtCol Samuel R. Shaw), 6th Service Bn (LtCol George B. Bell), plus the 6th Medical Bn (Cmdr John S. Cowan).

Training continued. They learned street fighting, more jungle fighting, and even how to set up villages. The troops were not told where they were next going, though Formosa was one place seriously considered; others under consideration were the Chinese coast, or back to Wake Island, but none save the senior officers knew that it would be Okinawa. Okinawa was an island in the prefecture of Tokyo, so the Americans were coming close to the end, and of course to where the fighting would be most horrific.

Okinawa was an island of approximately 400,000 poor farmers living in thatch-roofed huts, with a very few wealthy inhabitants in stone houses with tile roofs. Agriculture was the main production, and poverty was prevalent. Most crop growing was in the southern portion of the island. The northern part was primarily mountainous, accessible over narrow trails on which vehicular traffic could not move. Although the Okinawans were natives of the island, the Japanese considered them natives of Japan. Undoubtedly, historically the natives stemmed from early Japanese settlers. Naha, located near the southern end of the island, was the major city but there were many villages dotting the countryside. Training in house-to-house fighting would be very helpful.

OKINAWA

The invasion of this island was a major undertaking. The Joint Chiefs assigned it to the Tenth U.S. Army, commanded by LG Simon B. Buckner, Jr., USA. His subordinate commander was MG Roy S. Geiger, USMC, CG, the IIIMAC, which included three Marine divisions, the 1st, 2d, and 6th. The 1st MarDiv was commanded by MG Pedro del Valle; the 2d MarDiv's CG was MG Thomas E. Watson, and the 6th MarDiv, MG Lemuel C. Shepherd, Jr. In actual fact, the 2d MarDiv would never have the opportunity to show their stuff on Okinawa. More later on that touchy subject.

The rest of the Tenth Army was made up primarily of the 7th InfDiv, 27th InfDiv, 77th InfDiv, 96th InfDiv, plus assorted support services. These would generally, but perhaps with one exception, be as good as the best U.S. Army divisions serving in the Pacific Theater; had they not been, the entire campaign would have been a failure.

April Fool's Day was selected as ICEBERG DAY. It wasn't only the main island that was a target. There were separate groups of smaller islands that had to be taken to assure success on the main island. Two of these groups were left to the venerable 77th InfDiv, so effective on Guam, and a group from Tenth Army, which included some Marine units. The 2d MarDiv was aboard ships, and would remain so, but would make a demonstration on the southeastern portion of the island on Minatoga Beaches on L-day.

The actual landing force on the west coast would include, from the north to south: the 6th MarDiv, which would overrun the Yontan Airfield and move northward. Next would be the 1st MarDiv, which would cross the island to take the Katchin Peninsula. The 7th InfDiv would take Kadena Field and move across the island. Finally, the 96th InfDiv would proceed across the island to the east coast. No one expected that these would be the easiest parts of the campaign on the island. What was generally not known was the main Japanese army was all located in the southern portion of the island, dug in and waiting to be attacked. Numbers credited to the enemy were at least 100,000, which included 67,000 troops of the Japanese army, nearly 9,000 navy personnel and 23,000-plus Okinawan militia types. The U.S. divisions, plus attached units, might total 22,000 each, or 132,000 in all, not including the 2d MarDiv, which never landed. Odds for a successful invasion and attacking force were predicted as three to one at best, or a minimum of 2.5 to one. 1.3 to 1 was expecting a disaster at best.

Shortly before dawn on 1 April 1945 the great and small naval guns, plus numerous aircraft from nearby carriers, blasted the island. The 2d MarDiv was going to make a feint off Minatoga beaches. The reply was swift and deadly. Flights of Japanese aircraft began dropping in on transports and warships. The transport *Hinsdale* and LST 884, with members of 3/2 aboard, were standing by when struck. Eight Marines were killed, eight missing, and 37 wounded. It was not a good sign for the forthcoming major landings up north on the west coast.

On 1 April 1945, Marines of the 6th MarDiv landing on Okinawa's northernmost beach from Higgins boats.

At 0630, troops in APAs transferred to landing craft and began moving shoreward, as did LCMs with tanks. Two battalions, 2d (LtCol Horatio L. Woodhouse, Jr.) and 3d (LtCol Malcolm "O" Donohoo), of the 22d Marines were landed at Green Beaches 1 and 2 with 1/22 (Maj Thomas J. Myers) in support, while 1/4 (Maj Bernard W. Green) and 3/4 (LtCol Bruno A. Hochmuth) of the 4th Marines were landed at Red Beaches 1, 2, and 3, with 2/4 (LtCol Reynolds H. Hayden) in Division reserve. Their first target was the Yontan Airfield and the numerous small villages lying north of it. The landing was relatively unhampered and tanks were among the earliest elements ashore. This lack of machine gun, mortar and artillery fire surprised everyone, but, for a change, it was extremely welcome.

The accelerated pace of the assault on the left flank, however, soon caused the 22d to become overextended. Because 2/22 was forced to move toward their left, their right soon split from 3/22. This caused Col Merlin F. Schneider to quickly call in the reserve, 1/22, from offshore. By 1000 the 22d had moved rapidly inland but its left flank was considered to be dangerously thin. Gen Shepherd requested that IIIMAC release a battalion of the 29th Marines for his use.

Meanwhile, the 4th Marines (Shapley) were moving forward, meeting minimum resistance, and soon tied up with the 7th Marines from the 1st MarDiv on their right. Before noon they had taken Yontan field and by 1300 they had crossed the field and secured their objective to the east of it. Nonetheless, in so doing, they managed to create a wide gap between them and the 22d Marines to their left. Rapid progress was the name of the game and both regiments took advantage of their potential, soon passing first day objectives and moving toward the next. Objectives which were granted three days were taken on day one.

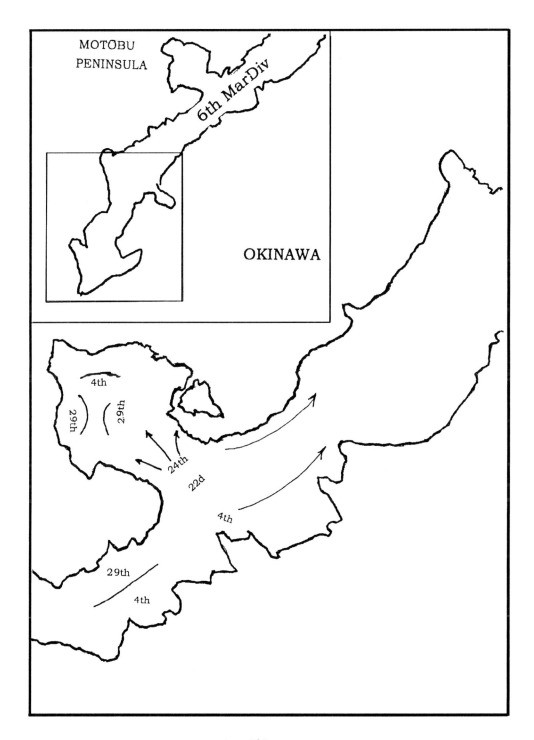

Okinawa

One Japanese aviator landed on Yontan, apparently not realizing that the Marines were in possession of the field. After he got out of the Zero he realized what he'd done and pulled his pistol from his holster. He was dead before he hit the ground. Equipment was being landed and the engineers were already building roads. By the evening of the first day, Col Bleasdale's 29th Marines, in Corps reserve, was already ashore and took up the division's left flank. Nevertheless, word was that the army divisions were having a tough time in the south, a harbinger of things to come.

The next day, 2 April, the division began the move northward. Except for occasional flourishes and combative isolated groups of enemy soldiers, the division was three days ahead of anticipated schedule. By 3 April the 22d and 4th Marines had crossed the mid-island watershed and worked down into the foothills on the opposite slope. Each regiment had met scattered elements of enemy soldiers but nothing substantial to hold them up.

On 4 April they reached the East China Sea and a point which planners had expected would take at least two weeks. They were now in a rolling grassy land with few trees and still running into scattered Japanese soldiers but nothing to hinder their forward motion. Within five days they were on the L plus 15 objective. IIIMAC was busy modifying plans to take advantage of this rapid forward movement. The 4th Marines were on the right going up the isthmus and the 22d on the left, with, until the 6th of April, the 29th in support.

On that date 3/29 (LtCol Erma A. Wright), accompanied by tanks, passed through the 22d Marines. The Division Reconnaissance Company (Maj Anthony Walker), with accompanying tanks, moved into Mobotu Peninsula and ran into what seemed like all the Japanese on Okinawa. The company had quite a few sharp actions and their reports indicated that this was probably where the 6th MarDiv could expect to find what they were looking for: the Japanese army. However, regardless of appearances, it was only a relatively small portion, though they would engage the Division for a few days.

Patrols from the 29th Marines were the first to enter the peninsula and managed to move in, and between 7 and 9 April ran into few of the enemy. The night of 9 April, 3/29's bivouac was hit by artillery and mortar fire, killing and injuring at least 10% the battalion. On 10 April Col Bleasdale sent out more patrols and found the enemy had retreated into numerous well-hidden caves. The next day, 11 April, Bleasdale's men had taken the wreck of the village of Manna, a mile northeast of the peninsula's dominating mountain peak, Yaetake, located near the southerly coast of Motobu. The enemy was well placed on the 700-foot rise and was engaged in shooting into Marine formations as they gathered around it. The 29th Marines tried several attempts to move up the height, to no avail. The enemy was too strong for anything but a massive and serious effort. Gen Shepherd decided he needed his tried and true 4th Marines to go up and take the mountain.

Shapley's men started up and soon ran into well-placed troops in the wild terrain and engaged in hand-to-hand fighting all the way up. The Japanese machine guns and mortars were efficiently situated and the Marines found themselves caught by their fire no matter where they were. The enemy was so fluid in their defense that they could fire, then withdraw. So well located were all the other guns that going after them in the brush was considered tantamount to self-sacrifice. As one Marine lieutenant told a Marine combat correspondent, "It was just one damned ambush after another."

Regardless of their losses, the 4th Marines and 3/29 continued on. Artillery support from the 15th Marines helped a great deal. They knocked out several artillery emplacements while the Marines were going on different trails in attempts to get behind obvious enemy locations. Col Victor F. Bleasdale was relieved of command of the 29th Marines on 14 April and was replaced by Col William J. Whaling. The latter, already with two Legion of Merit awards, would also be awarded a Navy Cross on Okinawa.

A scout from the 15th Marines, PFC Harold Gonsalves, a native of Alameda, CA,

Col Shapley's 4th Marines preparing to go up and take Mount Yaetake.

bravely faced the enemy artillery and machine guns to aid his Forward Observation Team to direct well-placed artillery fire. With an officer and another Marine, on 15 April Gonsalves went up again despite a slashing barrage of enemy mortar and rifle fire. As they reached the front, a grenade fell among them and Gonsalves dived on the deadly missile. He gave his life for his comrades, earning a posthumous Medal of Honor. Another loss that day was Maj Bernard W. Green, CO of 1/4, who was killed by a Japanese Nambu while he was in his observation post.

Caves were being sealed up with their occupants forever in residence. On 16 April, 1/4 (LtCol Fred D. Beans), supported by 3/29 (LtCol Erma A. Wright), finally made it to the hills surrounding Yaetake. The enemy had no new positions to fall back upon and the Marines got even for the punishment already taken. They used every weapon they owned, including BARs, and the Japanese were mowed down by the dozens. A native of Glasgow, KY, Corporal Richard E. Bush, a squad leader with 1/4, with indomitable courage rallied his men and led them forward through the slashing fury of the enemy's still formidable artillery and machine gun fire. He continued leading until seriously wounded. It was then that a grenade was tossed into the midst of his group. Without hesitation, Bush grabbed the live grenade and pulled it to him, absorbing the full blast with his own body. He managed to survive this terrible calamity and was awarded a Medal of Honor for his bravery.

Next day, the attack was resumed. In this final assault some Marine companies lost upwards of half their men. It was mainly hand-to-hand and, later, *Banzai* raids by the already disorganized Japanese. This latter mode of fighting was fine. That way the Marines could more easily kill off the Japanese while suffering fewer casualties themselves. The Japanese soldiers on Motobu died in the hundreds, making Mt. Yaetake a major grave site. As Col Shapley later said, "It was as difficult as I can conceive an operation to be. They had all the advantages of terrain ... an uphill fight all the way."

While the fighting on Motobu continued, 1/22 (Maj Thomas J. Myers, Navy Cross for Okinawa) and 3/22 had managed to continue the advance northward. In the meantime, LtCol Horatio C. Woodhouse and his 2/22, still relatively bloodless by 12 April, was way up ahead and took the farthest point on the island, Hedo Misaki. Nonetheless, it was still a fight until at least 28 April, when Marines caught the balance of Col Takehiko Udo's force, 123 men, and destroyed them near the village of Kawada, on the east coast. The northern end of Okinawa was considered secured.

The Division had a few days to catch their collective breath. The 1st MarDiv, which had been in Army Reserve and not involved in the drive south, except for the 11th Marines, was ordered on 4 May to the southern fighting line to replace the 27th InfDiv in line. The 11th Marines had been supporting the drive of the USA. In the 6th MarDiv everyone from Gen Shepherd to the line private knew the 6th MarDiv would be next.

While the 6th MarDiv was fighting in the north and taking the largest part of the island, the rest of the Tenth Army was fighting for its life. Gen Mitsuru Ushijima and his command had established a system of fortified cave defenses bordering both sides of the Asa Kawa River. Keystone of the Japanese defense was the ancient castle of Shuri, with caves running through each hill, with multiple openings, making it a veritable fortress. The Tenth Army's formation was as follows: on the east coast the 7th InfDiv; on its right the 96th InfDiv; followed on the extreme right along the western coast, the 27th InfDiv. On or about 18 April, Buckner replaced the 96th with the 77th InfDiv.

Between 6 and 15 April the three Army divisions had moved between 1,000 (on the east coast) and 1,500 yards forward, and by 30 April the entire line had advanced another 3,000 yards. It had been very slow going with numerous casualties. Buckner then ordered Gen Roy Geiger to assume command of IIIMAC, including the 1st and 6th MarDivs, and to bring the latter into line on the coast to flank the 1st MarDiv going south. That was accomplished by 7 May and there were now four divisions on line, two of which were Marines.

Shortly after dark on 9 May the engineers provided the 22d Marines with a footbridge across the Asa Kawa River. On 10 May, Company K, followed closely by Company I, of 3/22, started crossing the bridge. Company A of 1/22 began wading across the river and at 0530 two Japanese human "demolition charges" rushed the footbridge, destroying the south end. The engineers repaired the bridge and more suicide attacks blew up the repairs. The officers and men of the 22d, not to be hindered by the Asa Kawa inlet, pushed south, keeping pace with the 1st MarDiv. The major problem was trying to bring the wounded back across the damaged bridge.

While going south that day, the 22d Marines took very heavy losses trying to take Charlie Hill, located between the rivers Asa and Asato (see map on page 68). It fell to Capt Warren F. Lloyd's (Silver Star, Okinawa) Company C to take the hill. The enemy was so well entrenched in the limestone that though tanks were called up, they too were finding advancement near impossible. One platoon had seven men left of the original sixty-five, another had but twelve.

For Company C, the second day seemed worse. When the Marines killed Japanese soldiers in one cave opening they would draw fire from another. That went on all day, and they calculated their advance in inches. Regardless, at the end of the day, Company C clung

Discovering a Japanese grenade booby-trap on Motobu Peninsula.

to the ridge. Two men, Cpl Victor Goslin (Navy Cross) from Ashland, ME, and Pvt George Campbell of Philadelphia, held off a *Banzai* attack with grenades and rifle fire. In the morning the tanks came up once again, as did flamethrower tanks to pour in fire upon the inhabitants of pillboxes and tombs. The latter were used extensively by the Japanese soldiers on Okinawa. The assault upon Charlie Hill lasted most of the day and by the end of the day there was no more firing from it. The next morning Company C counted their losses: 35 killed and 68 wounded of the original 256. Examination of the terrain, especially the interior of the caves, spoke volumes. The whole area was a labyrinth of winding corridors, rooms of varied sizes, including those used as field hospitals, and many ammo dumps. The weapons were many and included field pieces mounted on railroad tracks run out of cave openings and, after firing, run back in.

Meanwhile 3/22 had been moving by the sea onto a ridge above the Asato River. From there they could look down upon the main city of Naha. Along the interior lines, the 4th Marines had been keeping pace with the 5th Marines, and in fact pushed ahead. The center of the U.S. advance was now a concave with the ends pushed ahead. The Americans were coming close to a town located quite close to Naha: Shuri, a place that would get much attention in the next few weeks. Part of the important Naha–Shuri–Yonaburu Line had been broken by the 22d Marines, and the enemy was well aware they would have to make a strong stand in the sloping hill northeast of Naha. The Marines named it "Sugar Loaf" for some reason, but taking it would be less than sweet. Arguably, this would be the site of the bloodiest of the Okinawa battles.

On the night of the 12th, LtCol Woodhouse ordered the CO of Company G, 1stLt Dale W. Bair, who earned a Navy Cross that night, Silver Star at Eniwetok, to take eleven tanks and assail the hill. The tanks went roaring up the hill and the Japanese, assuming this was a major attack, began to fall back. When they realized it was only company size they returned to their superb positions and the company was in rough territory. G was raked by a withering fire; Bair was wounded three times but continued the fight. Cradling a machine gun in his bleeding arms he tried to reach the crest but failed. The drivers of the amtracs, which came up to haul off the wounded Marines, were all dead. Only a heavy artillery barrage allowed G to free itself to withdraw.

Sugar Loaf was the apex of three hills in a triangle, and Woodhouse and his staff realized where the focal point was located. Their Marines had been driving between two hills and taking heavy fire from each. After they'd advised Gen Shepherd of their findings, the plans were changed from a frontal attack to a more strategic assault. On 14 May, Companies E and F worked all day upon the two outer hills, west and east of Sugar Loaf. Time after time each company was driven back, leaving dead and dying Marines on the slopes.

Between 14 and 17 May, a Marine Corporal from East St. Louis, IL, named James L. Day, fought a gallant battle against tremendous odds. He led his squad to a critical position forward of the front lines of Sugar Loaf amid intense mortar and artillery fire. They were quickly assailed by at least forty of the enemy. Day was outstanding during the fight, encouraging his men, hurling grenades, and directing his squad's deadly fire. Despite the loss of half his men he continued his fight and when reinforced by six men he then attacked the enemy. Faced with three sizable night assaults and the loss of five additional Marines, Day continued his valiant leadership and helped four wounded to safety in the rear, all while under intense enemy fire. Assisted by a wounded Marine, Day then held his position that night with a light machine gun, halting another attack. His weapon destroyed, and receiving personal wounds from phosphorous and fragmentation grenades, he managed to reorganize his position in time to halt a fifth attack. Three times the enemy closed upon him and yet he continued to kill them off. The following day the Japanese continued their numerous swarming attacks upon his exposed position. Seventy of the enemy were counted before his position. The following day, wounded and exhausted, he continued his defense and killed off at least thirty more of the enemy. It was considered, many years later, that Cpl Day had contributed greatly to the success of American arms on Okinawa. He was finally presented a Medal of Honor at the White House on 20 January 1998. By then Major General James L. Day had already been awarded a Navy Distinguished Service Medal (probably in Vietnam), three Silver Stars, one in Korea, two in Vietnam, and a Bronze Star with V.

Duluth, Minnesota's own Major Henry A. Courtney, Jr., Exec of 2/22, already wounded on 9 May, was now ordered to hold for the night in a static defense behind Sugar Loaf. He weighed the advantages of holding or counterattacking during the night of 14–15 May. Deciding for the latter, he received permission to begin. Courtney explained his plan to his remaining subordinates, then began a one-man attack up the slope, blasting caves with grenades, and neutralizing enemy machine guns as he went. His men got up and followed him. Soon, requiring more grenades, he waited for a LVT loaded with them and an additional 26 men. They started up again, and he led by example, up front. Throwing grenades into caves, blasting everyone in his way, he finally made the crest. There he came upon large numbers of Japanese forming up to attack. He and his followers went right for them, killing many and driving the balance into caves. He had his men dig in and then he began aiding the wounded. A mortar round blast caught him in the open, killing Courtney and ending his rush to glory. He was another posthumous recipient of the Medal of Honor. On the 15th, Maj Thomas J. Myers, CO of 1/22, and his runner, PFC Guido Conti, from Freeport, PA, died when a mortar round exploded in Myers' CP. Maj Earl J. Cook replaced Myers in command of the battalion.

One of Courtney's men, San Francisco's own Cpl Donald "Rusty" Golar, was another hero. In fact he was a self-proclaimed "Glory Hunter." His buddies added, "Keep your eye on that redhead." In the early hours of 15 May, Rusty gave the Marines something to watch. He had a "personal" light machine gun which he'd used effectively on Guam and now set up on this ridge for use on Sugar Loaf. He emptied his belts into the enemy and when they fired upon him from the flanking hill he switched to face the newcomers. Out of ammo, Rusty also found that only he and two other Marines of his group had survived and that ammo carriers coming up the hill had all been knocked off. He then began firing his pistol until it too ran dry. Golar then stood up and hurled his machine gun at the enemy. Next he gathered up all the grenades he could pry from the downed Marines and began hurling them at the enemy. The grenades ran out and he found a BAR. Up on his feet he began firing until that weapon jammed. Undaunted but now weaponless, Rusty got Don Kelly, one of the survivors, to help him carry some of the wounded. As Golar carried one man a sniper caught him. He carefully put his burden down and rolled over dead. His award for heroics was a Silver Star.

Private Harry (the Beast) Kizirian, from Providence, RI, earned a Navy Cross on Sugar Loaf. Three times wounded, but scorning evacuation, he continued to help other casualties down to safety. Then he led several rifle squads in assaults against Japanese strong points. With a BAR and later a machine gun, he personally eliminated three dozen of the enemy. The battle continued all night. The so-called Double Deuce (22d Marines) 2/22 had been at the forefront of the fight for Sugar Loaf. Eleven times they had gone up that hill and each time had been driven back. Their casualties numbered in the hundreds and the battalion was no longer in any shape to keep going. It wasn't just privates and corporals taking the deep six, any Marine up front was putting his life on the line, including battalion commanders.

After this great effort, 2/22 was relieved by elements of the 29th Marines and 3/22. The 22d's colonel, Merlin F. Schneider, was relieved in command of the 22d Marines by Col Harold C. Roberts (Legion of Merit, Guadalcanal). Roberts, while a Pharm Mate 3d Class, had served with the 5th Marines at Belleau Wood and was awarded a Navy Cross for bringing in wounded Marines on the night of 7 June 1918. LtCol Donohoo, CO, 3/22, was also wounded on 16 May. For the next several days the 29th tried and failed as had 2/22. Seven times the 29th went up the hill and seven times they were driven back, with heavy losses. On the 18th one more assault was launched and they finally made it. The enemy had been driven off Sugar Loaf and the wise-guy Marines were sarcastically calling for "PX Supplies" to be shipped up to them.

On the morning of the 19th, tanks were able to go over the saddle between Sugar Loaf and Half-Moon Hills and caught Japanese swarming out of their caves on the reverse slopes. Turning their guns on the exposed enemy, the tanks slew scores. The 29th Marines were relieved by the 4th Marines.

On the 20th of May the Japanese launched a counterattack in the vicinity of Crescent

Hill, southeast of Sugar Loaf. They ran into the tough 4th Marines, not a shattered 22d or 29th. They didn't make it. That night 500 or more Japanese, after a powerful artillery and mortar barrage, attempted to infiltrate the lines. Shapley called in counter-artillery, which kept more of the enemy from coming up. As the Aussies might say, the 4th Marines "gave 'em what for." In the morning nearly 500 bodies were counted lying before the lines of the 4th Marines. All-in-all, the Japanese had lost two infantry battalions (a third was torn apart), an antitank battalion, a service company and three hundred Japanese sailors, sometimes called Marines. Individual Marines performed outstanding deeds, with many dying in the process. The vaunted Naha–Shuri–Yonaburu Line, however, had been busted wide open.

By 22 May, the 4th and 22d Marines were sending patrols across the Asato River down into the outskirts of Naha. In the meantime there had been persistent rain for eight days and most roads on the island were now impassable. On 23 May there was an end to their waiting. Across the footbridges built across the Asato by the engineers went two battalions of the 4th Marines into Naha. From Shuri Heights came the Japanese, pushed by the 1st MarDiv, and furious fighting ensued in and around the city. Much of it was hand-to-hand. The 4th Marines took heavy casualties but they convinced the Japanese command to withdraw to a new defensive line beyond the Oroku Peninsula.

The fighting in and around Naha continued for days. During the course, many men were casualties, including such notables at LtCol Horatio C. Woodhouse, CO of 2/22, who was killed in action on 30 May. Meanwhile, the *Kamikazes*, both planes and suicide boats from Okinawa, were lambasting the offshore fleet, sending many into the deep or many more scattering away from the island. Those that supplied the Tenth Army would be sorely missed.

Though it was expected that the taking of Oroku would be bloody, the 6th MarDiv found, to its collective delight, that the Japanese decided not to defend it nor the airfield. On 4 June the landing was even better, almost, than that on L-day, 1 April 1945. By noon the airfield belonged to the 4th Marines. The rest of the five-day fight for the balance of the Peninsula was not easy. The 22d Marines crossed the Kokuba from the east, the 29th Marines pushed from the west and the 4th Marines from the south. Though the Japanese were in a box they fought an efficient and tenacious defense. Under each hill were numerous rooms, sometimes of three or even more floors, and each was home for hundreds of Japanese; six hundred were estimated in one such. Each had to be taken. Systematically, with the 15th Marines providing primary support, the 6th MarDiv went in and dug them out, eliminating the pocket.

On 7 June one Marine from Altoona, FL, Pvt Robert M. McTureous, Jr., a rifleman in 3/29, became a notable. He went to the aid of stretcher bearers caught in a slashing machine gun fire as they were attempting to evacuate wounded. Filling his pockets with grenades, he charged the cave openings from which the fire emanated. His furious one-man assault diverted most of the fire from the bearers to himself. Replenishing his stock of grenades, he dauntlessly returned several times to continue his work. While silencing a large number of the hostile guns he was badly wounded. Crawling over two hundred yards, he finally reached his own lines before receiving aid. He had effectively disorganized the enemy by neutralizing his fire, saving the lives of many Marines. His reward was a well-deserved Medal of Honor.

On 14 June, Oroku's end was near and the enemy fell to form. Huge numbers of Japa-

Heavy rains in May and June made equipment difficult to move for all Americans.

nese fell dead in many *Banzai* attacks. More died by their own hand when American inter-
preters tried talking them in. Nevertheless, a few Japanese did surrender, along with numerous Korean Labor troops. But this was only the end of part two of the fight for Okinawa.

For a few days the men of the 6th MarDiv had a chance to sleep and eat and write letters home telling their folks "I'm fine." But on 17 June the 6th MarDiv was on the move
once again. Elements were sent to relieve right flank units of the 1st MarDiv. Maj Earl J.
Cook, CO of 1/22, while leading his battalion on 18 June, was wounded. His replacement
was Weapons Company's CO, LtCol Gavin C. Humphrey. Col Roberts was killed while trying to get aid to a surrounded captain and his company. On the 19th the 4th Marines took
Kiyamu, and on the 22d, both the 4th and 29th Marines continued to mop up the remnants. By this date the Marines were actually taking in prisoners and their stockade of
POW's was soon loaded.

On 21 June the island was declared secured. After eighty-two days the Tenth Army
could finally look forward to a modest rest. The 6th MarDiv had managed, in its "very first
battle," to capture two-thirds of the land mass of the island; Naha, its capital city; and several airfields, and had eliminated about 20,000 enemy soldiers. However, great victories
do not fall into one's lap. The division paid a price: Over 8,200 casualties, of whom 1,700
were killed.

Order of Battle
Okinawa
(1 April to 22 June 1945)

Headquarters

MG Lemuel C. Shepherd, Jr.	CG (WIA 16 May *)
BG William T. Clement	ADC
Col John C. McQueen	CoS
Maj Addison B. Overstreet	G-1
LtCol Thomas B. Williams	G-2
LtCol Victor A. Krulak	G-3
LtCol August Larson	G-4 (To 16 May)
LtCol Wayne H. Adams	G-4

Headquarters Bn

LtCol Floyd A. Stephenson	CO
Maj Ralph W. Bohne	ExO
Maj Ralph W. Bohne	S-3
Capt Donald J. McCaffrey	CO Hdqs Co (To 5 Apr)
Maj John M. Downey	CO Hdqs Co
Maj Anthony Walker	CO Reconn Co (To 14 Jun)
1st Lt William J. Christie	CO Reconn Co
Capt Alfred C. Griffin	CO 6th ASCO Co
Maj John M. Downey	CO 6th MP Co (To 5 Apr)
Capt Donald J. McCaffrey	CO 6th MP Co
Maj George W. Carr	CO 6th Sig Co (To 4 Apr)
LtCol William C. Moore	CO 6th Sig Co
1stLt David Astor	CO 6th Amph Trk Co (To 30 May)
1stLt Murrel S. Hansen	CO 6th Amph Trk Co

Fourth Marines

Col Alan Shapley	CO
LtCol Fred D. Beans	ExO (To 14 Apr)
LtCol Fred D. Beans	ExO (From 1 May)
Maj Orville V. Bergren	S-3
Capt Robert B. Corey	CO H&S Co (To 26 Apr)
1stLt Russell A. Thompson	CO H&S Co
Capt Raymond L. Luckel	CO Wpns Co

1/4

Maj Bernard W. Green	CO (KIA 15 Apr)
LtCol Fred D. Beans	CO (To 1 May)
LtCol George B. Bell	CO (WIA 4 June *)
Maj Robert V. Allen	ExO
Capt Frank A. Kemp	S-3 (To 22 May)
Maj John R. Kerman	S-3
1stLt George Proechel, Jr.	CO Hdqs Co (To 5 Jun)
2dLt John M. Keeley	CO Hdqs Co
Capt Clinton B. Eastment	CO A Co (WIA 8 Jun)

1stLt David N. Schreiner	CO A Co (DOW 21 Jun)
1stLt Joseph I. Deal	CO A Co
1stLt Thad N. Dodds	CO B Co (KIA 2 Apr)
1stLt Charles E. James	CO B Co
1stLt James G. Washburn	CO C Co (WIA 15 Apr)
1stLt William H. Carlson	CO C Co (WIA 23 May, WIA 27 May & KIA 5 Jun)
1stLt Lawrence S. Bangser	CO C Co

2/4

LtCol Reynolds H. Hayden	CO (To 26 May)
Maj Edgar F. Carney, Jr.	CO
Maj Roy C. Batterton	ExO (WIA 15 Apr)
Maj Edgar F. Carney, Jr.	ExO (To 26 May)
Maj Lincoln N. Holdzcom	ExO
Maj Lincoln N. Holdzcom	S-3 (To 26 May)
Capt Wayne L. Edwards	S-3 (To 6 Jun)
1stLt James E. Brown	S-3 (To 19 Jun)
Capt Wayne L. Edwards	S-3
Maj Edgar F. Carney, Jr.	CO Hdqs Co (To 14 Apr)
2dLt Ernest L. Tongate, Jr.	CO Hdqs Co (To 7 May)
2dLt Gerald Fitzgerald	CO Hdqs Co (To 17 May)
Capt Wayne L. Edwards	CO Hdqs Co (To 26 May)
1stLt Merrill F. McLane	CO Hdqs Co
Capt Leonard W. Alford	CO E Co (To 24 May)
1stLt Robert J. Herwig	CO E Co (To 29 May)
Capt Leonard W. Alford	CO E Co (WIA 11 June, DOW 17 Jun)
1st Lt Robert J. Herwig	CO E Co (WIA 21 Jun)
1stLt Lester J. Markusen	CO E Co
Capt Eric S. Holmgrain	CO F Co
Capt Archie B. Norford	CO G Co (KIA 15 Apr)
1stLt Leo J. Gottsponer	CO G Co

3/4

LtCol Bruno A. Hochmuth	CO
Maj Thomas E. Beeman	ExO (To 16 Apr)
Maj Carl E. Conron, Jr.	ExO (KIA 20 May)
Maj Wilson B. Hunt	ExO
Maj Carl E. Conron, Jr.	S-3 (To 15 Apr)
Maj Rade Enich	S-3 (WIA 23 May)

Capt Martin J. Sexton	S-3 (From 1 to 14 Jun)
Maj Clay A. Bond	S-3
Capt Robert B. Corey	CO Hdqs Co (To 14 Jun)
Capt Robert G. McMaster	CO I Co (WIA 21 Jun)
Capt Martin J. Sexton	CO K Co (To 1 Jun)
Capt Vernon Burtman	CO K Co (To 13 Jun)
Capt Martin 3. Sexton	CO K Co (From 15 Jun)
Capt Nelson C. Dale, Jr.	CO L Co (WIA 2 Apr)
1stLt Marvin D. Perskie	CO L Co

Twenty-second Marines

Col Merlin F. Schneider	CO (To 16 May)
Col Harold C. Roberts	CO (KIA 18 Jun)
LtCol August Larson	CO
Col Karl K. Louther	ExO (To 16 May)
LtCol August Larson	ExO (To 17 Jun)
LtCol John B. Baker	ExO (To 20 Jun)
LtCol Samuel R. Shaw	ExO
LtCol John B. Baker	S-3 (To 17 Jun)
LtCol Walter H. Stephens	S-3 (To 20 Jun)
LtCol John B. Baker	S-3
Capt David B. Cruikshank	CO H&S Co
Maj George B. Kantner	CO Wpns Co (To 2 May)
LtCol Gavin C. Humphrey	CO Wpns Co (To 16 Jun)
Capt Francis D. Blizard, Jr.	CO Wpns Co

1/22

Maj Thomas J. Myers	CO (KIA 15 May)
Maj Earl J. Cook	CO (WIA 17 Jun)
LtCol Gavin C. Humphrey	CO
Maj Earl J. Cook	ExO (To 14 May)
Maj Edward G. Kurdziel	ExO (To 15 Jun)
Maj Norman R. Sherman	ExO
Maj Edward G. Kurdziel	S-3
Capt Charles P. DeLong	CO Hdqs Co (To 20 Apr)
Capt Eldon W. Autry	CO Hdqs Co (To 19 May)
Capt Alfred H. Benjamin	CO Hdqs Co
Capt Walter G. Moeling, III	CO A Co (WIA 15 May)
1stLt Thomas J. Bohannon	CO A Co (WIA 31 May)
1stLt Leland J. Gulligan	CO A Co (1 to 3 Jun)
2dLt Ralph R. Desso	CO A Co (WIA 9 Jun)
2dLt Robert T. Johnson	CO A Co (To 15 Jun)
1stLt Evan L. Wolcott	CO A Co
1stLt Ernest George	CO B Co (To 9 Apr)

1stLt Thomas Parran, Jr.	CO B Co (To 20 Apr)
Capt Charles P. DeLong	CO B Co (WIA 15 May)
1stLt Thomas Parran, Jr.	CO B Co
Capt Warren F. Lloyd	CO C Co (To 17 May)

2/22

LtCol Horatio C. Woodhouse, Jr.	CO (KIA 30 May)
LtCol John G. Johnson	CO
Maj Henry A. Courtney, Jr.	ExO (WIA 9 May, * KIA 14 May)
Maj Glenn E. Martin	S-3 (To 21 Jun)
Capt Charles S. Robertson	S-3
Capt John C. Deal, Jr.	CO Hdqs Co
1stLt Frank B. Gunter	CO E Co
Capt Maurice F. Ahearn, Jr.	CO F Co (WIA 13 May)
Capt William L. Sims	CO F Co (WIA 9 Jun)
1stLt Robert O. Hutchings	CO F Co
Capt Owen T. Stebbins	CO G Co (WIA 12 May)
1stLt Hugh T. Crane	CO G Co

3/22

LtCol Malcolm "O" Donohoo	CO (WIA 16 May)
Maj George B. Kantner	CO (To 19 May)
LtCol Clair W. Shisler	CO
Maj Paul H. Bird	ExO (KIA 11 Apr)
Maj George B. Kantner	ExO (To 15 May)
Maj Roy D. Miller	ExO (To 19 May)
Maj George B. Kantner	ExO
Maj Roy D. Miller	S-3
Capt Frank H. Haigler. Jr.	CO Hdqs Co (To 15 May)
1stLt Buenos A. W. Young	CO Hdqs Co (To 21 Jun)
2dLt Leo M. Humphrey	CO Hdqs Co
1stLt Arthur B. Cofer	CO I Co (To 20 Apr)
Capt John Marston, Jr.	CO I Co
Capt Joseph P. Dockery	CO K Co (WIA 10 May)
1stLt Reginald Fiacke, Jr.	CO K Co (KIA 15 May)
1stLt James D. Roe	CO K Co
Capt John P. Lanigan	CO L Co (WIA 16 May)
Capt Frank H. Haigler, Jr.	CO L Co

Twenty-ninth Marines

Col Victor F. Bleasdale	CO (To 14 Apr)
Col William J. Whaling	CO
LtCol Orin K. Pressley	ExO
LtCol Angus M. FraServ	S-3 (To 14 Jun)
LtCol George W. Killen	S-3
1stLt Robert B. Stinson	CO H&S Co
Capt James G. Petrie	CO Wpns Co

1/29

LtCol Jean W. Moreau	CO (WIA 16 May)
Maj Robert P. Neuffer	CO (TO 25 May)
LtCol Samuel S. Yeaton	CO (To 14 Jun)
LtCol Leroy P. Hunt, Jr.	CO
Maj Robert J. Littin	ExO (To 21 Apr)
Maj James H. Brock	ExO (To 26 May)
Maj Robert P. Neuffer	ExO
Maj James H. Brock	S-3 (To 23 Apr)
Capt Ernest P. Freeman, Jr.	S-3 (To 27 May)
Maj James H. Brock	S-3
Capt Ernest P. Freeman, Jr.	CO Hdqs Co (To 23 Apr)
1stLt Elliot L. Walzer	CO Hdqs Co (To 15 May)
Capt Ernest P. Freeman, Jr.	CO Hdqs Co (From 1 Jun)
1stLt Raymond J. Kautz	CO A Co (To 21 Apr)
Capt Jason B. Baker	CO A Co (From 24 Apr to 15 Jun)
1stLt Warren B. Watson	CO A Co
Capt Lyle E. Specht	CO B Co (WIA 17 May)
1stLt Charles P. Gallagher	CO B Co (To 22 May)
1stLt Griffith E. Thomas	CO B Co (WIA 28 May)
1stLt Robert H. Neef	CO B Co (From 1 Jun)
Capt Edwin H. Rodgers	CO C Co (WIA 8 Apr)
Capt George Heiden	CO C Co (WIA 15 May)
Capt Jack F. Ramsey	CO C Co (WIA 28 May)
1stLt Eugene T. Lawless	CO C Co (WIA 15 Jun)

2/29

LtCol William G. Robb	CO (WIA 19 Apr *)
Maj Thomas J. Cross	ExO
Maj Robert P. Neuffer	S-3 (To 16 May)
Capt Robert B. Fowler	S-3 (KIA 12 Jun)
Maj Wallace O. Fleissner	S-3
Capt Billie Musick	CO Hdqs Co (To 21 Apr)
Capt Martin J. Harrington	CO Hdqs Co (To 22 May)
Capt Ralph D. Porch, II	CO Hdqs Co (To 18 Jun)
Capt Howard L. Mabie	CO D Co (WIA 16 Apr *)
Capt Alan Meissner	CO E Co
Capt Robert B. Fowler	CO F Co (WIA 15 Apr *. To 15 May)
1stLt George S. Thompson	CO F Co (WIA 8 Jun)
1stLt Robert J. Sherer	CO F Co

3/29

LtCol Erma A. Wright	CO (To 14 Jun)
LtCol Angus N. FraServ	CO
Maj Crawford B. Lawton	ExO (WIA 9 Apr)
Maj Everett W. Whipple	ExO (To 21 Apr)
Capt Walter E. Jorgensen	ExO (WIA 16 May)
Capt Thomas P. Tomasello	ExO (To 22 May)
Capt Walter E. Jorgensen	ExO (From 1 to 13 Jun)
Maj Anthony Walker	ExO
Maj Everett W. Whipple	S-3 (To 8 Apr)
Capt James R. Stockman	S-3 (To 6 Jun)
Capt Richard M. Haynes	S-3 (To 13 Jun)
Maj Merlin Olsen	S-3
Capt James R. Stockman	CO Hdqs Co (To 8 Apr)
1stLt Leroy W. Noyes, Jr.	CO Hdqs Co (To 13 Jun)
Capt Walter E. Jorgensen	CO Hdqs Co
Capt Thomas J. Blanchet	CO G Co (To 17 May)
1stLt John J. Keatlng	CO G Co (To 22 May)
Capt William P. Tomasello	CO G Co (WIA 5 Jun *)
1stLt Robert M. Hontz	CO G Co (From 10 Jun)
Capt William P. Tomasello	CO H Co (To 16 May)
Capt William A. Gamble	CO H Co (WIA 5 Jun *)
Capt Walter E. Jorgensen	CO I Co (To 23 Apr)
Capt Philip J. Mylod	CO I Co (WIA 14 May)
1stLt Harvey F. Brooks	CO I Co (WIA 15 May)
1stLt John P. Stone	CO I Co

Fifteenth Marines

Col Robert B. Luckey	CO
LtCol James H. Brower	ExO
Maj William H. Hirst	S-3
1stLt Lawrence I. Miller	CO H&S Btry

1/15

Maj Robert H. Armstrong	CO
Maj William T. Box	ExO
1stLt William N. Larson, Jr.	S-3
1stLt Paul K. Lynde	CO H&S Btry
1stLt Benjamin S. Read	CO A Btry (To 19 Apr)
1stLt John J. Ó Connor	CO A Btry
1stLt James H. Boyd	CO B Btry
Capt Herbert T. Fitch	CO C Btry

2/15

Maj Nat M. Pace	CO
Maj Edward O. Stephany	ExO (To 13 Apr)
Maj William C. Roberts	ExO

Maj Robert P. Yeomans	S-3
2dLt Henry H. Lawler	CO H&S Btry (Rear Echelon)
1stLt Henry C. Schlosser	CO D Btry
Capt McCuthen G. Atkinson	CO E Btry (WIA 13 Apr)
1stLt Joseph A. Edwards	CO E Btry
Capt John L. Noonan	CO F Btry

3/15

LtCol Joe C. McHaney	CO
Maj Benedict V. Schneider, Jr.	ExO
Maj Hugh C. Becker	S-3
Capt Edward C. Ó Donnell	CO H&S Btry
Capt Harris H. Barnes, Jr.	CO G Btry
1stLt Charles F. Petet, Jr.	CO H Btry
Capt Louis D. Abney, Jr.	CO I Btry

4/15

LtCol Bruce T. Hemphill	CO
Maj Francis F. Parry	ExO
Capt Benjamin F. Spencer	S-3
Capt Robert D. Lackland	CO H&S Btry
1stLt Robert T. Patterson	CO K Btry
Capt John "T" Haynes, Jr.	CO L Btry
Maj Robert F. Irving	CO M Btry

6th Engineer Bn

Maj Paul F. Sackett	CO
Maj Robert S. Mayo	ExO
Capt James H. Cooper	S-3
1stLt William M. Graham, Jr.	CO H&S Co
Capt John W. McCuiston	CO A Co
Capt Noel E. Benger	CO B Co
Capt Burt A. Lewis, Jr.	CO C Co

6th Medical Bn

Cmdr John S. Cowan	CO
Lt Joseph M. Shelton	ExO
LCmdr Owen W. E. Nowlin	CO A Co
LCmdr Gerald Flaum	CO B Co (To 27 Apr)
Lt Burton V. Scheib	CO B Co
LCmdr Aaron A. Topcik	CO C Co (To 27 Apr)
LCmdr Robert J. Crawley	CO C Co (To 17 May)
Lt John C. Wilson	CO C Co (To 9 Jun)
LCmdr Robert J. Crawley	CO C Co
LCmdr Horace B. McSwain	CO D Co (To 18 May)
LCmdr Gerald Flaum	CO D Co (To 3 Jun)
Lt Michael T. Michael	CO D Co
Lt Charles M. Ihle	CO E Co

6th Motor Transport Bn

LtCol Ernest H. Gould	CO
Maj Robert E. McCook	ExO
1stLt Robert E. Wagoner	S-3
Capt Albert Hartman	CO H&S Co
Capt Hershel J. Hall	CO A Co
Capt William F. A. Trax	CO B Co
Capt Willis M. Williams	CO C Co

6th Pioneer Bn

LtCol Samuel R. Shaw	CO (To 10 May)
Maj John G. Dibble	CO (To 8 Jun)
LtCol Samuel R. Shaw	CO (To 18 Jun)
Maj John G. Dibble	CO
Maj Olin L. Beall	ExO (To 23 Apr)
Maj John C. Dibble	ExO (To 19 Jun)
Capt Harry B. Smith	ExO
1stLt Harold L. Manley	S-3
1stLt John G. Wintersohle	CO H&S Co
Maj John C. Dibble	CO A Co (To 23 Apr)
1stLt Charles T. Robertson, III	CO A Co
Capt Harry B. Smith	CO B Co (To 18 Jun)
Capt Richard J. Morrisey	CO B Co
Capt Russell J. Lutz	CO C Co

6th Service Bn

LtCol George B. Bell	CO (To 25 Apr)
LtCol Alexander N. Entringer	CO
1stLt William F. Ragan	S-3 (To 9 May)
Capt Charles A. Harper, Jr.	S-3
2dLt Warren A. Lee	CO Hdqs Co (To 26 Apr)
Capt Ira E. Hamer	CO Hdqs Co
Capt Oscar C. Miller	CO Ord Co
Capt William L. Batchelor	CO S&S Co

6th Tank Bn

LtCol Robert L. Denig, Jr.	CO
Maj Harry T. Mime	ExO
Maj Henry Calcutt	S-3 (WIA 18 May *)
2dLt Robert E. Wren	CO H&S Co (To 23 Apr)
1stLt James C. Vail	CO H&S Co
Capt Philip C. Morell	CO A Co
Capt Robert Hall	CO B Co (WIA 10 May)
Capt James R. Williams, Jr.	CO B Co (WIA 21 May *)
Capt Hugh Corrigan	CO C Co (WIA 15 May)
Capt John H. Clifford	CO C Co

GUAM

The 6th MarDiv was transported back to Guam and after a few days' "R&R" it began a new training program. It was for the planned assault upon Japan. The war, however, was over in mid-August, and the 4th Marines, selected to "invade" Japan, were at sea at that time. Therefore, on 30 August 1945, the regiment, under BG Clement, landed at Kurihama (Yokosuka) naval base.

CHINA

It wasn't until 1 October that the balance of the division boarded transports for a trip to North China for duty at Tsingtao. The two regiments, 22d and 29th, began disembarking on 11 October, and on 13 October Division CP opened for business in what was formerly the Japanese Naval Intelligence building. The arrival of the Americans quickly changed things. Not only did the Japanese troops surrender to MG Shepherd but prices quickly climbed to pre-war levels. The Marines could now go into town and walk on sidewalks while heading for something special and unobtainable for many months.

During the next few months the Division was systematically reduced until, on 1 April 1946, it was renamed the Third Marine Brigade. During its nineteen months of existence, the 6th Marine Division never served in the continental United States. Now just two divisions were on the Marine Corps rolls; the 1st and 2d Marine Divisions.

Bibliography

United States Government Publications

Annual Reports of the Navy Department for the Fiscal Years 1940–1950. Washington, D.C.: U.S. Government Printing Office.

Anon (William McCahill). *The Marine Corps Reserve, A History.* Washington, DC: Division of Reserve, Headquarters, U.S. Marine Corps, 1966.

Bailey, Major Alfred Dunlop, USMC (Retired). *Alligators, Buffaloes, and Bushmasters: The History of the Development of the LVT Through World War II.* Washington, DC: History and Museums Division, Headquarters, U.S. Marine Corps, 1986.

Clifford, Lieutenant Colonel Kenneth J., USMCR, ed. *The United States Marines in Iceland, 1941–1942.* Washington, DC: Historical Division, Headquarters, U.S. Marine Corps, 1970.

Condit, Kenneth W., and Edwin T. Turnbladh. *Hold High the Torch: A History of the 4th Marines.* Washington, D.C.: Historical Branch, G–3 Division, Headquarters, U.S. Marine Corps, 1960.

History of U.S. Marine Corps Operations in World War II. 5 vols. Washington, D.C.: U.S. Government Printing Office, n.d. (circa 1958)–1968.

Shaw, Henry I., Jr. *The United States Marines in the Occupation of Japan.* Washington, DC: Historical Branch, G–3 Division, Headquarters, U.S. Marine Corps, 1962 edition.

U.S. Marine Corps World War II monograph series (by publishing date)

1947. Stockman, James R. The Battle for Tarawa. Historical Section, Division of Public Information, Headquarters, U.S. Marine Corps.

1948. Rentz, John N. *Bougainville and the Northern Solomons.* Historical Section, Division of Public Information, Headquarters, U.S. Marine Corps.

1949. Zimmerman, John L. *The Guadalcanal Campaign.* Historical Division, Headquarters, U.S. Marine Corps.

1950. Hoffman, Carl W. *Saipan: The Beginning of the End.* Historical Division, Headquarters, U.S. Marine Corps.

1950. Hough, Frank O. *The Assault on Peleliu.* Historical Division, Headquarters, U.S. Marine Corps.

1951. Hoffman, Carl W. *The Seizure of Tinian.* Historical Division, Headquarters, U.S. Marine Corps.

1952. Rentz, John N. *Marines in the Central Solomons.* Historical Branch, Headquarters, U.S. Marine Corps.

1952. Hough, Frank O. and John A. Crown. *The Campaign on New Britain.* Historical Branch, Headquarters, U.S. Marine Corps.

1954. Heinl, Robert D., and John A. Crown. *The Marshalls: Increasing the Tempo.* Historical Branch, G–3 Division, Headquarters, U.S. Marine Corps.

1954. Lodge, O.R. *The Recapture of Guam.* Historical Branch, G–3 Division, Headquarters, U.S. Marine Corps.

1954. Bartley, Whitman S. *Iwo Jima: Amphibious Epic.* Historical Branch, G–3 Division, Headquarters, U.S. Marine Corps.

1955. Nichols, Chas. S., Jr., and Henry I. Shaw, Jr. *Okinawa: Victory in the Pacific.* Historical Branch, G–3 Division, Headquarters, U.S. Marine Corps.

Books

Alexander, Joseph H. *Edson's Raiders. The 1st Marine Raider Battalion in World War II.* Annapolis: Naval Institute Press, 2001.

_____. *Utmost Savagery: The Three Days of Tarawa.* Annapolis: Naval Institute Press, 1995.

Asprey, Robert B. *Once a Marine: The Memoirs of General A.A. Vandegrift, U.S.M.C.* NY: W.W. Norton & Company, Inc., 1964.

Aurthur, Robert A., Kenneth Kohlmia, and Robert T. Vance. *The Third Marine Division.* Washington, D.C.: Infantry Journal Press, 1948.

Blakeney, Jane. *Heroes, U.S. Marine Corps, 1861–1955: Armed Forces Awards & Flags.* Washington, D.C.: private printing, 1957.

Brown, Ronald J. *A Few Good Men. The Fighting Fifth Marines: A History of the USMC's Most Decorated Regiment.* Novato, CA: Presidio Press, 2001.

Burrus, L.D. *The Ninth Marines: A Brief History of the Ninth Marine Regiment.* Washington, DC: Infantry Journal Press, 1946.

Cass, Bevan G. *History of the Sixth Marine Division.* Washington, D.C.: Infantry Journal Press, 1948.

Clark, George B. *Heroes of the 4th Brigade: Awards and Citations.* Pike, NH: The Brass Hat, 2002.

_____. *Legendary Marines of the Old Corps.* Pike, NH: The Brass Hat, 2002.

_____. *Table of Organization of USMC Units and Associated USA Units in the Great Pacific War, 1941–1945.* Pike, NH: The Brass Hat, 2003.

_____, ed. *United States Marine Corps Medal of Honor Recipients.* Jefferson, NC: McFarland & Company, Inc., 2005.

Clifford, Kenneth J. *Amphibious Warfare Development in Britain and America from 1920–1940.* Laurens, NY: Englewood, Inc., 1983.

Conner, Howard M. *The Spearhead: The World War II History of the 5th Marine Division.* Washington, D.C.: Infantry Journal Press, 1950.

Croziat, Victor J. *Across the Reef: The Amphibious Tracked Vehicle at War.* London: Arms and Armour Press, 1989.

Curley, W.J.P., Jr. *Letters from the Pacific, 1943–1946.* N.p., private printing, 1959.

Del Valle, Pedro A. *Semper Fidelis: An Autobiography.* Hawthorne, CA: The Christian Book Club of America, 1976.

FitzPatrick, Tom. *A Character That Inspired: Major General Charles D. Barrett, USMC.* Fairfax, VA, private printing, 2003.

Hallas, James H. *The Devil's Anvil: The Assault on Peleliu.* Westport, CT: Praeger, 1994.

_____. *Killing Ground on Okinawa: The Battle for Sugar Loaf Hill.* Westport, CT: Praeger, 1996.

Heinl, Robert D. *Soldiers of the Sea: The U.S. Marine Corps, 1775–1962.* Annapolis: United States Naval Institute, 1962.

Hoffman, Jon T. *Chesty: The Story of Lieutenant General Lewis B. Puller, USMC.* New York: Random House, 2001.

_____. *Once a Legend: "Red Mike" Edson of the Marine Raiders.* Novato, CA: Presidio Press, 1994.

Hough, Frank O. *The Island War: The United States Marine Corps in the Pacific.* Philadelphia: J.B. Lippincott Company, 1947.

Hunt, George P. *Coral Comes High.* NY: Harper and Brothers, 1946.

Isely, Jeter A., and Philip A. Crowl. *The U.S. Marines and Amphibious War. Its Theory and Its Practice in the Pacific.* Princeton: Princeton University Press, 1951.

Johnston, Richard W. *Follow Me! The Story of the Second Marine Division in World War II.* New York: Random House, 1948.

Langley, Lester D. *The Banana Wars: An Inner History of American Empire 1900–1934.* Lexington: The University Press of Kentucky, 1983.

Leahy, Edward. *In the Islands.* Tucson: Hat's Off Books, 2002.

Letcher, John Seymour. *One Marine's Story.* Verona, VA: McClure Press, 1970.

Matthews, Allen R. *The Assault.* NY: Simon and Schuster, 1947.

McCrocklin, James H., comp. *Garde D'Haiti, 1915–1934.* Annapolis: The United States Naval Institute, 1956.

McMillan, George. *The Old Breed: A History of the First Marine Division in World War II.* Washington, D.C.: Infantry Journal Press, 1949.

Millett, Allan R. *In Many a Strife: General Gerald C. Thomas and the U.S. Marine Corps, 1917–1956.* Annapolis: Naval Institute Press, 1993.

_____. *Semper Fidelis: The History of the United States Marine Corps.* New York: Macmillan Publishing Co., Inc. and Collier Macmillan Publishers, London: 1980.

Munro, Dana G. *The United States and the Caribbean Republics, 1921–1933.* Princeton: Princeton University Press, 1974.

Musicant, Ivan. *The Banana Wars: A History of United States Military Intervention in Latin America from the Spanish-American War to the Invasion of Panama.* New York: Macmillan Publishing Company, 1990.

Paul, Doris A. *The Navajo Code Talkers.* Bryn Mawr, PA: Dorrance & Company, Incorporated, 1973.

Proehl, Carl W., ed. *The Fourth Marine Division in World War II.* Washington, D.C.: Infantry Journal Press, 1946.

Schmidt, Hans. *The United States Occupation of Haiti, 1915–1934.* New Brunswick: Rutgers University Press, 1971.

Schuon, Karl. *U.S. Marine Corps Biographical Dictionary.* New York: Franklin Watts, Inc., 1963.

Smith, Holland M. *Coral and Brass.* NY: Charles Scribner's Sons, 1949.

Willock, Roger. *Unaccustomed to Fear. A Biography of the late General Roy S. Geiger, U.S.M.C.* Princeton, NJ: privately published, 1968.

Index

(* indicates Medal of Honor recipients)